# Police Leaders in
the New Community
Problem-Solving Era

# Police Leaders in the New Community Problem-Solving Era

**Michael J. Jenkins**

UNIVERSITY OF SCRANTON

**John DeCarlo**

JOHN JAY COLLEGE OF CRIMINAL JUSTICE

CAROLINA ACADEMIC PRESS

Durham, North Carolina

Library of Congress Cataloging-in-Publication Data

Jenkins, Michael, 1984-
  Police leaders in the new community problem-solving era / Michael
Jenkins and John DeCarlo.
    pages cm
  Includes bibliographical references and index.
  ISBN 978-1-61163-590-4 (alk. paper)
  1.  Police--Supervision of--United States.  2.  Police-community
relations--United States.  I. DeCarlo, John.  II. Title.

  HV7936.S8J46 2015
  363.2068'4--dc23

                    2014032800


                CAROLINA ACADEMIC PRESS
                    700 Kent Street
              Durham, North Carolina 27701
               Telephone (919) 489-7486
                  Fax (919) 493-5668
                    www.cap-press.com

        Printed in the United States of America

# Contents

# Foreword

By the late 1970s and early 1980s, police leaders, policy makers, and researchers were confronted by the stark reality that "professional" policing—that is, the centralized, bureaucratic, factory, reactive model of policing formulated in the mid-20th century—had failed. It failed to control crime, it alienated minority communities, it created an isolated police culture hostile to outsiders, and, despite its emphasis on bureaucratic controls, it failed to maintain officer or management accountability. The evidence of the collapse of professional, or reform, policing abounded: the intervention of the Supreme Court in criminal investigation with its exclusionary rule and Miranda warning during the 1950s; the riots against police during the 1960s; police behavior in response to the civil rights movement of the 1960s; the research regarding its tactics—preventive patrol, rapid response to calls for service, and criminal investigation—during the 1970s; and the seemingly inexorable rise of crime starting in the 1960s.

During the same period, ideas about improving policing began to surface: police had to improve their relationship to the community; minorities and women needed to be hired and promoted in police departments; alternative tactics had to be devised; problems, not incidents, ought to be a basic unit of police work; enforcement of minor offenses is important to citizens; police, at all levels, use extensive discretion; foot patrol has value; citizen concerns are important in devising police priorities; and, civilians can play important roles in police work. Reconciling these ideas to the reigning police ideology was initially difficult. After all, did not opening police departments to citizen and political input run the risk of reopening the long-fought battle against police corruption and political interference in police matters? Was not arresting and ensuring prosecution of those who commit serious crimes the basic business of police? How could local neighborhood concerns about disorderly behavior be responded to in a highly centralized bureaucracy focused on responding to serious crimes? How could police officers be controlled without a strong semi-military command and control system?

Nonetheless, by the mid-1980s it was becoming clear that policing was not just entering a phase of improving its mid-century strategy, it was moving away from the reform strategy and entering a yet not fully understood era of policing most commonly referred to as community policing. At the core of emerging police thinking was the idea that police had to structure a new relationship with neighborhoods and communities. In many respects this was not a new idea. The community relations movement that started during the 1940s after riots in Detroit and Los Angeles, and which was endorsed by President Johnson's 1965 Commission on Law Enforcement and the Administration of Justice, attempted to bridge the gap between police and community, especially minority communities. It attempted this primarily through meetings with community leaders, recruitment of minorities, and officer training in race relations. The community relations movement had several problems, not the least of which was that many, if not most, police departments viewed community relations as an opportunity to "sell" policing as it was then. But more profound was the failure to understand that if one truly changes the relationship between police and community it has enormous impact on the total strategy of policing. And this is where it gets tough.

It is clear that it is one thing for police leaders, academics, and policy makers to have and understand new good ideas about policing, and to even understand that a basic shift in police thinking is afoot; it is something entirely else to implement the changes that such a shift implies and requires. It is not an exaggeration to write that if a police department shifts from the reform to a community strategy, every element of its strategy must change, from its sources of authority, to its structure and administrative processes, to its tactics and sought after outcomes. Complicating this situation enormously for police leaders is that they make these changes in the midst of their everyday work. There is no time out for retooling. Crime still happens; citizens still have emergencies; children get lost; and "cats still wind up in trees." Moreover they make these changes in the face of the "conventional wisdom" that often shapes media and community views of the police, e.g., that response time is a key metric of police performance.

Michael Jenkins and John DeCarlo have studied and herein present how four police departments have confronted these challenges: Boston, Massachusetts; Los Angeles, California; Milwaukee, Wisconsin; and Newark, New Jersey. Each has an interesting history both of successes and failures, but all are committed to move towards a genuine community/problem solving model. Moreover, the authors view these departments within the context of police and organizational literature. The question that the authors ultimately confront is how, in the complex political, organizational, and social world police exist in, does change survive.

George L. Kelling, Ph.D.
Professor Emeritus, Rutgers Newark University
Professor Emeritus, Northeastern University
Senior Fellow, Manhattan Institute

# Acknowledgments

The authors appreciate the assistance and support of a number of our personal, academic, professional, and practitioner friends and institutions. This book is based on the dissertation Jenkins completed under the following committee, chaired by George Kelling, Norman Samuels, Ronald Clarke, and Anthony Braga. Their insight and expertise were invaluable in helping to formulate and implement the research ideas. Their comments on early versions of this work undoubtedly improved the book you're reading today.

We are grateful to a number of personnel from within each of the police departments: Boston Police Commissioner Ed Davis, Milwaukee Police Chief Ed Flynn, L.A. Police Chiefs William Bratton and Charlie Beck, and Newark Police Director Garry McCarthy confidently opened their departments in support of the research. Desiree Dusseault and Jen Maconochie graciously helped to organize research visits to the BPD. A close friend and colleague, Eric Piza, assisted with visits to the NPD. We thank Sgt. Kristin Riestra and Anne Schwartz for their hospitality during visits to the MPD. Sergeant Jaime Marin and Sgt. Pinto and Officers Chao and Armando kindly assisted with research visits to the LAPD. We are indebted to the many people within each police department who took time out of their daily responsibilities to share their views and experiences.

We thank Teresina Gildea, Jessica Lloyd, John "Zack" Monahan, Joe Mosangkoun, Dana Raciti, and Michael Pristash for their superb, patient, and professional research, transcribing, and editing assistance. We appreciate Beth Hall, our acquisitions editor at Carolina Academic Press, for continuing to be a supportive, energetic, and responsive advisor. We're also indebted to both Ryland Bowman and Grace Pledger for lending their expertise during the production stages.

To our families, thank you for your support and understanding as we stuck to our stick-to-it-ness.

Finally, we greatly appreciate George Kelling's mentorship and decades of contributions to the policing field. More practically, without him, such widespread access to the police departments would not be likely. As students of policing and as a former chief (DeCarlo), Dr. Kelling's work has been transformative. We're honored to call him a friend.

Generous funding from the University of Scranton's Provost Office, the University of New Haven's Provost Office, and the Bodman Foundation supported this research. We thank, too, our current and past colleagues at these institutions and at John Jay College of Criminal Justice.

Of course, even with the mentorship, guidance, and support of the preceding sources, the opinions, findings, conclusions, and mistakes remain our own.

Michael J. Jenkins and John DeCarlo

# Introduction

What you'll read hereinafter is the result of a relatively open-ended exploration of the current state of urban policing as outlined by the elements of an organizational strategy in Boston, Los Angeles, Milwaukee, and Newark. Jenkins initially began this exploration as part of the requirements for completing his doctoral degree at Rutgers University under the mentorship of George Kelling. DeCarlo, a retired police chief, a police practitioner for 34 years, and a Ph.D. from John Jay College, brings both a practitioner's and an academic's perspective to the analysis and contemplation of the four departments' experiences presented here. We hope that by combining our perspectives in this book you'll get a unique view of how personnel within these police departments view the effect of a community problem-solving strategy on their work.

Chapter 1 introduces you to a brief history of modern policing in the United States. It also explores the concept of a police organizational strategy and breaks it down into its various elements. These elements will form the outline for Chapters 4, 5, 6, and 7, which present the findings from each of the respective departments. The elements prove useful for understanding the police profession as a product of a comprehensive organization.

Chapter 2 shares a little bit about the methods and methodology. You might find some of the discussions surrounding the strengths, weaknesses, and challenges of conducting such research helpful to your own studies of police and police organizations. Chapter 2 also describes the specific sources of data and the analytical process followed in building each of the cases in the subsequent chapters.

We set the stage in Chapter 3 by giving a brief overview of the departments' and the cities' histories, pointing out key developments that will prepare the reader for understanding the current research of each department. We also provide some statistics on the demographics and crime rates in each of the cities to help the reader picture the general context in which the departments operate.

The next four chapters, then, delve into the community problem-solving experiences of each of the departments. At best, we would like to think that the findings in each chapter represent the typical, unbiased police officer's view of police work and the police organization in the United States. At the very least we present the finest face of community problem-solving that some arguably top-notch police executives can offer. As you will see, even *that* promises to be quite telling. You will notice some lengthy direct quotations within these chapters. They are one of the main sources of data in building each case. It is our desire that you will see these for the richness they provide and for the thoughtfulness with which our police respondents approached this study.

We present each department's magnitude of change in Chapter 8, analyzing the change from where each department came to where they show signs of heading in the future. The designations of low, low-medium, medium, high, etc., are relative to each department and depend on the access and quality of the data we were able to collect. We also summarize some of the notable changes in each of the elements of the departments' organizational strategies. As in the four chapters that lead up to it, we use Chapter 8 to re-orient the reader with the current status of the police departments. The illustrations of each department are meant to give the reader a basis for comparison when examining their own best practices or research.

Chapter 9 closes with some key themes that emerged while placing the experiences of the study's departments into the greater body of literature and practice. The importance of police leadership and organizational structure bears repeating in our discussion. The nature of their uncovering and the robustness with which the data pointed to them warrant future attention by researchers and practitioners. Finally, the chapter and book close with the defining characteristics and challenges of policing in the new community problem-solving era as well as an explanation of why we believe the name fittingly describes the latest policing era.

# Police Leaders in the New Community Problem-Solving Era

# Chapter 1

# A Modern History of Police Organizational Strategies and Change in Policing

## A Brief History of Policing in the United States

A review of policing in the United States reveals a dynamic evolution in policing strategy, mission, technology, authorization, demand, function, structure, and relationship with the community (Kelling & Moore, 1988). Changing social, cultural, economic, and political environments punctuate various elements of policing, thereby altering each era's idea of what constitutes "policing." Police responsibilities and community expectations of their police change with the times. It is the police relationship with the community, however, that most conspicuously defines the history of policing in the United States.

From an era when every able-bodied townsman fulfilled the police function by responding to the hue and cry, to a time when a highly organized, well paid, educated, and professional,[1] full-time police force prevents and responds to all types of problems, crimes and criminals, the intimacy with which police and citizens work together has varied over the years. Each node in the evolution of policing represents police attempts to respond to the social, cultural, economic, and political environments in which the police and the community negotiate their relationship. For instance, indignation with the corrupting closeness of police, politicians, and the public during the Political era (in the latter half of the nineteenth century) sparked the drastic moves to "get the politics out of the police and get the police out of politics"

---

1. "Professional," when referring to the police, connotes the particular bureaucratic, para-military governance that arose in police organizations in response to corruption and general dissatisfaction with police.

during the Reform era (roughly the early 1900s to 1970) (Miller, 1977, p. 11). Police estrangement from the community that symbolized this era came to a head in the 1960s as riots (and police inability to successfully combat crime and to work with the community) challenged the police to find new ways of relating to the community.

Beginning in the 1960s rising crime rates, the fear of crime, and emerging research on the inefficacy of principal police tactics (i.e., preventive patrol and rapid response) demanded a reappraisal of the profession. Police officials, responding to academic research (e.g., Trojanowicz, 1982; Kelling, 1981), recalled the value of conducting neighborhood foot patrols and began to see a reduction in citizen fear of crime as an end in itself. Police administrators learned to appreciate line officers' broad use of discretion and began to question the primacy of the law enforcement function of police. The community problem-solving (CPS) era, as it has come to be known, followed.

## *Theoretical Framework*

Over the past thirty years police departments across the country have made strides in adopting aspects of CPS. The manifestations, magnitude, and maintenance of this shift in paradigm varies across departments and over time. The conceptions that police personnel have of CPS sometimes differ from researcher constructs of the same strategy. CPS represents different tactics, strategies, and philosophies to different people, sometimes even within the same police department. In conducting case studies, this research will explore police personnel's views of CPS through a broad lens of broken windows policing (a popular tactic used in community and problem-solving policing). A condensed explication of these separate ideas (i.e., community policing, problem-solving policing, and broken windows policing) follows.[2]

---

2. Police personnel, academics, policy analysts, and the public often conceive of and operationalize these concepts differently, leading to difficulties in implementing and studying the effects of each. Other terms used to discuss similar concepts include community-oriented policing, problem-oriented policing, CPS policing, neighborhood policing, team policing, zero-tolerance policing, and quality of life policing. These terms encompass various policing philosophies, strategies, and tactics. We use community policing and community-oriented policing interchangeably. CPS specifically describes the era of modern policing. The term captures both the policing strategy and the wide range of activities that we explore in this study.

## Community Policing

While the concepts overlap, each idea has a distinct meaning for police work. Skogan (2006, p. 28) states, community policing is "an organizational strategy that leaves setting priorities and the means of achieving them largely to residents and the police who serve in their neighborhoods.... [It] is a process rather than a product." Of the three terms (community policing, problem-solving policing, and broken windows policing), community policing most directly involves extensive and considerable change for police personnel and the organization for which they work. It is a philosophy that undergirds all aspects of police operations, including how the department is organized, how police spend their time, how police measure their performance, and how police view their relationship with the people they serve. Skogan's (1990, pp. 90–93) four community policing principles are:

1. Community policing assumes a commitment to broadly focused, problem-oriented policing.
2. Community policing relies upon organizational decentralization and a reorientation of patrol tactics to open informal, two-way channels of communication between police and citizens.
3. Community policing requires that police be responsive to citizen demands when deciding what are local problems and priorities.
4. Community policing implies a commitment to helping neighborhoods help themselves by serving as a catalyst for local organizing education efforts.

Though little evidence supports the crime prevention benefits of community policing, research examines the ability of a community oriented police department to improve their relationships with citizens and to assist them in community based activities. Furthermore, research shows that aspects commonly found in police departments implementing community policing (i.e., problem-solving and broken windows policing) have a more direct effect on the crime and disorder reduction outcomes of a police department. These are discussed below.

## Problem-Solving Policing

Research on the inefficacy of rapid response (Kansas City Police Department, 1977) and preventive patrol (Kelling, Pate, Dieckman, & Brown, 1974), James Q. Wilson's (1968) work on police discretion and the "varieties of police behavior," and Herman Goldstein's (1979) introduction of the idea of problem-solving mark the beginning of the CPS era. It also commenced a shift in how police viewed their success and provided a channel for police and community collaboration. According to the problem-solving model, police should use the number of problems solved, not response times, in measuring the success of their work (Goldstein, 1979). Moore (2002) describes this as a shift from outputs to outcomes. Eck and Spelman (1987) advanced and refined Goldstein's ideas in their research on the successful implementation of a problem-solving model that included scanning, analyzing, responding, and assessing (or, the SARA model). This model has become the most accepted understanding of how police departments implement problem-solving policing. Eck (2006, p. 117) lays out five premises of problem-oriented policing:

1.  The public demands much of police;
2.  The causes of these demands are often complex;
3.  The police serve the public better when they make systematic inquiries into these complexities;
4.  Knowledge helps build new approaches to police services; and
5.  Learning from successful and unsuccessful innovations makes police more effective in handling the demands of the public.

Whereas community policing offers a wide range of broad philosophical tenets for organizing and administering police services and working with the community, problem-oriented policing more narrowly focuses on the specific way police could work with the community to respond to problems and on the outcomes police should use in measuring their success. Problem-solving is a method used by a community-oriented department to respond to a variety of community needs; community policing is a driving philosophy for police departments that implement problem-oriented policing; broken windows policing is often part of a community oriented police department's repertoire of tactics, stemming from their implementation of a problem-solving exercise (Reisig, 2010). Clarke (2002) differentiates between community-oriented policing and problem-oriented policing; he notes, community policing "seeks to strengthen relationships with communities and engage their assistance in the fight against crime. Problem-oriented policing, on the other hand ... is mostly directed to reducing opportunities for crime through environmental changes and criminal or civil enforcement" (emphasis the authors', p. 3).

A variety of tactics, then, can be used with a problem-oriented approach to respond to any number of problems. Research confirms the success of police problem solving in a number of communities and for a range of crimes and problems (Braga, Kennedy, Waring, & Piel, 2004; Braga, Weisburd, Waring, Mazerolle, Spelman, & Gajewski, 1999; Hope, 1994; Sampson & Scott, 2000). Additionally, while a Campbell systematic review of the effectiveness of problem-solving policing (Weisburd, Telep, Hinkle, & Eck, 2010) found various forms of problem solving to have an overall statistically significant modest effect on crime and disorder, the authors found only ten evaluations rigorous enough to meet their inclusion criteria. They concluded that future implementations of problem solving should consider the specific problem-solving approaches that can best combat specific types of crimes. The current research adds to the knowledge of problem-solving policing by examining what (if any) problem-solving experiences distinguish each of the four police departments.

## *Broken Windows Policing*

Police researchers often credit broken windows policing as helping to usher in the CPS era and as giving CPS police departments a way to respond to a crime or disorder problem in their neighborhood. Kelling and Wilson first presented their broken windows theory of neighborhood crime in 1982. Their theory explored the psychological and normative effects of neighborhood in-civilities and disorder on criminal offending and the role that police could play in reconciling community norms to neighborhood order. Based on observations of police in the field, they urged police departments to return to what Kelling and Wilson argued was the historical responsibility of police: to maintain orderly communities. Though they were not the first to posit a link between disorder, crime, and fear of crime (see, Jacobs, 1961; Zimbardo, 1970; Glazer, 1979), their broken window metaphor and the increasingly popular community policing movement combined to make change more palpable to police departments looking to advance their spectrum of services. Kelling and Wilson's (1982) metaphor aided police administrators in understanding the relationship between disorder, crime, and the fear of crime. It also gave line-officer supervisors tangible tactics to employ in carrying out the theory and spoke to those line officers who had already been doing broken windows policing in fulfilling their day-to-day duties.

Kelling and Wilson's (1982) oft-quoted broken windows metaphor follows:

> If a window in a building is broken and is left unrepaired, all the rest of the windows will soon be broken. This is as true in nice neighborhoods as in run-down ones. Window-breaking does not necessarily occur on a large scale because some areas are inhabited by determined window-breakers whereas others are populated by window-lovers; rather, one unrepaired broken window is a signal that no one cares, and so breaking more windows costs nothing. (p. 30)

The one broken window (e.g., a persistent panhandler, a group of intimidating teens, excessive litter, graffiti, or individuals sleeping in public places) gives the impression to potential wrongdoers that no one cares how people act in or treat the neighborhood, opening the door to more serious law breaking.

In their empirical testing of broken windows policing, Wagers, Sousa, and Kelling (2008) further assess the main tenets of broken windows, giving greater insight into the theory's implications. They state:

1. Disorder and fear of crime are strongly linked;
2. Police (in the examples given, foot patrol officers) negotiate rules of the street. "Street people" are involved in the negotiation of those rules;
3. Different neighborhoods have different rules;
4. Untended disorder leads to the breakdown of community controls;
5. Areas where community controls break down are vulnerable to criminal invasion;
6. The essence of the police role in maintaining order is to reinforce the informal control mechanisms of the community itself;
7. Problems arise not so much from individual disorderly persons as it does from the congregation of large numbers of disorderly persons; and,
8. Different neighborhoods have different capacities to manage disorder. (p. 253)

People have perceived broken windows policing as zero-tolerance policing, where police officers are expected to formally intervene in all instances in which they suspect an individual has committed a low-level offense. Such an application of broken windows policing can sometimes hurt the police department's relationship with citizens (Gau & Pratt, 2008). Research on the effect of broken windows policing on crime often measure the policing tactic by numbers of misdemeanor arrests and citations, which, in some instances, neglects the informal ways that police also deal with citizens who are acting disorderly (e.g., Kelling & Sousa, 2001; Shi, 2009; Kubrin, Messner, Deane, McGeever, & Stucky, 2010). Nevertheless, many of these studies do in fact support the inverse relationship between proactively policing disorderly and misdemeanor offenses and rates of fear and crime.

Researchers variously differentiate among community policing, broken windows policing and problem-solving, and yet these concepts are often implemented in conjunction with each other. This current research traces the CPS efforts of police departments, paying special attention to their attempts at broken windows policing. An initial examination of the police departments, discussions with George Kelling (who had recently consulted with each of the police departments), and an understanding of the proven leadership abilities of the police departments' (then) recently appointed police executives led us to focus on the CPS strategy and broken windows policing tactic as a way of orienting the study of the police departments' organizational strategies. The elements of organizational strategy (explicated below) further help to manage, understand, and interpret the extensive amount of data collected for this study.

Conducting case studies of the four police departments offers insight into the factors related to the ebb and flow of a department's commitment to CPS policing. The analysis of the four police departments in this study shows how the police organizations moved toward a CPS strategy, how police personnel view the CPS strategy as fitting into their police department,[3] and the most salient inhibitors and facilitators of organizational change in the new CPS strategy.

## Organizational Change in Police Departments

The more restrictive term "corporate strategy" is commonly used when discussing:

> The pattern of decisions in a company that determines and reveals its objective, purposes, or goals, produces the principal policies or plans for achieving those goals, and describes the range of business the company is to pursue, the kind of … organization it is or intends to be, and the nature of the … contribution it intends to make to its … communities. (Andrews, 2003, p. 51)

"Organizational strategy" more aptly describes the business of public service agencies and will be used to discuss the policing organization.[4] Seven elements of a police organizational strategy, adapted from Kelling and Moore (1988), inform and guide this current research:

1.  legitimacy (or authorization) (*From where do police derive their power to influence society?*);
2.  police function (*What is the police role in society?*);

---

3. Hence, using community problem-solving (CPS) as an organizing theme.

4. For a brief discussion of how corporate strategy applies to public institutions, see Kelling, G. (1989). A Discussion of the Concept of Organizational Strategy for Use in 'Planning and Management' Sequence, unpublished manuscript.

3.  organizational structure (*How do orders and information flow through sections of the organization?*);
4.  administrative processes (*What activities are necessary to maintain the proper functioning of the organization and how are decisions made?*);
5.  external relationships (*What relationships do police have with their external environment?*);
6.  demand entrance and demand management (*How and to whom do the police market or sell their services? How does demand enter the organization and who controls this demand?*); and
7.  tactics, technology, and outcomes (*What are the main activities, programs, and tactics police use to achieve their mission? What are the specific measures police use to define success or failure?*).

Moore, Sparrow, and Spelman (1997) offer a similar typology, distinguishing between four types of innovations: programmatic, administrative, technological, and strategic. This study determines the extent and nature of the organizations' changing strategy by examining each organization holistically, looking at how Kelling and Moore's (1988) elements of organizational strategy fit into programmatic, administrative, and technological innovations; these innovations (in toto) evince strategic innovation and shifting organizational strategies in each police department. First, a discussion of the elements of organizational strategy follows. Though these terms refer to a multitude of possibilities within an organization, only the most striking parts of each element (as they arise from the data in each case) will be discussed in this research. Thus, some of the findings explore only a narrow portion of some elements.

## *Legitimacy*

A wide range of activities and factors relate to views of police legitimacy. Researchers examine police legitimacy by using objective and subjective measurements that include the police department's relationship to the community, their relationship with local politicians, the police personnel's and citizens' beliefs and behaviors, the education and training levels of departmental personnel, the representativeness of the police department, and the ways of recruiting, hiring, firing, promoting, and investigating police personnel. Data on citizens' perceptions of the police department and on citizens' compliance and cooperation with the police reflect the department's legitimacy in the community and suggest that how police perform their duties (e.g., procedural justice) is sometimes more important than the outcomes of their work (i.e., order maintenance or crime reduction) (Tyler, 2002; Fagan & Tyler, 2004). For police legitimacy, then, the traditional ways of measuring what police do and their effectiveness doing it do not account for its most pertinent aspect, the manner in which they fulfill their responsibilities.

Themes of legitimacy are central to the creation, discourse, and evolution of the broken windows theory (Walker, 1984). A more sophisticated understanding of how broken windows policing affects a police department's organizational strategy can offer suggestions on how to improve legitimacy in police departments as well as provide information on how best to facilitate citizens' co-production of order. Past research has shown that broken windows policing (sometimes misinterpreted by police departments as zero-tolerance policing) can hurt or help police efforts at gaining legitimacy. This depends on community and police understandings and perceptions of that type of policing and on the citizen and police definition of scope of the crime problem (Skogan, 2008; Gau & Pratt, 2008). Evidence of police legitimacy in the CPS strategy can include a decrease in citizen complaints against the police department, transparent processes within the police department (especially including the investigation of police personnel), increased efforts by the police to positively engage the community, support from relevant political bodies, and training officers in properly using their discretion to intervene with citizens upon reasonable suspicion of a low-level offense.

## *Function*

This chapter has discussed the changing functions and roles of policing in the United States. The police function changes with time and location and by police department and individual police personnel as personnel and their departments interpret and implement their own understandings of what is expected of them. The main functions of police throughout time are maintaining order, serving the community, and fighting crime. The "varieties of police behavior" that departments use to fulfill those functions are the "watchman style," the "legalistic style," and the "service style" (Wilson, 1968). Initial conceptions of the broken windows theory discuss the need for the police function to shift from one focused on crime control to one in which the police and community work together to reduce disorder, crime, and fear of crime. The function of a police department within a CPS strategy manifests in their successful establishment of positive working relationships with citizens and other community groups, response to lower-level offenses (i.e., quality of life offenses, violations of city ordinances, or motor vehicle violations), and in connecting these relationships and responses to reductions in crime, disorder, and fear. As discussed below, the CompStat process is one way that police organizations try to connect their crime, fear, and disorder strategies to their efforts at community building, broken windows policing, and problem solving. This study explores four police departments' experiences in implementing the broken windows theory within the context of CPS and offers data to help police departments and researchers move beyond traditional "zero-tolerance" applications of the broken windows theory and better understand these connections.

## *Organizational Structure and Administrative Processes*

The form of an organization should be directly related to the function it fulfills. The traditional quasi-military structure of police organizations is intended to enhance the ability of supervisors to control police behavior, to manage the allocation of resources and personnel, and to deliver the crime fighting services of police departments by delineating clear lines of supervision and authority. This structure dominates the history of modern policing in the United States. Other types of organizational structures will have a less stringent hierarchy of authority and varying degrees of flatness (that is, they will include more personnel within the decision-making and administrative processes).

Administrative processes refer specifically to the opportunities for and mechanisms by which decisions are made and processed through the organization. Traditionally, the police executive (e.g., police chief or police commissioner) consults with his or her administrative personnel to create orders and send them down through the ranks. Standardized decisions on how to allocate resources and deploy personnel are made at headquarters and are founded on equalization. Investigative personnel are based in a central location and responsible for their content area of specialization (i.e., robbery, burglary, homicide, shootings) across the entire city. This research examines changing relationships between patrol and investigations units, department reorganizations, new task forces, criteria for decisions dealing with personnel, training, the role of leadership, the CompStat process, and the police subculture to discuss changes in the organizational structure and administrative processes.

Sixty percent of police agencies with 100 or more sworn personnel claim to follow some version of a CompStat process (Weisburd, Mastrofski, Greenspan, & Willis, 2004). Police departments use CompStat in various ways (as a management tool, as a problem-solving exercise, to transmit the executive leader's values to command staff, and to hold personnel responsible for using their own problem-solving skills to respond to data-derived crime and disorder problems) (Willis, Mastrofski, & Weisburd, 2007). The CompStat process, then, can directly relate to a police department's implementation of community, problem-solving, and broken windows policing. In addition to integrating these ideas into their CompStat process, a police department in the CPS era should exhibit signs of decentralization, shared leadership, investigative and patrol maintenance of a limited geographic area, and training and personnel decisions that support the department's move toward such a strategy.

## External Relationships

The police department's relationship to its external environment refers to the department's economic, political, and social situation (specifically, the police department's access to economic resources, the political context in which the department operates, and the department's relationship with the community, the union, and other law enforcement agencies). These relationships most conspicuously define discussions of the CPS strategy and inevitably arise when studying most of the other elements of organizational strategy.

Any number of socio-political and socio-economic combinations can exist at a given time. Discussions of a police department's external environment commonly include the department's relationship with the union, the community, and other governmental bodies, the economic strength of the organization, and social or cultural movements that challenge or promote police authority. A police department in the CPS era should have sustained, sincere, and productive working relationships with citizens and other community groups as well as support from local politicians. The police and the community, under the CPS strategy, would be viewed as co-producers of reduced levels of crime, disorder, and fear of crime. Ideally, as with any other type of policing, a department would also have the benefit of a healthy economic situation.

## Demand Entrance and Demand Management

The avenues in place for an organization to receive demand for its service and how the organization interprets and manages that demand speak to how the police department views its relationships with the groups mentioned above. Again, the form of those avenues should relate to the stated nature of the police department's relationships with citizens, community groups, and politicians. Demand enters the police organization through contacts with citizens while on patrol or in the precinct house, formal meetings (and collaborations) with community groups, citizen calls to 9-1-1, and local politicians. As such, that demand can be managed by upper-level command staff, other police personnel, politicians, the police department's communications division, or strategic crime units.

In a CPS strategy, demand enters the organization at all levels; line and mid-level police personnel have the authority and resources to work within limited geographic areas to manage and respond to that demand in a neighborhood-specific way. Additionally, under this strategy, police should increase contacts with citizens and community groups and prioritize calls for service based on seriousness and time since occurrence. Finally, avenues should be put into place by which line personnel are free from responding to non-emergency calls for service and can use that time to partake in other, community building and problem-solving activities.

## *Tactics, Technology, and Outcomes*

Although multiple tactics and technologies can be used to fulfill any number of outcomes, functions, missions, or strategies, understanding how a police department employs specific ones further evidences the type of strategy underlying a police department. Tactics can include preventive patrol, investigative operations, and rapid response to calls for service. Broken windows policing within a CPS strategy can incorporate many possible tactics including zero-tolerance policing, police-community meetings, foot patrol, arrests for misdemeanor offenses, and the use of a number of technologies. Braga and Bond (2008) and Braga et al. (1999) discuss other effective tactics used by police implementing broken windows policing as part of a problem-solving process (e.g., dealing with problem properties, civil remedies, collaborations with community groups, and environmental design changes). Police operations should include these tactics and evidence the proper use of technologies in support of them (such as, at CompStat). Though CompStat aids police departments in creating and holding commanders accountable for problem-solving strategies at the highest levels of the police organization, problem-solving at the line level often takes a different form (e.g., interacting with citizens, community groups, and other law enforcement or city agencies to respond to geographic hotspots of crime and disorder as determined by multiple data sources).

Broken windows policing is a tactic used by many departments to achieve reduced levels of crime, disorder, and fear and to increase citizen satisfaction with the police within a CPS strategy as assisted by a CompStat process. In addition to the usual outcomes of police work (i.e., crime control), a police department doing broken windows policing should also be concerned with citizens' views of the police department, crime, disorder, and the overall quality of life in their community.

The preceding elements of organizational strategy will be used to frame the analysis of each case, which includes how police personnel view their police organizations and the inhibitors and facilitators to change in each police department. A review of the literature on organizational change in police departments implementing the current strategy of policing follows.

# Organizational Change in Departments Implementing Community Problem-Solving

The literature on organizational change in police departments discusses the inhibitors (Moore, Thacher, Hartmann, Coles, & Sheingold, 1999; Zhao, Lovrich, & Thurman, 1999) and facilitators (Zhao et al., 1999; Mastrofski, 2006) of police innovation, generally, and as it regards CPS, specifically. Researchers use a variety of methods in studying this organizational change, including panel data collected from mailed surveys, a single case study, literature reviews, quasi-experimental analyses of secondary data, and comparative case studies. Researchers also explore the various macro-level and micro-level effects of the seven previously-listed elements on a changing organization and officers' perceptions of those effects. For instance, Zhao and Gray et al. (1995) relate post-materialist societal values to trooper, command staff, sergeant, and public support of community policing. Others examine how leadership, technology, resources, officer attitudes and education, organizational structure, and police culture facilitate or inhibit organizational change in police departments. Facilitators (training, organizational restructuring, and police leadership) and inhibitors (ineffective leadership, the police subculture, and a lack of resources) of change in police departments are discussed below.

## *Facilitators*

Comparing survey data from 1993 and 1996, Zhao et al. (1999, p.79) find four aspects of training that facilitate the implementation of community policing ("enhancement of overall performance skills, police-citizen collaboration in crime prevention efforts in the community, improvement of middle management skills, and improving police-community relations"). Their findings reveal a progression in training for community policing from 1993 to 1996, suggesting that the police departments surveyed continued to recognize the value of training for community policing. Similarly, in their case studies of ten police departments receiving Community-Oriented Policing Services (COPS) grants, Moore et al. (1999) note the importance of recruiting, hiring, training, and promotional procedures in thoroughly implementing community policing. Organizational restructuring enhances the benefits of these new human resource and personnel changes at both the organizational and the individual level.

Kim and Mauborgne (2003) demonstrate the New York Police Department's experience with redistributing officers' shifts, refocusing in what activities police spent their time, creating new bureaus, and pushing responsibility and authority down to the precinct commanders. A prominent feature of CPS policing is the decentralization of authority and responsibility. Departments that prudently restructure the organization (e.g., placing the right people in the right positions) reinforce the department's commitment to community policing as an organizational strategy. Research into organizational restructuring emphasizes the importance of such change to a successful adoption of community policing. Moore et al. (1999) show how re-designing the organizational, physical, and information-sharing infrastructure aids police departments in their move toward CPS. This restructuring not only provides the material resources and framework but also authenticates for police personnel the department's commitment to CPS policing. The value of line officer and supervisor beliefs that their leaders are authentic in their community policing undertaking becomes apparent when discussing the police subculture as a barrier to community policing implementation.

Police executive leadership is key to effective restructuring (Appelbaum, Everard, & Hung, 1999). As Skolnick and Bayley (1986, p. 9) discovered, "administrative leadership, an animating philosophy of values, can indeed effect change ... [altering] both the structure of police organization and the performance of street patrolmen." The bureaucratic, paramilitary organizational structure[5] of most police departments offers the chief executive officer (e.g., the police director, commissioner, chief) the authority to direct the actions of department personnel. Acting as both political representative to the community and decisive leader of their police organization, and by gaining the authority and trust of both groups, police leaders can institute radical changes in police departments (to include organizational restructuring, reallocation of resources, and revising the organization's mission) (see Skolnik & Bayley, 1986; Moore et al., 1999; Kim & Mauborgne, 2003). A savvy leader creates the logistical and cultural environments that inure department personnel to the CPS strategy.

---

5. Interestingly, the same bureaucratic, paramilitary structure that community policing challenges is helpful for police leaders trying to implement community policing strategies. As with other government institutions, leaders of an authoritarian structure can choose to democratize at will, but it also takes buy-in from personnel at all levels for lasting change to occur. See Wilson, J. (1989). *Bureaucracy: What Government Agencies Do and Why They Do It*. United States: Basic Books.

Committed and energetic leadership, the strategic use of technology, increased resources, personnel, and community buy-in, and restructuring the organization, recruiting, hiring, training, and promotional procedures facilitate change in police departments implementing CPS. Deficiencies in these areas will inhibit a police department's move toward community policing. For instance, research finds the internal structure of police departments, inadequate training in community policing values, a police leader's lack of clear vision for the department, insufficient resources, inefficient means of evaluating their community policing experiences, and a subculture resistant to change contribute to police departments' difficulties in implementing CPS (Skolnick & Bayley, 1986; Moore et al., 1999; Zhao et al. 1999).

## *Inhibitors*

While a bureaucratic, paramilitary organization aids police administrators in the initial push for CPS, the nature of the change (i.e., giving subordinates the freedom to innovate and holding them accountable for delivery of services to their precincts) demands widespread acceptance and buy-in from a range of department personnel.[6] As just mentioned, an insightful and persuasive leader can assist the department in making the necessary changes to facilitate the organization's move to community policing.[7]

Skolnick and Bayley (1986) discuss how the lack of a courageous, executive visionary can effectively stall any propensity an organization may have to CPS. The dual role of many current police chiefs as chief executive officer and political figure requires the police chief to balance their own convictions with a clear and compelling vision, while also ensuring an adroit rapport with their department as well as the wider community. Police leadership also influences other possible inhibitors to organizational change, including confusion over what is community oriented policing, organizational culture, "internal structure and operational impediments," a lack of resources, and unions (Zhao et al., 1999, p. 8).

Research often cites the police subculture as the most impenetrable element to change in a policing organization (Sparrow, 1988). Researchers, however, disagree defining police subculture and how it might affect personnel beliefs

---

6. See Kim & Mauborgne (2003) and Bratton & Knobler (1998) for the role of police leadership in working with limited acceptance of (and scant resources for) such change.

7. As already suggested, each of the facilitating and inhibiting elements interacts with the others to create differences in the speed and magnitude of an organization's successful adoption of CPS.

about organizational changes. In one of the most popular ethnographic studies of police subculture, Reuss-Ianni and Ianni (1983) discuss the two distinct cultures that arose in the New York City precinct they studied (i.e., street cop culture and management culture). Their research uncovers the social organization of police work at the precinct level, how formal policies and informal understandings interact to influence police behavior, and how each culture relates to their environments and negotiates their sometimes differing values to bring about change in the organization. Chan (1996), in her review of the police subculture literature, reconceptualizes the relationship between Reuss-Ianni and Ianni's cultural dichotomy and situates police work within a greater cultural, environmental, and socio-political environment.

Regardless of the strength researchers give to the police subculture, penetrating that subculture and using it to facilitate change is a key task for effective organizational change. The organization's ability to change and the manner of that change will depend on how police administrators perceive and mediate the gaps between street cop culture, management cop culture, and command culture. Fortunately, the structural changes and the philosophies that drive the CPS strategy (i.e., participatory decisionmaking and a transformation of command and control) are also stimulants for breaking down obstinate police subcultures and are facilitated by a strong police executive. Therefore, CPS-minded leaders should presumably be open to working with the other levels of police personnel in a manner most conducive to organizational and cultural change. Instead of viewing the subculture as a barrier to change, crafty police leaders should use that subculture as a conduit for their change (Appelbaum et al., 1999). Chappell (2009) holds that organizational restructuring should occur before, and therefore, instigate, cultural change—build it, and they will come.

Police chiefs can create the material conditions (i.e., organizational and information processing structures) that are best equipped to execute a CPS strategy. Even with such change, however, Zhao et al. (1999) mention civil service rules, police officer perceptions of community policing as too soft, and police union and line officer resistance as impeding an organization's change to community policing. Yet, a bright and politically astute police executive anticipates such difficulties and responds to them in a manner that illuminates his or her plan for the department and encourages union, police personnel, and community support for their innovation.

Kim and Mauborgne (2003) document how William Bratton, during his tenures as head of a number of policing agencies, successfully brought about rapid organizational change by overcoming cognitive, political, motivational, and resource hurdles. This type of leadership does more with less. Despite a lack of support from many line officers and managers, limited resources, and less than optimal enthusiasm from police personnel, William Bratton exemplified what Kim and Mauborgne call "tipping point leadership" (2003, p. 64), as he led the Massachusetts Bay Transit Authority, the Boston Police, the New York Transit Police, and then the New York Police Department.

One explanation of how police leaders may do more with less is that they more wisely and efficiently expend the resources they have. For instance, Chappell's (2009) observations of police officers on patrol revealed line officers' concerns that they could not do community policing because of a lack of personnel in their department. A successful police leader, however, works with their organization and citizenry to determine the most resourceful way to meet the most pressing needs of the community. Restructuring the organization and refocusing its mission results in a more efficient and effective use of resources and creates buy-in from department personnel and the community. Moore et al. (1999) demonstrate the merit of strong leadership in helping to overcome cultural and resource impediments in their case studies (see also, Sparrow, 1988).

Often cited as the element most resistant to change in the police organization, the police subculture can be influenced by each of the factors already mentioned (recruiting, hiring, training, promotional standards, organizational, restructuring, external grant money, and the strategic use of technologies to support the change). Getting police personnel to understand why changes are being made, how that change will occur, why change is beneficial to them and their organization, choosing an array of officers to include at all the stages of the change, and assuring them (through action) that change is real will help drive change in an organization otherwise characterized by an obstinate police subculture (Adams, Rohe, & Arcury, 2002). The organization must walk the talk. Clearly communicating the purpose and nature of the organizational change also facilitates that change. For instance, research into multinational corporations and other private organizations discusses the pivotal role of effective communication in combating rumors, reducing uncertainty, and maintaining trust to bring about change in those organizations (Appelbaum et al., 1999; DiFonzo & Bordia, 1998).

Police leaders can reinforce their commitment to change by realigning police performance and outcome measures (Alpert & Moore, 1997). A police organization may state their commitment to a specific philosophy or strategy (and the organization may even make moves toward that new strategy) but if the organization does not set up the avenues by which the department's and officers' performance will be measured, lasting change is unlikely. Instituting new ways of measuring police performance signals to police personnel that change is real and establishes channels for departments to reward officers who embody the new values, further affirming the new organizational philosophy.

# Summary

This section has outlined the central policing ideas that are discussed in this research and has explained past research on the policing experience as it relates to the various elements of a CPS organizational strategy. Facilitators and inhibitors to police organizational change in the CPS era were also discussed and give insight into this study's findings on the four departments' experiences with the CPS strategy. A useful way to explore how an organization adapts to specific strategies and tactics is by conducting case studies of police departments implementing such changes. The current research intends to better understand how the above-mentioned factors facilitate or impede organizational change and how each element works together in the CPS strategy. Since researcher and police interpretations of how best to implement certain strategies change in response to the times and environments in which they serve, the current examination of four police departments experiences will further add to the body of knowledge on police organizational change and the strides police departments have made in the CPS era. The following chapter describes the methods and methodology behind how we conducted this research.

# References

Alpert, G. & Moore, M. (1997). Measuring police performance in the new paradigm of policing. In R. Dunham, &. G. Moore (Eds.), *Critical Issues in Policing*, 3rd edition, pp. 265–281. Prospect Heights, Illinois: Waveland.

Andrews, K. (2003). The concept of corporate strategy. In N. Foss (Ed.), *Resources Firms and Strategies*. New York: Oxford.

Appelbaum. S., Everard, A., & Hung, L. (1999). Strategic downsizing: Critical success factors. *Management Decision*, 37:7, pp. 535–552.

Braga, A. & Bond, B. (2008). Police crime and disorder hotspots: A randomized controlled trial. *Criminology*, 46, pp. 577–607.

Braga, A., Kennedy, D., Waring, E., & Piehl, A. (2004). Problem-oriented policing, deterrence, and youth violence: An evaluation of Boston's Operation Ceasefire. *Journal of Research in Crime and Delinquency*, 38, 3, pp. 195–225.

Braga, A. & Weisburd, D. (2006). Problem-oriented policing: The disconnect between principles and practice. In D. Weisburd & A. Braga (Eds.), *Police Innovation: Contrasting Perspectives* (pp. 133–154). New York, NY: Cambridge.

Braga, A., Weisburd, D., Waring, E., Mazerolle, L., Spelman, W., & Gajewski, F. (1999). Problem-oriented policing in violent crime places: A randomized controlled experiment. *Criminology*, 37, pp. 541–580.

Bratton, W. & Knobler, P. (1998). *Turnaround: How America's top cop reversed
the crime epidemic*. New York: Random House.

Chan, J. (1996). Changing police culture. *British Journal of Criminology*. 36:1,
pp. 109–134

Chappell, A. (2009). The philosophical versus actual adoption of community
policing. *Criminal Justice Review*, 34, 1, pp. 5–28.

Clarke, R. (Ed.) (2002). Problem oriented policing, Case studies. National
Criminal Justice Research Services. Washington, D.C.: U.S. Department of
Justice.

DiFonzo, N., & Bordia, P. (1998). A tale of two corporations: Managing uncertainty during organizational change. *Human Resource Management*, 37,
3 & 4, pp. 295–303.

Eck, J. (2006). Science, values, and problem-oriented policing: Why problem-
oriented policing? In D. Weisburd & A. Braga (Eds.), *Police Innovation:
Contrasting Perspectives* (pp. 117–132). New York, NY: Cambridge.

Eck, J., & Spelman, W. (January 1987). Problem-solving: Problem-oriented
policing in Newport News. Research in Brief. Washington, D.C.: National
Institute of Justice Research in Brief.

Fagan, J. & Tyler, T. (2004). Policing, order maintenance and legitimacy. *Policing in Central and Eastern Europe: Dilemmas of Contemporary Criminal
Justice*, In G. Mesko & M. Pagon (Eds.), Slovenia: University of Maribo.

Gau, J. & Pratt, T. (2008). Broken windows or window dressing? Citizens'
(in)ability to tell the difference between disorder and crime. *Criminology
and Public Policy*, 7, pp. 163–194.

Glazer, N. (1979). On subway graffiti in New York. *Public Interest*.

Goldstein, H. (1979). Improving policing: A problem-oriented approach.
*Crime & Delinquency*, 25, 2, pp. 236–258.

Hope, T. (1994). Drug-market locations: Three case studies. In R. Clarke (Ed.),
*Crime Prevention Studies* (Vol. 2, pp. 5–32). Monsey, NY: Willow Tree.

Jacobs, J. (1961). *The death and life of great American cities*. New York: Vin-
tage Books.

Jenkins, M. (2011). The organizational strategies of police departments implementing
broken windows policing (Doctoral dissertation Rutgers University).

Kansas City Police Department (1977). Response time analysis: Executive summary. Kansas City, MO: Board of Commissioners.

Kelling, G. (1981). The Newark foot patrol experiment. Washington, DC: Police Foundation.

Kelling, G. (1989). A discussion of the concept of organizational strategy for use in 'planning and management' sequence, unpublished manuscript.

Kelling, G., & Moore, M. (November 1988). The evolving strategy of policing. Perspectives on Policing. National Institute Justice.

Kelling, G., Pate, T., Dieckman, D., & Brown, C. (1974). The Kansas City preventive patrol experiment: Technical report. Washington, DC: Police Foundation.

Kelling, G., & Sousa, W. (2001). Do police matter? An analysis of the impact of New York City's police reforms. *Civic Report*. New York: Manhattan Institute for Policy Research.

Kelling, G. & Wilson, J. (1982, March). Broken windows: The police and neighborhood safety. *The Atlantic Monthly*, pp. 29–38.

Kim, W. & Mauborgne, R. (April 2003) Tipping point leadership. *Harvard Business Review*.

Kubrin, C., Messner, S., Deane, G., McGeever, K., & Stucky, T. (2010). Proactive policing and robbery rates across U.S. cities. *Criminology*, 48, pp. 57–98.

Mastrofski, S. (2006). Police organization and management issues for the next decade. National Institute of Justice Policing Research Workshop: Planning for the Future. Washington, D.C.

Miller, W. (1977). *Cops and Bobbies: Police authority in New York and London, 1830–1870*. Chicago: University of Chicago.

Moore, M. (1992). Problem-solving and community policing. *Crime and Justice*. 15, pp. 99–158.

Moore, M., Sparrow, M., & Spelman, W. (1997). Innovations in policing: From production lines to job shops. In A. Altshuler, & R. Behn (Eds.), *Innovations in American Government: Challenges, Opportunities, and Dilemmas*. Washington, DC: Brookings Institute.

Moore, M., Thacher, D., Hartmann, F., Coles, C., & Sheingold, P. (1999, March). Case studies of the transformation of police departments: A cross-site analysis. (Harvard University) Retrieved from http://www.hks.harvard.edu/criminaljustice/publications/cops_csa.pdf.

Reisig, M. (2010). Community and problem-oriented policing. *Crime and Justice*, 39, pp. 1–53.

Reuss-Ianni, E, & Ianni, F. (1983). Street cops and management cops: The two cultures of policing, in Newburn, T. (Ed.), (2005). *Policing: Key Readings* (pp. 297–314). Portland: Willan.

Sampson, R. & Scott, &. M. (2000). Tackling crime and other public-safety problems: Case studies of problem-solving. Community Oriented Policing Services. Washington, D.C.: U.S. Department of Justice.

Shi, L. (2009). The limits of oversight in policing: Evidence from the 2001 Cincinnati riot. *Journal of Public Economics*, 93, pp. 99–113.

Skogan, W. (1990). *Disorder and decline: Crime and the spiral of decay in American cities.* Los Angeles: University of California.

Skogan, W. (2006). *Police and community in Chicago: A tale of three cities.* New York, NY: Oxford University Press.

Skolnick, J., & Bayley, D. (1986). *The new blue line: Police innovation in six American cities.* New York: The Free Press.

Sparrow, M. (November 1988). Implementing community policing. *Perspectives on Policing*, 9, pp. 1–12.

Trojanowicz, R. (1982). An evaluation of the Neighborhood Foot Patrol Program in Flint, Michigan. East Lansing, MI: Michigan State University.

Tyler, T. (2002). A national survey for monitoring police legitimacy. *Justice Research & Policy*, 4 1, pp. 71–86.

Wagers, M., Sousa, W., & Kelling, G. (2008). Broken windows. In R. Wortley, & L. Mazerolle (Eds.), *Environmental Criminology and Crime Analysis* (pp. 247–261). Portland: Willan.

Weisburd, D., Mastrofski, S., Greenspan, R., & Willis, J. (2004). Growth of compstat in American policing. Washington, D.C.: The Police Foundation.

Weisburd, D., Telep, C., Hinkle, J., and Eck, J. (2010). Is problem-oriented policing effective in reducing crime and disorder? *Criminology and Public Policy*, 9, 1, pp. 139–172.

Willis, J. J., Mastrofski, S. D., & Weisburd, D. (2007), Making sense of CompStat: A theory-based analysis of organizational change in three police departments. *Law & Society Review*, 41, pp. 147–188.

Wilson, J. (1968). *Varieties of police behavior: The management of law and order in eight communities.* Cambridge, MA: Harvard University Press.

Wilson, J. (1989). *Bureaucracy: What government agencies do and why they do it.* United States: Basic Books

Zhao, J., & Gray, K.(1995). Moving toward community policing: The role of postmaterialist values in a changing police profession, *American Journal of Police*, 14, 3/4, pp. 151–172.

Zhao, J., Lovrich, N., & Thurman, Q. (1999). The status of community policing in American cities. *Policing: An International Journal of Police Strategies and Management*, 22, 1, pp. 74–92.

Zimbardo, P. (1970). The human choice: Individuation, reason, and order versus deindividuation, impulse, and chaos. In W. Arnold & D. Levine (Eds.), 1969, *Nebraska Symposium on Motivation*. Lincoln, NE: University of Nebraska.

# Chapter 2

# Methods and Methodology

## The Purpose of This Research

Scholars debate the role of CPS and broken windows policing in lowering crime rates, but few can dispute the role that these have had on the policing world. A large majority of police departments have implemented or are implementing some form of CPS (Skogan, 2006; Hickman & Reaves, 2001; Erickson, 1998). An understanding of how police departments (and police personnel) interpret the current era of policing and the ways in which they use CPS to drive their departments forward is useful in clarifying the nebulous idea of CPS.

The current study presents the findings of in-depth case studies of four medium-to-large police departments. As stated in Chapter 1, police respond differently to shifting environments. A study conducted on innovations in community policing in the first decade of the twenty-first century (i.e., in a post-9/11 world) will offer different insights into the concept of CPS than studies conducted in the 1980s or 1990s. The conditions to which police respond and the environments in which they work change over time. This study, then, offers a snapshot of four police departments' recent experiences in this new CPS strategy.

While previous research has "disregarded the importance of history, process, and the temporal dimensions of organizations," (King, 2009, p. 213) the current study's review of past research and a retrospective analysis of the four departments' experiences enhances this study's contribution to the field by "including time and process," (King, 2009, p. 229) and "introducing an historical and temporal element to organizational studies" (King, 2009, p. 232). Quantitative data and one-time surveys and questionnaires alone do not fully portray the contextualized experiences of police departments implementing CPS policing.

This book, rooted in previous research on organizational change in police departments, explores how police departments implement broken windows policing as part of an adaptation of a CPS organizational strategy, describes how police personnel view the effect of this shift on police work, and suggests barriers and facilitators to a successful implementation of CPS policing. This study focuses on three major research questions:

1. What are the organizational shifts in a police department as it moves into the new CPS strategy (as evidenced by changes in their legitimacy, function, organizational structure, administrative process, external relationships, demand, technologies, tactics, and outcomes)?
2. How do police personnel view the effect of this shifting strategy on the work they do?
3. Which elements in the police organization facilitate or inhibit such an implementation?

# Methods

This study uses mixed methods to:

1. focus on in-depth interviews, personal observation, surveys, and archival data;
2. report on and interpret in detail the perspectives of key police personnel as they relate to the shifting organizational strategy; and
3. triangulate personal observation, archival data, interview data and survey data (Creswell, 1998; Miles & Huberman, 1994; Yin, 2003).

We follow the case study methodology. This is appropriate because the primary concern is obtaining detailed, in-depth analyses and multiple, multifaceted perspectives within a particular setting. This approach will be helpful in investigating discrepancies between the police departments' stated values and actual organizational changes (Sjoberg, Williams, & Sjoberg, 1991; Stake, 1995; Creswell, 1998; Weisburd, Mastrofski, McNally, Greenspan, & Willis, 2003; Yin, 2003; Weisburd & Braga, 2006).

## *Sampling Strategies*

The purposive and convenience sample in this study consists of four medium-to-large, urban police departments. The four departments (Boston, Los Angeles, Milwaukee, and Newark) were purposely chosen based on knowledge of their varied experiences with implementing broken windows policing as part of a wider departmental move toward CPS, an understanding of the leadership capabilities of their police executives, and a reasonable expectation of access to department personnel and data.[1] Characteristics of the four departments and the cities they serve add to the strength of this study's findings. While each department polices within an urban setting, their cities are distinguished by geographic, demographic, and socio-economic factors.[2,3]

Though the purposive and convenient sample of police departments in this research does not offer itself to the same levels of generalizability as more rigorous random sampling techniques, past research on police organizations demonstrates the merit of conducting case study research on such a sample. The extensive accessibility of the departments and the time and resource constraints of having only one researcher to collect data at each of the cities justify the use of these methods in this study. Similarly, this research uses convenience, purposive, and snowball sampling techniques to obtain interviews with the police departments' high-ranking personnel.

The main data collection source is face-to-face interviews with key personnel within the police departments (each lasting between twenty-five and ninety-five minutes). With initial assistance of our department contact, a purposive and snowball sampling method was used to select interview participants from each of the police departments based upon their history with (and the positions held within) the department. From the beginning, the contact persons within the department asked the researcher to please inform them of any personnel he was interested in interviewing. The researcher and contact person, together, created a list of key personnel with whom to speak. These personnel presumably have greater insight into the institutions' histories and are in positions that give them knowledge of the departments' organizational strategies.

A semi-structured interview guide focused on specific questions concerning the shifting organizational strategy of the police department and on respondents' views of the effects of broken windows policing on their organizations and communities. Using a convenience sampling method to obtain interviewees lends itself (initially) to the whim and agenda of the contact person within each department. Arguably, this person may wish to present the police department in a favorable light. However, the methods discussed above and the use of snowball sampling help to offset this possibility by giving the researcher

---

1. Knowledge of these departments' experiences with broken windows policing in the CPS strategy comes from guidance given to the author by his dissertation advisor, Dr. George Kelling, who has worked as a consultant for each department.

2. These differences are explained in more depth in the following chapters.

3. See Willis, Mastrofski, & Weisburd (2004) for a further discussion of their choice of similarly situated cities (Lowell, MA; Minneapolis, MN; and Newark, NJ) as case studies for their research on the role of CompStat on organizational change.

the opportunity to choose interviewees and to have interviewees refer other personnel to participate in the semi-structured interview. Furthermore, the triangulation of archival data from within and outside the police department, a survey of sworn personnel, adherence to the chain of evidence, and maintenance of proper documentation of the coding rationale assist in systematically portraying each case.

## Survey Methodology

Surveys were administered in Milwaukee and Newark police departments[4] to obtain personnel's views of their mission. Because the survey data is used to triangulate data in this study and response rates in the police departments were low, the survey reports results from a non-probabilistic (convenience) sample and, consequently, no significance tests were run. Thus, conclusions from this survey data represent only this study's sample of personnel's interpretations of their police departments' missions.

The survey content (intended to measure respondents' views of their police departments' missions) included tenets of broken windows policing offered by Wagers, Sousa, and Kelling (2008). These items measure the individual beliefs about the various elements of their police departments' CPS strategy. The first question is the only open-ended question on the survey and assessed the respondents' unfiltered views of their missions. The remaining closed-ended, Likert scale questions helped to determine the extent to which sworn personnel agree with or view as important to their police department's mission specific assumptions and tactics relevant to the study. Because many of the data sources in this study (i.e., interviews, observations of crime strategy meetings, and departmental archives) relate more to command level views of the police department, efforts were made to gather mid- and low-level personnel's (i.e., police officer's) views in this survey. Therefore, the researcher administered the survey online (in both Milwaukee and Newark) and at shift roll calls (in Newark).

Despite the cooperation of the police departments and the researcher's best efforts (e.g., attending all three shifts' roll calls for five days straight in Newark), the response rates for this survey are not ideal. Theoretically, all sworn personnel had access to the survey in either paper format or via a link to an online survey. In Milwaukee, the link to the survey was sent to the work e-mail accounts of all sworn personnel and posted on both physical and virtual roll

---

4. A lack of cooperation from police unions in Boston prevented a survey to that department's personnel. We could not survey those in the LAPD.

call boards in the department. Surveys in Newark were administered at various roll calls and sent to all sworn-personnel above the rank of police officer. In all instances, respondents were reminded of their police executive's support of the study. The samples' respondents account for about 5% and 10% of the sworn personnel in the Milwaukee and Newark police departments (respectively), and a majority of the sample's respondents from each survey were from the rank of patrol officer (52.3% in Milwaukee; 66.1% in Newark).

Apart from logistical challenges to administering a department-wide survey, researchers discuss the suspicions that police personnel may have about how such a survey may be used (Paoline, 2001). However, a concise statement regarding the purpose of the survey, an assurance that the survey is completely confidential and anonymous, and the use of a focused survey tool (in some instances, administered online) help to allay these suspicions. Furthermore, although the researcher's efforts to reach the lower levels of the organization in Newark (by attending roll calls) resulted in a greater response rate, one must consider the implications of the different collection methods on responses. For instance, Newark police officers filling out paper surveys at the end of their roll calls (many times while standing in front of a supervisor's roll call desk) might be less forthcoming than officers in Milwaukee who had the option to fill out an online survey in the privacy of their own homes. To respond to this potentiality, the researcher (and the police officer supervisors in Newark) did give officers the option to take the paper survey with them and return it at the end of their shift. Along those same lines, although the online survey format can facilitate more honest responses, it may preclude personnel who are not as comfortable giving information on a computer. The final sections of this chapter discuss how these data sources help to build the case in each site and how the cases are analyzed.

## *Building the Cases*

Because of the sensitive nature of some of the data (i.e., chief's memos, general orders, observations of command staff meetings, and personal accounts of officers) and to protect participant confidentiality, all hardcopies, audio recordings, and other electronic documents are stored in a locked office on a password-protected computer. Furthermore, audio recordings and typed computer documents are identified by an alphanumeric code (i.e., BOS-01). Except for the police executives themselves, all names in here are pseudonymous. We did attempt to reflect the *overall* representation of respondent sex and ethnicity.

Initial site visits oriented the researcher to the physical and social layouts of this study's four police departments and included ride-alongs with police officers and sergeants, observations of intradepartmental meetings, and introductory conversations with personnel within the department. Two more visits to each police department followed and consisted of more intensive interviews and focused data collection. Throughout all visits, the researcher was cognizant of his presentational strategy and mostly balanced the roles of the "socially acceptable incompetent" and "selective competence" in response to the corresponding interactions.[5] These strategies are important in gathering the most accurate qualitative data (especially in police departments) (Lofland, Snow, Anderson, & Lofland, 2006 p. 68–70).

This study includes a total of eighty-six interviews conducted with the open-ended, semi-structured interview guide. Of those, seventy were also audio-recorded with the respondents' explicit permission. There are nearly 40 hours of audio recordings from these interviews. The remaining semi-structured interviews do not have recordings for various reasons that include one respondent's refusal to give permission, technological difficulties, and circumstances in which the researcher did not request to have the interview recorded due to a noisy environment (i.e., a crowded restaurant at lunch time), or because he believed that doing so might inhibit the respondent's candidness (for example, when interviewing the police director). In all of these cases, notes were taken during the interviews or immediately following the interview and coded in the same manner as the other interview data. Conversations with other police department personnel (including discussions with police officers during ride-alongs and with non-sworn personnel while in between appointments) provided additional insight into the departments and are used to contextualize and corroborate the police department-assigned interviews. These conversations were less formal, more organic, and every bit as rich as the more formal, planned interviews. They took place in a variety of settings (e.g., restaurants, bars, and police cars), and there are no audio recordings. These data sources, along with the ability to request formal interviews and the snowball sampling technique, strengthen the initially convenient interview sample.

We attempted to administer surveys to all current, sworn personnel. The survey gauges respondents' views on their police departments' missions by asking respondents to assign a level of importance or agreement to beliefs, tactics,

---

5. Such presentations help both the researcher and police personnel to negotiate their data collecting and information-revealing relationship. The researcher must have enough understanding about the environment he studies to ask the right questions and to maintain his appropriate place as an outside researcher in the police department. The researcher must be selective in portraying his knowledge, however, so as to not inhibit the police personnel from offering information that they might assume the researcher already knows.

and understandings commonly discussed in research of community problem-solving and broken windows policing. The survey was administered using already established avenues (for example, on the internet at Surveymonkey.com in the Milwaukee Police Department and at roll calls in the Newark Police Department). Documents (i.e., general orders, chief's bulletins, memoranda of understanding, newspaper articles, annual reports, directives, and strategic action plans), personal observations, and survey data corroborate and rebut interview and survey data, and, with the semi-structured interviews, demonstrate: (1) from where police receive their authorization; (2) the police function; (3) the organizational structure; (4) the administrative processes; (5) how police relate to the community; (6) from where the demand for police service arises and how that demand is managed; and (7) the tactics, technology, and outcomes used by the departments.

The researcher was granted what is perceived to be a great amount of access to a variety of documents. In each site, he was given hours of access to sit alone on a department computer and explore the departments' intranet files or in a room with cabinets filled with historical and current internal documents. In many instances, he could take the files with him in hardcopy and/or electronic format; at other times, the department contact put information on CDs to make the data more portable. The interview schedules were initially set up by the police department contact person, which can presumably lead to biased samples of interviewees. However, the contact person also assisted the researcher in obtaining interviews with other department personnel at the researcher's request (for example, when respondents suggested other personnel with whom to speak or when the researcher thought a certain perspective would enrich his study).

The case study of the Newark Police Department (hereafter, NPD) was built using 21 audio-recorded semi-structured interviews, semi-structured interviews without audio-recordings, informal conversations with department personnel, an online and paper-pencil survey of 128 sworn personnel, observations of two CompStat meetings and one Intelligence Meeting, over 230 General Orders, approximately 5,000 online news and blog articles, and other department documents (e.g., draft community relations handbook and gun and violence strategies Powerpoint presentations). Intensive research visits to the NPD took place from 18 January 2010 to 22 January 2010, from 24 May 2010 to 26 May 2010, and from 15 September 2010 to 19 September 2010.

The Boston Police Department (hereafter, BPD) case study consists of twelve audio-recorded semi-structured interviews, semi-structured interviews without audio-recordings, informal conversations with department personnel, observations on ride-alongs with patrol car units, walk-alongs with the Safe Streets Team, an IMPACT meeting and meetings of captains and commanders of the

BPD's Safe Streets Teams, nearly 1,500 online local news articles, and unrestricted access to the BPD archives (which include annual reports, chiefs' memos, community presentations, and strategic planning committee reports). Disagreement among the various unions prompted the police commissioner to prohibit this researcher from administering a survey to their personnel. Though the Office of the Police Commissioner was willing to assist, union representatives cite two reasons for not allowing the researcher to administer surveys (a fear that the information obtained from a survey can be used negatively against their personnel and a desire to keep their personnel from becoming "survey monkeys," expected to assist with the many requests they receive for survey data). A field orientation was held at the BPD from 27 April 2009 to 28 April 2009 and intensive research visits took place from 17 August 2009 to 19 August 2009 and from 27 May 2010 to 28 May 2010.

The Milwaukee Police Department (hereafter, MPD) case study consists of 17 audio-recorded semi-structured interviews, semi-structured interviews without audio-recordings, informal conversations with department personnel, an online survey of 99 sworn personnel, observations on ride-alongs with patrol car units and of two CompStat meetings and morning crime briefings, just under 5,000 online local news articles, and unrestricted access to the MPD intranet (which included annual reports, chiefs' memos, a police personnel blog, brainstorming papers, and CompStat and strategy Powerpoint presentations). A field orientation was held at the MPD from 18 March 2009 to 22 March 2009 in which the researcher was introduced to key MPD personnel, became acquainted with the structure of the MPD within the city, and became familiarized with the sources of archival data that would be made available. Intensive research visits took place from 20 July 2009 to 24 July 2009 and from 16 June 2010 to 18 June 2010.

The case study for the Los Angeles Police Department (hereafter, LAPD) is made up of 20 audio-recorded semi-structured interviews, semi-structured interviews without audio-recordings, informal conversations with department personnel, observations of automobile patrol, foot patrol, and horseback units, a CompStat meeting, a community meeting with the Watts Gang Task Force, a meeting of the Board of Police Commissioners, online local news articles, and access to the LAPD intranet (which included annual reports, chiefs' memos, and brainstorming papers). A field orientation was held at the LAPD from 25 February 2009 to 28 February 2009 in which the researcher was introduced to key personnel within the LAPD, became acquainted with the structure of the LAPD within the city, and became familiarized with the sources of archival data that would be made available. An intensive research visit took place from 5 December 2010 to 11 December 2010.

## *Analyzing the Cases*

After building each of the four cases in Chapters 4, 5, 6, and 7, Chapter 8 explores the magnitude and manner of change within each police department. Chapter 9 then presents an overview of the current policing landscape (what we refer to as the New Community Problem-Solving era) and offers implications for police departments and insight into the common facilitators and inhibitors to the implementation of the New Community Problem-Solving strategy.

Data from each case are organized within the framework of the elements of organizational strategy and then are analyzed for the magnitude of change that the department demonstrates within each. This model borrows from Eck and Stern (1992) (as used in Moore, Thacher, Hartmann, Coles, & Sheingold [1999], in their analysis of ten police departments). Eck and Stern (1992) (in Moore et al., 1999, p. 5) argue that improved problem-solving efforts and "improved efforts at developing and sustaining 'community partnerships'" demonstrate a departments' move toward CPS. Moore et al. (1999, p. 5) characterize the magnitude of change "in terms of how likely it seemed that the changes would be sustained over time." Our study applies their framework to each of the elements of organizational strategy to determine a department's observed magnitude of change and gives specific examples of each element's change within the four police departments.

The interview transcripts were analyzed using the coding and node schemes offered by NVivo 8.0 (a computerized qualitative data-management program). The NVivo 8.0 software facilitates the management, coding, and querying of electronic data. It is used in place of filing cabinets, folders, highlighter markers, and sticky notes to organize the multiple sources of data for each case, to electronically highlight patterns, themes, and/or areas of interest (as recognized by the researcher's understanding of the data). The software also allows for electronic searches of documents within and among each case.

The data analysis process includes a coding scheme that derives from a provisional start list of codes stemming from research questions and the areas of inquiry (i.e., legitimacy, function, structure and process, etc.). Initial readings of the interviews, onsite observations, and the organizational strategy framework revealed a number of "nodes" to the researcher. They include administrative processes, broken windows policing, community, community-oriented policing, data, demand for services, discretion, external relationships, ineffective strategies, internal affairs, leadership, legitimacy, patrol and investigative divide, personnel, police function, political context, resistance to change, resources, restructure, scandal, technology, training, and a general interest node.

Text searches for each node and coding any missed, relevant material into their corresponding nodes served to clean the data. Then, again using NVivo 8.0, the researcher ran a query to include all places coded at "broken windows" and any of the other nodes (for example, a query for all Newark interview data coded at "broken windows" and "CompStat" or "culture" or "internal affairs"). For ease of reading and analysis purposes, data were queried in groups of five (such as the grouping in the previous example) for each case. A query of places coded at only "broken windows" was also conducted and those few results were placed in the other queries. In Newark, for example, this process resulted in a collection of approximately 273 pages of interview data. The researcher then went through each interview and copied and pasted each relevant section into a word processing document, color-coded by interview code and organized in an outline form. This returned a word processing document of 136 pages for Newark. After further analyzing these data, the researcher pared down the interviews to a 33-page word processing document that serves as the immediate base for these research findings. A similar analysis of internal and external documents (i.e., general orders, strategic plans, online newspaper articles, and blogs[6]) and survey data (except in Boston and Los Angeles) are used to triangulate the interview data. Pattern coding helps to "understand the patterns, the recurrences, the plausible whys ... [and] identify an emergent theme, configuration, or explanation" (Miles & Huberman, 1994, p. 69). The codes were used to make contrasts and comparisons among data sources, summarize themes, provide varying explanations of those patterns, and, in particular, analyze how departments adapt their organizational strategies to accommodate and implement broken windows policing within the CPS era. Even with the NVivo 8.0 software, the researcher is still responsible for translating "raw information into interpretation, combining evidence with insight" (Agranoff & Radin, 1992, p. 215).

## *Strengths and Weaknesses of the Current Research*

Methodologists across fields recognize the value of using mixed methods and offer frameworks for conducting rigorous (qualitative and quantitative) case studies (see, Yin, 1981; Agranoff & Radin, 1991; Rossman, 1993; Ander-

---

6. While the use of blogs and online users' comments sections might raise methodological concerns for some researchers, this study uses them much like the use of lie detector tests in police hiring decisions. That is, not as definitive sources of inherently reliable information, but rather, as an indicator of other possible areas of inquiry in building a case.

son, 1996; Clarke, 1997; Moore et al., 1999; Shadish, Cook, & Campbell, 2002). The organizational, public administration, and policing literature discuss the advantages and possible disadvantages of conducting this type of research. Many of these studies cite Yin's (2003) seminal work that describes the value of the case study design and methods when asking "how" and "why" questions.

Yin (2003, p. 13) defines the case study as "an empirical inquiry that investigates a contemporary phenomenon within its real-life context." As the definition suggests, an advantage of conducting a case study includes the ability to contextualize a phenomenon (Yin, 2003). For example, as the gold standard, randomized experimental design may be useful in finding statistically significant relationships between variables but does not reveal the manner in which two variables might interact. Similarly, complex statistical testing attempts to ferret out relationships between multiple variables (separate from the phenomenon studied) and fails to describe or anticipate the social and contextual phenomena that affect those relationships. As Shadish et al. (2002, p. 478) argue, qualitative methods and the case study methodology "have unrivaled strengths for the elucidation of meanings, the in-depth description of cases, [and] the discovery of new hypotheses." The case study firmly embeds its data in the context of the case material, and, therefore, necessarily includes a richer understanding of the relationships between variables (Agranoff & Radin, 1991). The current study responds to others' concerns for "context sensitivity," unwraps the elusive "black box" that often arises in evaluations of police activities and, in so doing, suggests areas of inquiry for future researchers (Eck, 2010, p. 863; Braga, Kennedy, Waring, & Piehl, 2004).

Case study research gives the researcher access to in-depth knowledge and understandings of personnel within specific contexts and allows the researcher to use a site's original documents to look beyond respondents' interpretations of certain phenomena to gain a more accurate picture of the phenomena studied (Agranoff & Radin, 1991). DiFonzo and Bordia (1998) used two case studies to examine organizational change in the private sector; Agranoff and Radin (1992) champion the use of the comparative case study for research in public administration; and a number of rigorous and compelling case studies have been conducted in the policing arena, specifically with regard to innovation and change within police departments (Skolnick & Bayley, 1986; Kelling & Coles, 1996; Greene, 1999; Moore et al., 1999; Clarke, 2002; Willis et al., 2004; Chappell, 2009). The case study methodology suits the current study of shifting organizational strategies within four police departments. As Yin (2003) notes, the multiple case design (within the case study methodology) makes the findings even more robust.

Finally, researchers champion a cross-case analysis in the synthesis of "general patterns, themes, metaphors, and images across the cases through the processes of comparison and contrast" (Rossman, 1993, p. 11). Anderson (1996) employs Rossman's analysis process in his cross-case analysis of curriculum reform (similar processes are discussed in Yin, 1981; Agranoff & Radin, 1991; Moore et al., 1999). Yin (1981) analogizes both the single case and cross-case analysis to (appropriately enough) detective work:

> Presented with the scene of a crime, its description, and possible reports from eye-witnesses, the detective must constantly make decisions regarding the relevance of various data ... the adequate explanation for the crime then becomes a plausible rendition of a motive, opportunity, and method that more fully accounts for the facts than do alternative explanations. (p. 61)

Regarding the cross-case analysis, he continues:

> Modification may be necessary in applying the explanation to the second case, and the detective must learn to ignore irrelevant variations from case to case. How the detective carries out this work in (a) constructing an adequate explanation for each case singly, and (b) knowing the acceptable levels of modification in the original explanation as new cases are encountered is analogous to a researcher conducting a cross-case analysis. (Yin, 1981, p. 63) (see also Agranoff & Radin, 1991, p. 219)

Yin's analogy illustrates the task of conducting a cross-case analysis and implies the immense amount of rigor, critical analysis, and impartiality required of the researcher.

Such reliance on the capabilities of the researcher is one of the possible weaknesses of qualitative case study methods, as the researcher holds certain biases, loyalties, preconceptions, and analytic constraints. Other possible disadvantages of case study research include the perception that case studies do not follow rigorous, standardized and unbiased procedures, the inability to generalize case study findings (i.e., external validity), and the large amount of time it takes to conduct adequate case studies that usually end up as lengthy, unreadable documents (Yin, 2003). While the findings of the current research may not be statistically generalizable, they are analytically generalizable and, therefore, useful to police departments and their leaders when deciding among possible paths on which to move their organizations (Yin, 2003).

# Summary

We present a snapshot of the vast activities of the organizations (as observed by the researcher) during a few points in their recent experiences of change (Manning, 2008). While the findings from this research cannot offer ironclad prescriptions for police administrators, the rigorous and comprehensive (yet specific) case study and cross-case analysis clarify for researchers and administrators how police department personnel view a CPS strategy, offer a contextualized look into implementing such change, and explain ways that four departments adapted their organization to the Community Problem-Solving Era. Though this study does not offer findings from a random sample of police departments (or even of the personnel within those departments), the in-depth exploration of these four departments' experiences within the CPS strategy allows readers of this analysis to consider their own experiences in relation to those presented here and to adapt these findings to their organization as they see fit. This is, after all, the way that police and the citizenry have always negotiated their relationships and responsibilities to each other.

# References

Agranoff, R., & Radin, R. (1991). The comparative case study approach in public administration. Research in Public Administration, 1, pp. 203–231.

Anderson, R. (October 1996). Study of curriculum reform. U.S. Department of Education, Office of Educational Research and Improvement. Retrieved from http://www2.ed.gov/pubs/SER/CurricReform/title.html.

Braga, A., Kennedy, D., Waring, E., & Piehl, A. (2004). Problem-oriented policing, deterrence, and youth violence: An evaluation of Boston's Operation Ceasefire. *Journal of Research in Crime and Delinquency*, 38, 3, pp. 195–225.

Chappell, A. (2009). The philosophical versus actual adoption of community policing. *Criminal Justice Review*, 34, 1, pp. 5–28.

Clarke, R. (Ed.). (1997). *Situational Crime Prevention: Successful Case Studies*, 2nd edition. Monsey, NY: Criminal Justice Press.

Clarke, R. (Ed.). (2002). Problem oriented policing, Case studies. National Criminal Justice Research Services. Washington, D.C.: U.S. Department of Justice.

Creswell, J. (1998). *Qualitative inquiry and research design: Choosing among five traditions*. Thousand Oaks: Sage.

DiFonzo, N., & Bordia, P. (1998). A tale of two corporations: Managing uncertainty during organizational change. *Human Resource Management,* 37, 3 & 4, pp. 295–303.

Eck, J. (2010). Policy is in the details: Using external validity to help policy makers. *Criminology & Public Policy,* 9, pp. 859–866.

Eck, J. & Stern, D. (1992). Revisiting community policing: A new typology, paper presented to the National Institute of Justice.

Erickson, T. (1998). Community policing: The process of transitional change. *The FBI Law Enforcement Bulletin,* 67, 6, pp. 16–21.

Greene, J. (April 1999). Zero tolerance: A case study of police policies and practices in New York City. *Crime and Delinquency,* 45, 2, pp. 171–187.

Hickman, M., & Reaves, B. (February 2001). Community policing in local police departments: 1997 and 1999. Bureau of Justice Statistics. Washington, D.C.: U.S. Department of Justice.

Kelling, G., & Coles, C. (1996). *Fixing broken windows: Restoring order and reducing crime in our communities.* New York: Free Press.

King, W. (2009). Toward a life-course perspective of policing organizations. *Journal of Research in Crime and Delinquency,* 46, pp. 213–244.

Lofland, J., Snow, D., Anderson, L., & Lofland, L. (2006). *Analyzing social settings: A guide to qualitative observation and analysis.* Belmont: Wadsworth.

Manning, P. (2008). *The technology of policing.* New York: NYU.

Miles, M. & Huberman, A. (1994). *Qualitative data analysis,* 2nd ed. Thousand Oaks: Sage.

Moore, M., Thacher, D., Hartmann, F., Coles, C., & Sheingold, P. (1999, March). *Case studies of the transformation of police departments: A cross-site analysis,* Harvard University. Retrieved from http://www.hks.harvard.edu/ criminaljustice/publications/cops_csa.pdf.

Paoline, E. (2001). *Rethinking police culture: Officers' occupational attitudes,* New York: LFB Scholarly.

Rossman, G. (1993). Building explanations across case studies: A framework for synthesis, a report for the Curriculum Reform Project, US Department of Education.

Shadish, W., Cook, T., & Campbell, D. (2002) *Experimental and quasi-experimental designs for generalized causal inference.* New York: Houghton Mifflin.

Sjoberg, G., Williams, N., Vaughan, T., & Sjoberg, A. (1991). The case study approach in social research. In J. Feagin, A. Orum, & G. Sjoberg (Eds.) *A Case for Case Study* (pp. 27–79). Chapel Hill: University of North Carolina.

Skogan, W. (2006). The promise of community policing. In D. Weisburd & A. Braga (Eds.), *Police Innovation: Contrasting Perspectives*. Cambridge: Cambridge University Press.

Skolnick, J., & Bayley, D. (1986). *The new blue line: Police innovation in six American cities*. New York: The Free Press.

Stake, R. (1995). *The art of case study research*. Thousand Oaks, CA: Sage Publications.

Wagers, M., Sousa, W., & Kelling, G. (2008). Broken windows. In R. Wortley, & L. Mazerolle (Eds.), *Environmental Criminology and Crime Analysis* (pp. 247–261). Portland: Willan.

Weisburd, D. and Braga, A. (2006). Introduction: Understanding police innovation. In D. Weisburd and A. Braga (Eds.) *Police Innovation: Contrasting Perspectives*. Cambridge: Cambridge University Press.

Weisburd, D., Mastrofski, S., Greenspan, R., and Willis, J. (2004). Growth of compstat in American policing. Washington, D.C.: The Police Foundation.

Weisburd, D., Mastrofski, S., McNally, A., Greenspan, R., and Willis, J. (2003). Reforming to preserve: CompStat and strategic problem solving in American policing. *Criminology and Public Policy*, 2, 3, pp. 421–456.

Yin, R. (March 1981). The case study crisis: Some answers. *Administrative Science Quarterly*, 26, 1, pp. 58–65.

Yin, R. (2003). *Case study research, design and methods*, 3rd ed. Newbury Park: Sage.

# Chapter 3

# The History of Community Problem-Solving in Each Department

## The Recurring Renaissance: Newark's Community Problem-Solving History

Newark, NJ, rests just ten miles from New York City, on the Port of Newark, and is accessible by the Passaic River. Its history is intertwined with the growth and decline of industry that arose from Newark's convenient and accessible metropolitan location. The constant challenges that mark Newark's history and its attempts to face them are described in various terms—renaissance, re-birth, resurgence, and revitalization. Among those challenges are a declining economy, rising violent crime rates, race riots, and incompetent governance.

Settled by the Puritans in the seventeenth century, Newark welcomed set-tlers of a variety of Christian backgrounds. Visitors to Newark in the 1830s describe Newark as "'wonderfully altered ... [and as a] strong arm of indus-try'" and speak of its people as "'remarkably industrious,'" always in the shadow of the world's greatest big city—New York City (*History of the City of Newark*). As Newark continued to grow, its diverse populations (i.e., Italians, Germans, Jews, Poles, and Lithuanians) settled in different areas of the city. While many of these distinct neighborhoods survive today, their diversification includes Blacks, Portuguese, Brazilian and other Hispanic groups. The most drastic change in Newark's demographics took place in the 1960s when newly arriv-ing Blacks from the South began to recognize their disenfranchised and infe-rior position in Newark's socio-economic-political system.

The 1967 race riots in Newark, as in other cities, marked a clear distinction in the trajectory of Newark's history. Middle-class and White residents fled the turmoil of Newark's streets for the safer suburbs, taking with them their social and economic investments. This began a steady decline in the quality of life for

Newark's citizens. A 1968 Report for Action commissioned by then-governor Richard Hughes suggested reforms in police-community relations as a way to prevent future disorder in the city (Liebman, 2007). However, incorrigible, incompetent leadership hurt Newark's ability to rebound from the traumatic experiences of the 1960s. As this study demonstrates, Newark has yet to implement some of the forty-year-old suggestions.

In 1975 *Harper's Magazine* named Newark "the worst American city" (Louis, 1975, p.67). As business and police ventures[1,2] attempted to gain ground in Newark, themes of "Resurgence," "Rebirth," "Revitalization," and "Renaissance" continued to frame Newark's struggles to undo its past. By the early 1990s, Newark was commonly referred to as the "stolen car capital of the country" (Nieves, 1993). In 1996, *Time* described Newark as the most dangerous city in the United States (Fried, 1996). Contrasting the city's Puritan roots, numerous police officials and politicians have been found guilty of various levels of corruption. Five of the last seven mayors have been indicted on criminal charges, with the recent mayor Sharpe James serving a two-year sentence in federal prison. At the close of the twentieth century, however, the criminal justice community, spurred by successful demonstrations of CPS in Boston, Chicago, Indianapolis, and Memphis, began laying the groundwork for the Greater Newark Safer Cities Initiative. This network opened the doors for collaboration and cooperation among a wide range of law enforcement agencies, community and religious groups, and academics (Kelling, 2005). By 2009 Newark was off the list of the twenty-five most dangerous cities and drawing national attention for its crime reduction strategies (*Safest and Most Dangerous*, 2009).

As the city continued its progress, an enthusiastic young mayor and a director of police (who played a pivotal part in the 1990s turnaround of crime in New York City) implemented new strategies to meet community needs and to fight crime and disorder. Figures 3.1a and 3.1b track crime in Newark and the other cities in this study for the past ten years and reflect the successes of Newark Police Department (NPD) under Director McCarthy. Efforts by the NPD acknowledge the contentious racial divides and political corruption that has defined Newark's recent history.

In this study, the NPD is the only one located in the Mid-Atlantic region and serving a predominantly Black population. The NPD represents a police

---

1. See Skolnick and Bayley (1986) for a case study of policing innovation in Newark, NJ during the early 1980s.

2. George L. Kelling's work with the Newark Police Department informed his "Broken Windows Theory" (Kelling & Wilson, 1982). Kelling also published work on the Newark Foot Patrol Experiment during this time.

department fighting to control violent crime and to change perceptions of political corruption within the city and its police department. The chapter on the NPD demonstrates the police department's move into the CPS era against the pull of sources of legitimacy and authorization that reflect the Political era of policing and despite a culture that values methods of policing (i.e., random patrol and rapid response to calls for service) more in line with a reform strategy.

## Community Problem-Solving V2.0: Boston's Community Problem-Solving History

During our nation's nascent years, the Puritans settled on the Shawmut Peninsula and founded the town of Boston—Massachusetts' capital city and the twenty-first most populous city in the nation (*Boston Successfully*, 2009; Banner, 2009). In this study, Boston represents the Northeast region of the United States and is one of the nation's most densely populated big cities. Despite (or perhaps because of) its strict, Puritan roots, a number of riotous episodes (i.e., the Boston Tea Party, the Boston Massacre, the birthing of our nation's Revolutionary War, the Great Boston Fire, the Boston Police Strike, the 1970s busing riots, and a precipitous rise and fall in youth homicide rates) represent the varied problems to which the Boston Police Department (BPD) and its citizens have responded.

Boston's prominence in the foundation of the United States and its serving as one of the main ports for newly arrived immigrants made Boston a likely place for the formation of the first organized police force in the United States in 1838. The history of the Boston police force mirrors that of the evolution of American policing as discussed in Chapter 1. Throughout its history, the Boston police have served and focused on a variety of community needs including public safety, order maintenance, law enforcement, and public service. They have employed a variety of strategies and tactics to respond to the various problems they faced and have operated under varying levels of authority and legitimacy.

Described by many as a "city of neighborhoods" and reflecting the diversity of the city's history, Boston maintains distinct subsections distinguished by race, ethnicity, and culture, demarcated by geographic boundaries and landmarks. Whites make up nearly half of the residents in Boston's more than twenty neighborhoods, with substantial Black and Hispanic numerical minorities. Racial tensions in Boston, similar to those in other U.S. cities, came to a head in 1974 when a federal court ordered the city to desegregate its public school system (Bratton, 1998). The city answered the order by busing Black and White students; the public reacted riotously. For nearly six years, Boston

Figure 3.1a Property Crime Rates in the Four Cities*

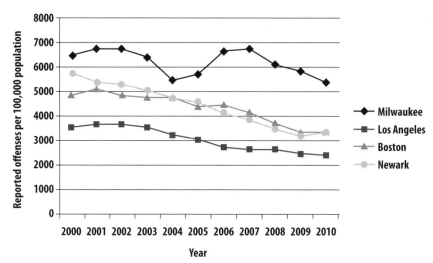

Figure 3.1b Violent Crime Rates in the Four Cities**

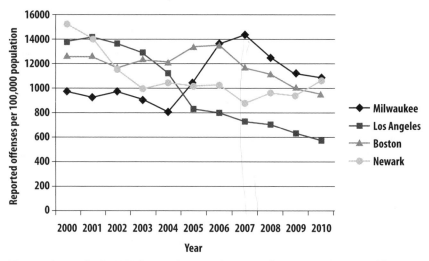

*Due to changes in the MPD's reporting practices, 2005 figures are not comparable to previous years' data.

**Due to changes in the LAPD's reporting practices, 2005 aggravated assault figures are not comparable to previous years' data.

Sources: FBI, Uniform Crime Reports, prepared by the National Archive of Criminal Justice Data.

police worked to quell these outbursts, while responding to racially driven assaults and addressing the routine calls for service (Bratton, 1998). The busing riots, as they came to be known, underscored police-citizen hostilities that arose from the police department's and citizens' mutual alienation, thus moving the BPD closer to its CPS era.

Though calls for the BPD to become more involved in the community followed, harsh police tactics and corrupt practices in the department continued to strain police-citizen relations (Braga, Hureau, & Winship, 2008). In May 1991, Mayor Raymond Flynn, under increasing pressure from the media, requested a review of the BPD's management and supervisory systems. The St. Clair Report outlined the pervasive culture of corruption that enabled instances of citizen mistreatment and contributed to disparate hiring and promotional practices for ethnic minorities. The commission recommended an overhaul of the department's strategic planning capabilities, technological innovation, CPS policing, case management, internal affairs, and leadership, hiring, training, and promotional practices (St. Clair, 1992).

The St. Clair Report proved to be the gadfly the BPD needed for wide-reaching and lasting change within the department. An increase in funding from local and federal government sources helped police administrators implement many of the structural, technological, and community-oriented changes recommended by the St. Clair Report (Bratton, 1998). Although then-Mayor Raymond Flynn did not follow the Report's suggestion to allow the much-maligned Commissioner Mickey Roache's term to expire, he did appoint William Bratton as Superintendent-in-Chief of the BPD. This appointment led to the eventual selection of William Bratton as BPD commissioner in 1993, helping to lay the groundwork for the BPD's successful implementation of the community policing philosophy. Then, beginning in 1995, Commissioner Evans oversaw the creation of a "locally-initiated, neighborhood-driven" strategic plan for neighborhood policing, which included input from police personnel, citizens, and other stakeholders (*Strategic Plan for Neighborhood Policing*, July 1996, p. 2). The "Boston Miracle" embodies the value of these changes and is discussed below.

The "Boston Miracle" refers to the period in the 1990s when Boston successfully implemented their Operation CeaseFire and Ten Point Coalition programs to dramatically reduce rising juvenile violent crime rates. Operation CeaseFire was a "carrot and stick approach" in which community groups offered services to seriously involved gang members, while numerous criminal justice agencies collaborated to provide assured punishment if said gang members continued on their criminal path. The Ten Point Coalition was an unprecedented collaboration between the BPD and leaders of relevant Black clergy, which lent legitimacy in the historically strained Black communities to the crime-fighting and community-building efforts of the BPD.[3] These efforts, in conjunction with the citizen-initiated neighborhood-based policing strategic plan, formed the organizational and functional bases by which the police began to work with citizens to respond to an array of neighborhood-specific and city-wide problems.

As a result of these programs, and subsequent to a steep rise in youth homicides (both as victims and perpetrators), Boston saw an even greater decline in the number of overall homicides (consisting overwhelmingly of a drop in youth and adolescent violence). Part of this decline is contributed to the aforementioned collaborative efforts of academics, community groups and federal, state, and local law enforcement agencies (Kennedy, Piehl, & Braga, 1996). While this rise and fall reflected similar trends occurring across the nation's urban centers, some scholars contribute the "Boston Miracle" to this unprecedented coalition between law enforcement and community groups during the height of the community policing era (Winship, 2002; Braga et al., 2008). These collaborations and shared understandings about the crime problem in Boston signified a renewed emphasis on police and community relations (Kelling, Hochberg, Kaminska, Rocheleau, Rosenbaum, Roth, & Skogan, 1998).

The BPD was at the forefront of the community-oriented policing movement in the early 1990s, and, by the mid-90s, exemplified a CPS strategy by working with a number of community and religious groups to produce a precipitous and sustained decline in (youth) homicides. These collaborations fell off at the turn of the twenty-first century, however, and an alarming rise in homicides followed as the BPD turned its attention to securing its city against a terrorist attack. Figures 3.1a and 3.1b present Boston's crime rates in the first decade of the twenty-first century, as the police and community reestablished their working relationships and drove down crime. This study examines the BPD's most recent experiences with the CPS strategy, considering the BPD's CPS history and their use of sophisticated policing technologies.

# From Detection to Prevention: Milwaukee's Community Problem-Solving History

Milwaukee represents, in this study, the police experience in the Midwest region of the United States. Called Mahnawaukee-Seepe by the Native Ameri-

---

3. For further reading, see numerous articles by policing scholar and current Boston Police Department chief policy advisor, Anthony Braga (e.g., Braga et al., 2008; Kennedy, Piehl, & Braga, 1996).

cans who inhabited the 97 square miles of land bordering Lake Michigan and three rivers, Milwaukee's history reflects the promise that America's manufacturing roots offered to a diverse group of immigrants from Europe and the southern United States. In the decade following 1840, Milwaukee's population increased over 1,000%, and in 1855, Milwaukee established their first official police force. Milwaukee consists of distinct ethnic neighborhoods and is described by one Milwaukee police official as a "big, small town." Policing firsts in technology (and in instituting systems to prevent and detect corruption), labor riots, and race riots accent Milwaukee's policing history.

As immigrant groups jockeyed for political and economic power, riots erupted, marking disputes between workers and factory owners and between Blacks and Whites. While Milwaukee welcomed immigrants from a variety of ethnic and racial backgrounds, the political and socioeconomic structures that arose in Milwaukee incorporated Blacks differently than their European peers. Competition for power and employment meant racial distinctions would continue to divide Blacks and Whites, as each group attempted to increase its lot in the burgeoning metropolis. Very racist toward Blacks.

As in other city police departments at the time, Milwaukee created a Police and Fire Commission to respond to the corrupting influence that politics had on policing standards. In 1888, John Janssen became the first chief to serve under the commission; he served for 33 years and was known as the "Father of the Milwaukee Metropolitan Police Force" (*History of MPD*; *John Janssen 1888–1921*). The new commission, the police department's introduction of (for the first time in the United States) fingerprinting, a motorized patrol, and police training academy could not keep Milwaukee from becoming a "city of officially sanctioned vice" (*Milwaukee Historical Society*; *John Janssen 1888–1921*; *Jacob Laubenheimer 1921–1936*). Nearly 100 years later, after Chief Harold Breier's 20-year tenure, legislation required term limits of police chiefs, gave the Police and Fire Commission more power over the police department, and required the Police and Fire Commission to conduct annual policy reviews of the police department.

Following Chief Breier's "law and order" reign, Milwaukee acknowledged the need for their police department to respond to shifting demographics by appointing its first Hispanic, Black, and female chiefs of police beginning in 1989 (*goMilwaukee*, 2011). During this period, the police department attempted to address increasing crime rates and improve community relations by employing various forms of CPS. Scandals arising from the Jeffrey Dahmer[4] and

1970 ended Political

Went from Reform era to Community

---

4. The MPD was criticized for mishandling a run-in with Jeffrey Dahmer, in which two police officers returned a naked and drugged 14-year-old Laotian boy to Dahmer after they

Frank Jude, Jr.[5] cases, however, strained the Milwaukee Police Department's (MPD) relationships with the significant Laotian, Hmong, and Black communities. Figures 3.1a and 3.1b reflect Milwaukee crime rates, which often landed Milwaukee on the list of the ten most dangerous cities its size in the United States and include within them Milwaukee's 23-year low murder rate in 2008.

The MPD faces many big city problems, within a small city culture (both within the police department and the city). The city's growth has made it ethnically diverse and culturally rich. However, one cannot separate the city's historical industrial, manufacturing, and employment undulations or its newly arrived immigrants' struggles for socioeconomic and political power from the challenges Milwaukee police face today. In response to failed leadership within the police department, and subsequent to the tenure of the MPD's first Black, Hispanic, and female police chiefs, the Fire and Police Commission brought in an East Coast police chief to respond to rising violence and weakened community ties. From the beginning of his tenure, Chief Edward Flynn put forth a neighborhood-based, data-driven approach to fulfill his mandate.

# The Pursuit of Professionalism: Los Angeles' Community Problem-Solving History

Mexico ceded *El Pueblo de la Reyna de Los Angeles* to the United States after the Mexican-American War in 1848. Two years later, in 1850, California was admitted into the Union and the city of Los Angeles was incorporated. Anglo Americans soon rose to power, and hopeful Americans and immigrants alike flooded the nation's fledgling land. The Los Angeles Rangers, LA's first police force, was created in 1853 in response to the murder of a prominent city resident (*The LAPD, 1850–1900*). More and less organized (and sometimes no) police forces attempted to manage the restless remainder of the nineteenth century. By the turn of the century, and under the early leadership of the Los Angeles Police Department's (LAPD) first long-serving Police Chief John Glass, the LAPD had gotten through those first few decades, hired its first African-

---

had encountered the boy in the street, thinking that Dahmer and the boy were lovers. Dahmer killed the boy and four others before he was caught again by the MPD.

5. In this case, White police officers were accused of beating Jude, Jr., a biracial male, after they accused him of stealing one of their police badges during a party held at one of the off-duty police officer's homes. MPD officers who responded to the call were also accused of beating Jude. Three of the officers were later found guilty of violating Jude's civil rights.

American police officers and was perched on the forefront of police professionalism. While overcoming near-disastrous scandals and corruptions, the LAPD would prove to be the vanguard in many policing movements through the twentieth and twenty-first centuries.

As often occurs following a police department's trajectory through different eras, the LAPD's move toward the professional era of policing was not without its throwbacks to political era strongholds. The progenitor of professional policing, August Vollmer (himself an LAPD outsider) led the department for one instrumental year in 1923 and laid the foundation for the LAPD's dilatory move into the professional era of policing. By 1938, corrupted Los Angeles Mayor Frank Shaw became the first mayor in the US to be recalled (Cannon, 1997). His thoroughly-earned ousting was a result of years of overt graft and unhindered police brutality that culminated with the assassination attempt of a former police officer, targeted for his role in investigating LAPD corruption (Gates & Shah, 1992). Less than a decade after the scandals of the late 1930s, the grotesque mutilation of the Black Dahlia, the Zoot Suit Riots, and grand jury investigations into LAPD vice detectives' shake downs of prostitutes and drug addicts forced an end to Chief Clemence B. Horrall's eight-year tenure and instigated calls for police reform (Domanick, 1994; Cannon, 1997).

The LAPD answered those calls by bringing in an outsider, devoted reformer, and retired Marine, Chief William Worton, to serve as interim chief. Civil service rules and political gaming kept Chief Worton from permanently assuming the position. In 1950, the LAPD appointed to Chief of Police a 23-year insider and inaugural head of the LAPD's Internal Affairs unit, William Parker. He would serve in this position until his death sixteen years later. Authors describe this period in the LAPD as: helping to "mold the LAPD into the world-recognized, aggressive police force that it is today" (Gates & Shah, 1992, p. 30) and "the most productive and renowned in the history of American municipal law enforcement" (*LAPD: Chief Parker*). Another author refers to Chief Parker as "the godfather—*il capo di tutti capi*—of the New Centurions" (Domanick, 1994, p. 103).

Building on former Chief Vollmer's earlier attempts to reform the LAPD, Chief Parker instituted more stringent hiring standards, a demanding academy training, and mechanisms for strict discipline. He embarked on a public relations campaign that, together, created the pristine, crime-fighter image of the LAPD that set the tone for the Los Angeles police organization for almost the next five decades (Cannon, 1997; *LAPD: Chief Parker*). A superficial scratch of the gild, however, revealed a tarnished image of the LAPD as heavy-handed, invasive, racist, and practically (and eminently) free from outside oversight (Cannon, 1997). These realities culminated with the Watts Riots of 1965, in which 34 people were killed, and roused the LAPD's apperception that minorities matter. In 1968 Chief Edward Davis commenced his nine-year service as Chief of the LAPD. He learned, however, from Chief Parker's experiences (in which Davis played a key role). Citing the LAPD's contemporary clashes with the community, Davis began a program of community policing that emphasized officer responsibility for limited geographic areas (in patrol cars) and encouraged relationships between the LAPD and its citizens (i.e., putting police officers in high schools) (Gates & Shah, 1992; Cannon, 1997; *LAPD: Chief Davis*).

In 1978, Chief Daryl Gates took over the LAPD, chosen over a top-scoring outsider (Domanick, 1994). He, with the support of then-Mayor Bradley, ended the LAPD's move toward community policing and reverted to its insular and sovereign path (Cannon, 1997). The LAPD's response to the rise of gangs and illicit drugs in the 1980s was forcefully proactive and abnormally deadly and yet also included Gates' brainchild, the Drug Abuse Resistance Education (D.A.R.E.) program. Community perceptions of police officers' abuses, however, alienated the community. The Rodney King incident and the subsequent L.A. Riots typified for many the years of separation the LAPD had from its community. These events instigated Chief Gates' departure from the LAPD and ended the Parker era. By 1992, the LAPD appointed its first African American Police Chief (and first outsider in fifty years), Willie Williams. Years of perceived police brutality and strained relationships with minority communities readied the LAPD for a new trajectory of serving its citizens. A proven community policing and affirmative action advocate during his time as chief of the Philadelphia Police Department, Chief Williams' stint with the LAPD would last only one term (five years) (*The LAPD: Chief Williams*). Though enjoying the confidence of Black Angelenos and the mandate of the Christopher Commission Report, Chief Williams lacked the necessary support of majorities of other ethnic groups, politicians and, ultimately, the Police Commission (Cannon, 1997). He resigned his position in 1997, the first year of his predecessor's (Bernard Parks) single term as LAPD Chief of Police.

By instituting an early CompStat-like process (called FASTRAC), reorganizing the LAPD and revamping the citizen complaints process, Chief Parks' erected a platform by which the LAPD's current move toward the community problem-solving era was reconceived (*Chief Bernard C. Parks*, 2002). During his oversight, however, a few high profile corruption and abuse incidents and his handling of the subsequent investigations into his department hampered his contest for a second term as Chief. The most notorious and involved of the scandals occurring under Parks' became known as the Rampart Scandal, in

which officers and detectives from the LAPD-prized anti-gang unit, Community Resources Against Street Hoodlums (CRASH) Rampart Division, mis-
used force (including deadly force), stole drugs from evidence rooms,
manufactured probable cause, and committed other criminal acts violating
individuals' due process rights (Kirk, 2001). After the physical abuses of minority groups in the 1980s and the worldwide infamy garnered by the Rodney
King and Rampart incidents, one wonders what the tipping point would be
for Los Angeles and the LAPD to institute real, radical and lasting organizational change.

It would take a United States Department of Justice Consent decree and
America's self-proclaimed "top cop" (Bill Bratton) to put the LAPD on a new
path of professionalism, service, and improved police-community relations.
As the third largest local police department in the United States, and serving
a population of over four million people (in a city of almost 500 square miles),
the analysis of the LAPD offers the reader an unparalleled instruction of police organizational change. This West Coast police department typified the reform and "professional" police department in the U.S. until a number of
egregious incidents uncovered another side of the LAPD. The violent and property crime rates for Los Angeles can be found on Figures 3.1a and 3.1b. Table
3.1 presents some basic characteristics of each of the police departments and
the cities and citizens they police.

Table 3.1
*Setting the Stage: Characteristics of the Four Sites*

|  | NPD | BPD | MPD | LAPD |
|---|---|---|---|---|
| 2010 Population* | 277,140 | 617,594 | 594,833 | 3,792,621 |
| City area (sq. mi.) | 26.0 | 89.6 | 96.9 | 503.0 |
| Education (% Bachelors+)* | 12.5% | 43.4% | 27.7% | 63.2% |
| % Unemployed** | 15.7% | 7.7% | 13.0% | 13.7% |
| City race/ethnicity*◊ | 52.4% B | 24.0% B | 40.0% B | 9.6% B |
|  | 33.8% H | 17.5% H | 17.3% H | 48.5% H |
|  | 11.6% W | 47.0% W | 37.0% W | 28.7% W |
| Sworn police personnel | 1,316 | 2,099 | 1,940 | 9,830 |

* U.S. Census Bureau
** For comparison purposes, we adapted these data from rates in March 2010 as found on
www.homefacts.com.
◊ W=White, non-hispanic; B=Black; H=Hispanic, of any race

# Summary

The following chapters portray the moves each department made on the CPS trajectories presented here. Chapter 4 reveals the promising ways the NPD responds to their history by implementing a CPS strategy in a technologically advanced, post-9/11, economically recessed environment. Attention to the NPD's mission, community relationships, and structure highlights the necessary political and community-based authority a police leader needs to successfully bring their organization into the twenty-first century. Chapter 5 examines how the BPD allocated personnel, created CPS teams, instituted new ways of managing demand for their services, and renegotiated community collaborations. In doing so, it offers unique insights into how a traditionally innovative (but recently stagnant) police department reignited its CPS strategy. It reveals a police department that builds on the CPS capital it had created during the last decade of the twenty-first century to reinstitutionalize the CPS strategy within its police department and its city. The current research will continue Boston's policing narrative to better understand the police organizational role in responding to citizens' needs. The drastic changes in the MPD are portrayed in Chapter 6. They include a reorganization of the Criminal Investigations Bureau, a reworking of weekly CompStat meetings (and a concomitant patrol supervision process), daily citywide crime briefings, and using new technologies to guide police discretion. This section examines these changes and shows how they imbued the organization with a CPS focus, seeking to change the detective-heavy culture of the MPD. The current study locates the MPD's changing organizational strategies within the diverse history of the city and builds on this history to better understand the police undertakings in such a city. The final case study, in Chapter 7, examines the LAPD during the end of Chief Bill Bratton's turnaround of the LAPD through the beginning of Chief Beck's tenure, demonstrating how the changes chiefs Bratton and Beck made helped to bring the LAPD into the CPS era.

# References

Banner, D. (2009). Boston history: The history of Boston, Massachusetts. Retrieved from http://www.searchboston.com/articles/history.html.

Boston successfully wins census challenge (30 November 2009). Retrieved from http://www.boston.com/news/local/massachusetts/articles/2009/11/30/boston_successfully_wins_census_challenge/.

Braga, A., Hureau, D., & Winship, C. (October 2008). Losing faith? Police, Black churches, and the resurgence of youth violence in Boston. Retrieved from http://www.hks.harvard.edu/rappaport/downloads/braga_final.pdf.

Bratton, W. J. (11 May 2006). LAPD Chief Bratton: We've changed. *Los Angeles Times* [Online]. Retrieved from latimes.com/news/opinion/commentary/la-oe-bratton11may11,0,7078215.story

Cannon, L. (1997). *Official negligence: How Rodney King and the riots changed Los Angeles and the LAPD.* New York: Random House.

Domanick, J. (1994). *To protect and serve: The LAPD's century of war in the city of dreams.* New York: Pocket Books.

Fried, C. (November 27, 1996) America's safest city: Amherst, N.Y.; The most dangerous: Newark, N.J. *Money* [Online]. Retrieved from http://money.cnn.com/magazines/moneymag/moneymag_archive/1996/11/27/225088/index.htm.

Gates, D. & Shah, D. (1992). *Chief: My life in the LAPD.* New York: Bantam.

goMilwaukee (2011). Harold Breier 1964–1984. Retrieved from http://city.milwaukee.gov/Police/Breier.htm

goMilwaukee (2009). Jacob Laubenheimer 1921–1936. Retrieved from http://www.milwaukee.gov/ContentMgmt/Blocks/Freeform_FCK/Support/editor/router.asp?docid=13130.

goMilwaukee (2009). John Janssen 1888–1921. Retrieved from http://city.milwaukee.gov/Police/Janssen.htm.

History of the city of Newark New Jersey: Embracing two and a half centuries 1666–1913. (1913). Vol. 2, Lewis Historical Publishing: New York. Retrieved from http://genealogytrails.com/njer/essex/timeline.html.

History of the Milwaukee Police Department. Retrieved from http://www.milwaukee.gov/history779.htm.

Kelling, G., Hochberg, M., Kaminska, S., Rocheleau, A., Rosenbaum, D., Roth, J., & Skogan, W. (June 1998). The Bureau of Justice Assistance comprehensive communities program: A Preliminary report. Washington, DC: National Institute of Justice.

Kelling, G. & Wilson, J. (1982, March). Broken windows: The police and neighborhood safety. *The Atlantic Monthly*, pp. 29–38.

Kennedy, D., Piehl, A. & Braga, A. (1996). Youth violence in Boston: Gun markets, serious youth offenders, and a use-reduction strategy, *Law and Contemporary Problems*, 59, pp. 147–96.

Kirk, M. (Producer and Director). (2001). *L.A.P.D. Blues* [Motion picture]. United States: Frontline.

*LAPD, 1850–1900.* Retrieved from http://www.lapdonline.org/history_of_the_lapd/content_basic_view/1107.

*LAPD: Chief Davis.* Retrieved from http://www.lapdonline.org/history_of_
the_lapd/content_basic_view/1112.

*LAPD: Chief Parker.* Retrieved from http://www.lapdonline.org/history_of_
the_lapd/content_basic_view/1110.

*LAPD: Chief Williams.* Retrieved from http://www.lapdonline.org/history_of_
the_lapd/content_basic_view/1116.

Liebman, S. (21 June 2007). Report for action. Retrieved from http://
blog.nj.com/ledgernewark/2007/06/report_for_action.html.

Louis, A. (January 1975). The worst American city. *Harper's Magazine,* pp.
67–71.

Milwaukee Historical Society. The Making of Milwaukee: Milwaukee's History. Retrieved from http://www.themakingofmilwaukee.com/history/
index.cfm.

Nieves, E. (21 September 1993). Joy rides turn deadly in New Jersey, *The New
York Times* [Online]. Retrieved from http://www.nytimes.com/1993/09/21/
nyregion/joy-rides-turn-deadly-in-new-jersey.html?pagewanted=all&src=pm.

Skolnick, J., & Bayley, D. (1986). *The new blue line: Police innovation in six
American cities.* New York: The Free Press.

St. Clair, J. (1992). Report of the Boston Police Department Management Review Committee. A report submitted to the City of Boston.

Strategic Plan for Neighborhood Policing (July 1996). Citywide Strategic Plan,
a report prepared for the City of Boston.

Winship, C. (March 2002). End of a miracle? Crime, faith, and partnership
in Boston in the 1990's. Retrieved from http://www.wjh.harvard.edu/soc/
faculty/winship/End_of_a_Miracle.pdf.

# Chapter 4

# The Newark Police Department

## Introduction

The Newark Police Department (NPD), like the other police departments in this study, has seen more than a fair share of controversy. Keep in mind the corrupt (not-so-distant) history and racial tensions so closely associated with New Jersey's largest city. This chapter (and each of the next three) discusses the community problem-solving (CPS) organizational strategy of the police departments, specifically focusing on how their mission, relationships with the community, and structure (all part of the elements of an organizational strategy) signal a move to the CPS era. In Newark, Police Director Garry Mc-Carthy (former Deputy Commissioner of the New York Police Department and now superintendent of the Chicago Police Department) helped bring the NPD into the twenty-first century by establishing working relationships with the community and implementing necessary technologies that helped to organize and account for police activities. It is important to note how the NPD dealt with past and ongoing controversies to legitimize itself with its citizens. Through determined and persistent leadership, and a tenacious approach to preventing violence, the NPD made in-roads in their community. The progress, however, is tenuous, and the future has yet to determine if such changes will last.

## The NPD Mission

*"You change the quality of life, you eliminate conditions that foster crime."*

### Function

The function of the NPD is to prevent violent crimes by maintaining order and enforcing quality of life violations. The mission statement of the NPD as articulated by a majority of respondents in this study's survey and as printed in the department's Community Relations Strategy reads, "The Newark Police Department is dedicated to eliminating crime and improving quality of life while fostering mutual trust and respect with our community" (*Office of Police and Planning*, 2010, p. 4). NPD official statements, publications, and survey responses specify this three-pronged function (eliminating crime, improving quality of life, and fostering positive relationships with the community). Interview data and online news archives, however, focus most explicitly on preventing violent crime and enforcing lower-level quality of life offenses. This section discusses these two functions and explains the subtleties of police personnel's views of their department's function.

**If you change the quality of life, you eliminate conditions that foster crime.** When Director McCarthy took office in late 2006, he described Newark as a city "held hostage by crime for at least three decades" (Erminio, 2006). This dramatic belief about Newark's crime problem, coupled with Director McCarthy's previous post as chief crime strategist for the NYPD (where he successfully implemented strategies to reduce violence and drug dealing in a high crime area), manifests in the NPD's portrayal of Newark's triune crime problem — violence, drugs, and quality of life.

Upon taking office, Director McCarthy offered his "three-pillar strategy to bring down the city's crime rate—" crackdown on quality of life crimes, computerize the crime-tracking system (to more efficiently allocate resources to the precincts) and create a narcotics unit to control mid-level drug dealing (Schuppe, 2006a). More explicitly, Director McCarthy states, "If you change the quality of life, you also eliminate conditions that foster crime" (Schuppe, 2006). Many in the NPD compare the underground drug trade to a free market where (gun) violence is used to squelch competition and collect debts. It follows, then, that any potential to reduce crime in Newark would have to include efforts to respond to the multitude of crimes and disorders associated with drug use and drug distribution. This discernment of the crime problem is reflected in the department's narcotics strategy, gun violence reduction strategy, and quality of life initiative and is supported by interview and survey data from this study and the Center for Collaborative Change.

When asked, "what issues should the NPD focus on in your neighborhood," the large majority of residents chose "Youth-Gangs-Drugs," with "Robberies-General Safety," "Community Relations," and "Violent Crime" (respectively) following distantly; typical order-maintenance concerns are at the bottom of the list (Center for Collaborative Change, 2010). This finding can be interpreted many ways. It supports, however, the idea that the NPD and community are on the same page when it comes to defining the general crime problem in Newark and suggests a disjoint between community expectations and police actions regarding how to respond to crime. The NPD believes paying attention to minor crimes and other signs of disorder can reduce the more serious crimes. Citizens prefer the NPD to spend their time on more serious offenses without the mediating influence of attacking lower-level crimes.

Though the NPD works to both fight crime and enhance citizen quality of life, stopping the next crime is undoubtedly the more prized of the two functions. As Captain White states, everything else the NPD does "is just the road to get there [crime reduction]." Similarly, Lt. Crossin offers, "Everything else for me is cake on top of that!" Another lieutenant (Lt. Brown) reports the ultimate focus of the new administration is "reducing the shooting, reducing the murders." Online news coverage of NPD and its functions also overwhelmingly favors stories of the NPD's efforts at reducing violent crime.

Interview data reveal NPD's multi-pronged approach to stemming violent crime and an understanding of the need to comprehensively respond to crime by employing problem-specific solutions that concentrate on the violence, guns and quality of life triumvirate. Deputy Nolan offers his interpretation of the Director's mantra, "It's not one thing that reduces crime, it's everything." He cites quality of life enforcement, NPD's first-ever centralized narcotics enforcement unit, the criminal intelligence unit, and the gun enforcement, gang enforcement, and street level narcotics teams. He relays, "All those things together have brought a major reduction in our violent crime."

Most officers in the NPD are cognizant of the need to respond to problems of crime and disorder. Many also recognize the necessity of quality of life enforcement in preventing more serious crime and enhancing the quality of life for Newark's citizens. A majority of respondents in this sample agree or strongly agree with statements on the positive relationships between disorder, fear of crime, and the breakdown of community controls. Nearly 90% agree that there is a positive relationship between the breakdown of community controls and crime. The majority agrees that the breakdown is a result of untended disorder. They also agree the NPD is working to bring order to its neighborhoods. As Table 4.1 reflects, of those personnel responding to the only open-ended question in our survey ("What is the current mission of your police department, as you understand it?"), 63% explicitly cited preventing (and/or eliminating) crime and improving quality of life.

Table 4.1

*The Current Mission of the NPD: What is the current mission
of your police department, as you understand it?*

| Response | N | Percent (%) |
|---|---|---|
| Prevent crime and improve QOL | 20 | 24.7 |
| Eliminate crime | 21 | 25.9 |
| Improve QOL | 10 | 12.3 |
| Protect and serve | 13 | 16.0 |
| Other | 17 | 20.1 |
| Total | 81 | 100 |

The interview respondents add perspective to these views. As Deputy Nolan explains:

> We are focused on intelligent policing, responding to those indicators that show us where our problems lie, dealing with those things up front, before they become a major problem. Handle the small problems, and then the big problems go away.

Capt. Phillips uses the NPD's new narcotics strategy to demonstrate his understanding:

> For a while, narcotics enforcement was placed really low on the ladder; it wasn't a priority. Today our focus as far as narcotics has definitely changed. Patrol's task is pretty much locking down that location and making sure that what we took out there doesn't come back, and the condition is gone, and we keep the condition gone.

Yet another respondent, Chief Thomas, states, "The little job is the stepping stone to preventing further acts of criminality or even violence, depending on the person you lock up." These findings reveal an important aspect of the CPS strategy: a police department must work to improve residents' quality of life, to reduce crime. They also suggest that personnel throughout the NPD grasp Director McCarthy's official mission for the NPD.

The NPD uses their newest computerized crime tracking, mapping, and analysis systems to create problem specific solutions for low-level offenses and to prevent more serious crimes. Capt. Green suggests CompStat is useful in helping to "redirect our sources to give more quality of life. The Director's big on getting our hands on people, interacting with people—good people, bad people." Lt. Dodd notes also, "[the] stress on field interviews, the stress on quality of life is huge at this point." Police recognize that contacts with individuals for lower-level offenses (via NPD's "blue summonses") provide the entrée needed to conduct field interviews and to glean information on the person's knowledge of or participation in more serious crime.

Given Newark's notorious spot near the top of all lists violent, it is not surprising to find prevention of violent crime as the first priority of its police department. In line with a CPS strategy, the NPD tries to enhance the quality of life for Newark's citizens and creates the conditions necessary for a reduction in violent crime. Succeeding in both of these functions, in turn, helps to foster trust and respect within the community. This is the third leg of the NPD's stated mission and an important part of a CPS strategy. The next section looks at the tactics and technologies used to fulfill these functions and investigates what the department's outcomes reveal about their crime prevention and quality of life efforts under Director McCarthy.

## Tactics, Technology, and Outcomes

As this study demonstrates, each of the elements of the police organization interacts with the others. Articulating these interactions gives a clearer picture of the workings of the police department and can provide confirmatory evidence to findings on each element. This allows the researcher to distinguish between the police leaders' stated and actual changes in each element. This section explores the various tactics and technologies used in the NPD, describes the outcomes used to measure their efforts, and discusses discrepancies among the function, tactics, technologies and outcomes in the NPD.

**An emphasis on putting your hands on people.** With an understanding of Newark's crime problem as one fueled by the drug market, the NPD uses a variety of tactics (i.e., patrol in cars, park-and-walks, rapid response to serious and in-progress calls for service, community meetings, field inquiries, and information sharing) and takes advantage of a number of technologies (computerized records management, GIS mapping, surveillance cameras, Crime Stoppers and Gun Stoppers Hotlines, Livescan and Shotspotter) to increase their contact with the community and to respond to violent crimes. There is little doubt that those in the upper echelon of the NPD believe that increasing the number of police-citizen interactions will reduce levels of crime in Newark. These interactions take the form of community meetings, field inquiries, knocking on doors, and stopping citizens upon reasonable suspicion of lower-level offenses.

Though intended to increase contacts with both "good people and bad people," evidence suggests that more positive police-citizen encounters occur in those areas less frequently plagued by violence. For example, the successful knock-and-talk initiative, discussed below, occurred in one of the more socioeconomically advantaged sections of Newark where property crimes were citizens' biggest problem. Citizens in these neighborhoods are already more likely to have more positive views of the police (Albrecht & Green, 1977). Other structured, positive contacts with citizens include: precinct commanders and executive officers attending community meetings, a Police Clergy Alliance, Police Citizen-Clergy Academy, and the Senior Citizen Police Academy. These are part of NPD's still evolving efforts to enhance community relations. An explication of the more routine and consequential citizen-police interactions follows.

Observations of Director McCarthy at CompStat and an in-depth interview reveal his strongly held conviction that quality of life contacts with citizens reduce serious crime. He states, "There's an absolute correlation between quality of life, field interrogations, and guns on the street. They are important for crime reduction." He then offers a scenario to demonstrate his point. He tells of an officer who stops a person for public consumption of alcohol. The officer subsequently finds the individual in illegal possession of a gun. The Director argues that the officer prevents a possible homicide that could have occurred with the convergence of a criminal, alcohol and a firearm. These scenarios play out in a number of ways to help prevent a variety of crimes. He asks and responds, "Are shootings up? Look at your quality of life offenses and they'll always be down." As he leads CompStat he demonstrates his view on the relationship between quality of life and violence. While grilling one precinct commander on his area's burglary problem, the Director asks to see on the projection screen the burglary events overlaid with quality of life stops and field inquiry reports. He then instructs his commanders to make sure those activities are occurring in the crime-dense areas of their precincts. During a subsequent CompStat meeting, he again stresses quality of life summonses and field interrogations and adds "We need to get people's hands on the wall," implying the need to stop and search those individuals whom police reasonably suspect are in violation of an offense.

Interviews with (and survey data from) other NPD personnel also exhibit this idea of increasing contacts with citizens to prevent crime. Lt. Brown refers to the focus on quality of life at CompStat meetings as the "cornerstone to preventing the larger issues." Capt. Green affirms the belief that CompStat looks at summonses to see if they are bringing down crime. Lt. Crossin states:

> We start with the smaller stuff, like urinating in public and drinking in public. Those are the people that maybe after a few beers are gonna hit somebody. So you get them because a lot of them have warrants, once you make contact with them, it winds up getting them off the streets.

And yet another respondent, Capt. Moran, describes the contact the NPD has with citizens as, "Putting our hands on people,[1] how many touches do we have with individuals, whether it's a friendly visit, whether it's not a friendly visit, we gotta be in contact with the community."

Additionally, survey data from this research reflect that the majority of this sample agrees that both patrol officers and detectives establish positive relationships with citizens within their precincts (an important element in the CPS strategy). A higher percentage (69%) agree that patrol officers establish positive relationships with citizens. Only 53% agree that detectives do the same. The survey data also demonstrate the NPD's mixed understandings of specific tactics used to fulfill their mission. For example, while the overwhelming majority of surveyed personnel view aggressive enforcement of quality of life offenses, community meetings, community collaboration, the CompStat process, and crime mapping as at least somewhat important to the mission of the NPD, a large majority also viewed traditional (i.e., Reform era) policing tactics as somewhat important or very important to the NPD's mission. Comparisons of the numbers show greater relative percentages for the traditional tactics of patrolling (i.e., in a car) than on foot or other non-traditional mode of patrolling. The relatively high percentage (67%) viewing rapid response as very important reflects a continued faith in traditional modes of policing. While these tactics are not at all mutually exclusive, prima facie distinctions between the numbers of personnel viewing some tactics as "very important" at higher rates than other tactics suggests this sample might view traditional policing tactics as more important to the NPD mission. This is a noteworthy hurdle that Director McCarthy (and any police leader) will encounter when bringing their police into the twenty-first century. Routine car patrol and rapid response to calls for service still hold a valued place in many police departments' repertoires of tactics.

Another issue that arises when bringing policing into the twenty-first century is getting police to understand the relationship between responding to lower level offenses and reducing serious crime. NPD personnel acknowledge a relationship between the two but suggest differing mechanisms by which the relationship occurs: detection, deterrence, and incapacitation. Most personnel who discuss this effect contribute it to an increased likelihood that interacting with individuals will necessarily increase the amount of wanted individuals, guns, and knowledge of other crimes that officers will uncover. For instance, Deputy Nolan argues:

---

1. "Putting our hands on people" is a unique, recurring phrase used by NPD personnel that represents the department's desire to increase the number and variety of contacts they have with citizens.

Quality of life summonses put the officer in contact with a lot more people. We've taken guns off the streets, simply because there has to be a lot more contact with people. In the process of warrant-checking those guys out, checking their identification, you find out this one's got a warrant, this one's holding a gun, this one's got drugs, so it's made us more effective in the smaller things, as opposed to just looking for the big, major crime.

Lt. Dodd describes such interactions as a "research tool," and argues for more, formal avenues for patrol and detectives to share their research findings.

The tactic of "touching" citizens or "putting hands on people" occurs within an overall crime reduction strategy that involves other tactics and technologies. These include rapid response to serious and in-progress calls for service, an electronic records management system, surveillance cameras, ShotSpotter, LiveScan, and crime hotlines (Crime Stoppers and Gunstoppers). As many respondents echoing Director McCarthy say, "It's not one thing that reduces crime, it's everything." These tactics, taken together, seek to focus resources on those people and places that account for clusters of crime and disorder.

The most valuable and effectively used tools in monitoring behavior and deploying resources include, Violent Enterprise Strategy Taskforce (VEST) meetings, a High Risk for Violence (HRV) list, a Fugitive Apprehension Team (FAT), geographic information systems (GIS), and the mapping and analysis of "blue summonses" and field inquiry reports. Chief Soren discusses FAT:

A database of individuals who we monitor very closely. We use the term 'touch.' We either attempt to arrest them when there's probable cause, vehicle stops when there's reasonable suspicion, field interrogations. These are the chronic offenders, people who have been arrested at least two or more times with a gun and a violent crime.

To facilitate this interaction, in 2007 Director McCarthy instituted the Title 23 summons in lieu of arresting an offender for quality of life offenses (i.e., aggressive panhandling, public consumption of alcohol, noise violations, and motor vehicle repair). These became known as the "blue summons" (for the color of the top carbon copy page of the summons) and aided officers in responding to lower-level offenses. Whereas in the past officers would have to arrest individuals for such offenses, these summonses give the officers a more efficient way to respond to quality of life violations, freeing time for them to remain on patrol to interact with the community. Though facilitating a patrol officer's intervention in such situations, the NPD's emphasis on "touching" citizens is not without its concerns. The following section shows how Director McCarthy sought to change management and cultural issues that arose as the NPD moved toward the CPS strategy.

**Don't just do 'em to do 'em.** The interview data reveal two recurring inhibitors to police officers enforcing quality of life offenses—managers bean-counting (which is a measurement issue) and police officers believing that conducting such stops is not real police work. Sgt. O'Shea discusses how the emphasis on blue summonses at CompStat leads commanders to make overtime decisions based on the number of summonses written by individual officers, since more summonses result in more overtime. By valuing numbers alone, supervisors devalue the role of the police officer as investigator, since spending time with the individual (asking questions that could lead to information on further criminality) takes time away from writing more summonses. Lt. Brown mentions a move in the department away from simply counting summonses and field inquiry reports:

> The point that we're trying to drive through from the upper echelon down to the guys in the street is not just do them to do them. In the past, it was just numbers for the sake of numbers. It's not just numbers now to do them, but the numbers are certainly a gauge. But if you listen to our police director long enough, you'll hear it's not just to do it just to do it; it's to do it at the times and the places with the people who are committing these offenses ultimately to use it as a tool to drive down the crime.

The challenge for the NPD is to get this belief through the ranks of the supervisors in charge of tracking and managing police performance. One high-ranking NPD official, Mr. Craft, notes:

> I really have to capture the minds and spirits of the precinct commanders and some of their execs (the lieutenants, the squad commanders, the special operations lieutenant, the platoon commander). They have to be the ones who carry the message down to the troops and get those sergeants really actively engaged.

Director McCarthy, through the CompStat process instills the quality-over-quantity mentality in his commanders with the hopes of having that view pushed down to what many consider the most important managers in a police department (the first line supervisors).

Interviews and survey data also suggest a need to change how police officers view their responsibilities. Officers and the public often associate police with fast-paced crime fighting, even though most police-citizen interactions can be better described as maintaining order. When police officers hear they are expected to intervene in situations where they witness someone committing a low-level offense, they may view such actions as not worthy of their time. Lt. Vance notes:

> Police officers don't believe that quality of life summons are real police work; they'd rather be catching a burglar, they'd rather be doin' narcotics, they'd rather be gettin' firearms. We've tried to explain to them that they wouldn't have to focus on robberies so much, or focus on narcotics so much, if they were focused on the quality of life sentences.

This excerpt highlights some officers' attitudes toward responding to low-level offenses. He also points out the dangers of police officers misinterpreting such responses as "zero tolerance." He states, "We went through a period where they were bein' overzealous, givin' out too many to the same people, and that causes backlash from the community because they think you're just bein' extremely petty." Survey data reflect a similar attitude toward the blue summonses and the role they play in the everyday responsibilities of police officers. Almost 75% of this sample believes an officer should issue a summons if they observe a quality of life violation. Nearly 65% of respondents view that stop as an effective way to garner information about crime or criminals in the area. Almost 55% believe that police officers have the time to issue a summons for quality of life violations. A discussion of the outcomes of the NPD's work and how they measure police performance follows. These measurements and outcomes support the NPD's claims as to their mission to reduce crime and disorder and enhance the quality of life but also uncover areas in which the NPD can improve.

**The bottom line is the level of crime; everything else is just the road to get there.** NPD personnel agree that the number one outcome of their efforts is crime reduction, as measured by index crime reports. To this end, supervisors view arrests made, summonses and blue tickets written, and field interviews conducted as reliable indicators of an individual police officer's crime fighting performance. Capt. White admits, though each of those categories is a measure of a police officer's activity, "The only true measure ... the bottom line is just the level of crime."

A few statistics highlight tactical changes in the NPD. For instance, from 2006 to 2009 the NPD reports a 60.73% increase in parking and moving summonses, quality of life summonses, and field inquiries, with quality of life summonses and field inquiries accounting for the largest percentage increases. This indicates the NPD has indeed amped-up their focus on lower-level offenses and that they are using quality of life and field inquiry contacts with citizens as a major tactic. There is a 14,099% increase in recorded quality of life offenses and a 232% increase in field inquiry reports from 2006 to 2009. Undoubtedly, this increase is due in part to the NPD now having a way of quickly citing someone for such offenses and measuring those offenses (i.e., through "blue summonses"). For the same period, however, arrests increased 6.62% and crime complaints decreased 19.63%. Data from the NPD Compstat Unit, as presented in Table 4.2 (below), reflect relatively constant levels of non-quality of life summonses, arrests, and crime complaints, and a distinct increase in field inquiries and quality of life summonses since Director McCarthy assumed his position. The Collaborative Change survey supports this finding. Citizens in the survey reported nearly 50% of their contacts with the NPD were a result of police-initiated stops or questioning.

### Table 4.2
*Totals of NPD police activities, 2006–2009*

| Activity | 2006 | 2007 | 2008 | 2009 |
|---|---|---|---|---|
| Moving Summons | 45,199 | 48,483 | 60,910 | 68,203 |
| Parking Summons | 88,657 | 100,095 | 120,387 | 94,772 |
| QOL Summons | 258 | 42,468 | 27,923 | 36,635 |
| Field Inquiry | 9,103 | 38,225 | 28,835 | 30,248 |
| Arrest | 26,413 | 28,336 | 30,582 | 28,162 |
| Complaint (i.e., reported index crime incidents) | 14,389 | 13,005 | 12,706 | 11,564 |
| Total | 184,019 | 270,612 | 281,343 | 269,584 |

NPD personnel agree the above-mentioned measurements relate to the police role. They caution that as "a good supervisor, you'll certainly be looking beyond the sheer numbers in evaluating personnel," examining where, when, and with whom those interactions occurred (Lt. Brown). The department must be mindful, however, of anti-quota laws that prohibit the use of mandated quotas and of the union's preference of using such evaluations for training (not disciplinary) purposes. A formal annual evaluation of sworn personnel up to and including the rank of lieutenant stemmed from their Community Relations plan. It began in June 2010 and proposes to do just that. The NPD believes this will allow them to more effectively respond to their mission to reduce crime, enhance the quality of life, and improve police-community relations. The NPD, under Director McCarthy, is just beginning to attend to their other stated functions of enhancing citizens' quality of life and fostering relationships with the community.

While valuing crime numbers that indicate actual crime decline, NPD police personnel also recognize that citizens' perceptions more directly influence how citizens view the outcomes of the NPD. Capt. Phillips states, "It's their perception, they don't have crime as we track it (by the seven index crimes). They're more quality of life offenses." Chief Thomas adds, "If they don't see a difference in their neighborhood, the numbers mean nothing to them." A respondent in the Homicide Unit uses numbers of homicides in Newark to establish the point that, "Sometimes perception is harder to overcome than the actual numbers." As he states:

> In 2007, we had 99 murders and in 2008 we went down to 67. That was a pretty big drop. Now, 2008, we went from 67 up to 77. Now all of a sudden 'Ahh! See! The murders are back up, ten more murders than last year, that's unacceptable.' But we're still 22 murders down from two years ago. You didn't hear a peep from anybody when it went from 99 to 67, nobody was sendin' us fruit baskets to the precinct congratulating us.

The lieutenant displays the conundrum police face as they balance the need to reduce violence (as perceived by reduced numbers) with the reality that citizens often make qualitative judgments about the outcomes of police (oftentimes regardless of the relative numbers).

This section has shown the various mechanisms by which the NPD has both positive and negative contacts with citizens, and how CompStat and technology complement relational and information-gaining interactions. It also showed that though the NPD is in fact increasing the numbers of contacts they have with citizens, although not all personnel buy into the idea that stopping individuals for quality of life offenses is an important part of their police department's mission. A discussion of the NPD's moves to gain legitimacy (and build relationships) with the public follows.

# Working with the Community

*"Legitimacy is a tough road to hoe."*

## *Legitimacy and External Relationships*

An inquiry of the question "from where do Newark police receive the authorization to act?" points most directly to the police department's relationships with citizens and politicians. Along with defining the three eras of modern policing in the United States, these relationships also concern today's CPS police departments. Newark's recent history demonstrates fluctuations in the source (local political and community support) and magnitude of the police department's legitimacy.

After the 1967 riots, the governor's commission (acknowledging the complicity of police-citizen relations) made a number of recommendations to the police. They include taking the politics out of hiring and promotional considerations, increasing salaries, recruiting Black and Spanish-speaking personnel, placing Blacks in operational command positions, civilianization, and residency requirements (Liebman, 2007). Currently, these groups make up the largest proportions of Newark's citizenry, though they are underrepresented at the highest levels of the NPD. The (combined) patrol officer and detective level of the NPD more proportionally represent ethnic and racial numerical minorities.

While strides have been made in recruiting and promoting racial and ethnic minorities, there is room in today's police department to increase their legitimacy with the community. There are even suggestions that the NPD could improve their legitimacy within their own ranks. Internal documents aimed at new community relations strategies, interviews with police department personnel, observations of the police director during CompStat meetings, and online news articles exhibit these continuing challenges to (and successes in) the police department's efforts to gain legitimacy and reveal how a police department can use technology and professionalism to secure a more legitimate image in the eyes of the public.

**Legitimacy is a tough road to hoe.** A call for federal monitoring of the NPD resulted from a lawsuit brought by the American Civil Liberties Union (ACLU) alleging NPD civil rights abuses of citizens and subsequent Internal Affairs cover-ups of citizens' complaints (Giambusso & Megerian, 2010). The Superior Officers' Association followed with an unanimous vote of no confidence in the city's police director, with the president of the Fraternal Order of Police suggesting his group might do the same (Queally, 2010). The situation highlights the ongoing tenuous relationships the NPD has with citizens, politicians, and its own personnel and raises questions about the magnitude of the NPD's legitimacy regarding these groups.

The legitimacy of a police department is sometimes caught in the fickle love triangle of police, politicians, and citizens. This is due, in part, to the historical role police-citizen relations has played in the success or failure of a police department and to the closeness of police and politics (both throughout history and into today[2]). Like all passionate love affairs, a duo's amorous rela-

---

2. The NPD police role in influencing the 2002 mayoral election in which incumbent Mayor Sharpe James defeated Cory Booker is documented in a 2005 film, *Street Fight*.

tionship often comes at the cost of an afflicted third party, and in some cases, with an illegitimate child. In Newark, close relations between longtime Mayor James and his NPD mean some citizens could potentially view the newest mayor's police department as illegitimate. Interviews conducted with police personnel (incidentally, but importantly, during the 2010 mayoral election season) suggest a slow road to legitimization for the NPD, at least in the minds of Mayor Booker's political opponents. Capt. Phillips replied in response to a question about the community's response to new strategies:

> It depends who you talk to. The majority of the people that I go to community meetings with, they love what we're doin' and they see a major reduction within their community of perceived crime, of actual crime. Since we're goin' into a political year, if you talk to somebody with a political agenda, you may get a different answer.

Since the mayor appoints the police director and the two often appear together publicizing their new crime strategies or touting their crime declines, citizens' anti-incumbent feelings towards the mayor might surface as beliefs of an illegitimate police department.[3] Director McCarthy, himself, is a plaintiff in a lawsuit in which he alleges a political flier in support of three candidates (for city council and mayor) defames his character (Giambusso, 2010). Sgt. Kelly views the legitimacy of the department differently and points to the local city council as the source of police authority:

> It's so volatile, we probably can't approach the public. They hate our guts right now.... Things are pretty bad for people in Newark to call a councilman to say 'I'm fed up with this guy dumpin' his garbage down the block.' Then the councilman calls the police department and it gets down through channels. Well, why can't that guy get a hold of the precinct commander, or the precinct cop?

Clearly the NPD understands there is a group of citizens who do not view the NPD as a legitimate organization and who warrant significant attention from the NPD.

Interviews with NPD personnel suggest reasons why some people do not support the NPD—a belief that police are not doing their job successfully and perceptions that they act unprofessionally when interacting with citizens. One NPD commander explains how the factors interact to produce even less citizen support. Capt. Goodman reports:

---

3. While this research cannot conclude that this process is occurring here, the divisive nature of Newark's recent political culture make such an exploration worthy of inquiry.

> They have genuine resentment for the police. Because, imagine this, when you call for the police, we don't get there, or we get there late, after the fact. But now they encounter the police sometime in the future; we stop them and issue them a blue summons for something. Imagine how you would feel as a citizen. When I needed you, you weren't there, and now you're gonna hit me with something as trivial as maybe I was smoking a cigarette and I threw it on the side walk.

The commander acknowledges the importance of responding to low-level offenses (e.g., issuing a blue summons), but also understands the necessity of the officer's professional response to such a violation. She also notes the need to respond first to those other, more serious complaints, thereby assuring citizens of the NPD's standards of professionalism and concern for the safety of their citizens.

Capt. Goodman goes on to discuss her doubt of the crime reductions, saying, "I see the calls for service. This is my job, this is where everyone complains, and we get repeat calls. If crime is reduced, I don't see it." This perception of illegitimate police numbers is supported by an internal survey of NPD that found 34% of sworn personnel believe citizens "have a point" when they say, "The murder rate and overall crime rate is much higher than the stats reported by the Department" (Office of Policy and Planning, 2010, pp. 15–16). This contrasts to a community survey that reveals only 14% of respondents, when presented with Newark's murder statistics from 2006 through 2009, "don't believe the stats" (Center for Collaborative Change, 2010, p. 41). Nonetheless, an implementation of the CPS strategy depends on the citizenry viewing the police department as legitimate. Perceptions that the police department misrepresents crime statistics do not assist in creating positive views of the NPD. Citizens' impressions that police do not professionally respond to incidents only exacerbate this issue.

Personnel perceptions of a lack in professionalism of the NPD are reflected in Sgt. Kelly's comment, "We're despised by a lot of people because of the stupid shit that some of our people are doin', from the leadership down to the newest guys." Capt. White offers an example of that "stupid shit":

> Sometimes there's a fine line between [safety and individual rights]. I think the public sometimes needs to understand that there's information they don't know. That's not to say some of these things aren't legitimate violations. Cops stoppin' somebody for absolutely no reason is uncalled for, but it's not always what it seems to be.

Police officers must always walk that fine line of public safety and individual rights, lest the public perceive police actions as unprofessional harassment.

Capt. White suggests that citizen misperceptions of police-citizen interactions may arise when citizens lack certain information that the police officer may have on the individual being stopped. This and other police personnel views of NPD legitimacy are discussed later, but first, more findings from a community-based survey are discussed.

A survey of community and NPD personnel perceptions of the NPD, administered by The Center for Collaborative Change in Newark, suggests generally positive feelings toward the NPD (Center for Collaborative Change, 2010). One pertinent finding from the community survey regards issues, problems, and concerns that community members have with the NPD's conduct, performance, and responsiveness. It found that nearly 31% of those responding to the question had "no problem" with the NPD or believed the NPD was "Doing well." The top two concerns of the remaining 70% of respondents who answered the same question addressed issues of "rudeness, respect, or attitude" and "harassment, profiling, or racism." Whites accounted for the largest proportion of those with the former concern; Latinos made up the largest percentage of respondents who cited the latter (Center for Collaborative Change, 2010). This finding confirms personnel perceptions of unprofessionalism in police work and highlights the need for the NPD to improve their handling of citizen interactions. Other survey findings supplement the later discussion of personnel's favorable perceptions of the NPD.

Perhaps more important than perceptions of illegitimacy is that Director McCarthy is leading the NPD in a way that will encourage stronger support of their department. At one CompStat meeting in March of 2009, Director McCarthy adjures those in attendance to, "Get your [city] council people here." He discusses the importance of maintaining the quality of life in areas where police have ended street drug markets. He believes these should occur for "the legitimacy and integrity of the agency, for the good order of the agency." He concludes, "The road to legitimacy is a tough road to hoe," (that is, getting politicians and citizens on the same page as the NPD).

That tough road includes such advancements as the Senior Citizen Academy, a Clergy-Citizen Academy, an enduring reduction in crime, a survey of community and personnel perceptions of the NPD, revamping certain Internal Affairs policies and training procedures, and holding a number of community meetings aimed at improving the department's image. During the same time, however, two videos of what appears to be police use of excessive force (one instance on a 15-year-old) and the revelation of discrepancies in the number of Internal Affairs investigations support citizen suspicions that improvements in the NPD are lacking.

Newark's excessively divisive political landscape and perceptions of police harassment, along with a belief that police are not responding to the appropriate, immediate concerns of their citizens, contribute to negative citizen and personnel views of the NPD. These views suggest the NPD does not receive its mandate from the people they police. This is contrary to the ideals of CPS. The following section discusses positive views of the NPD, explains affirmative actions that NPD is taking to increase their legitimacy with the community, and cites the Collaborative Change study in arguing that, overall, the NPD is viewed as a legitimate source of police service in Newark.

**At the end of the day, it's about how you treat people.** While the previous section discussed the mechanisms by which people might view the NPD negatively, other data reveal favorable views of the NPD and suggest ways the NPD can and does continue to cultivate those opinions. Relatively low (though still high) violent crime rates, increasing the number of constructive interactions with citizens, and using technology (i.e., intelligence and mapping software) to allocate resources and to suggest tactics assist the NPD in maintaining legitimacy in the community.

Most interviewees relayed the delicate relationship the community has with the police department. Police personnel understand the community generally views the NPD as legitimate, but realize one negative interaction can suddenly reverse public opinion. Deputy Sanchez discusses a situation in which his team helped to reduce violent and drug activity in a high crime public housing complex, resulting in mixed reviews for the police. He states:

> It depends who you ask. I'll give you an instance; [the] unit did a hell of a job in guarding the housing complex always plagued with violence. We have now given it back to the residents, to the hard workin' resident, and it's funny because I go there, and the old people, senior citizens are like, 'Thank you so much, this is a long time coming.' Then I hear of people tellin' me that their experience is a lot different. They're sayin', 'You guys locked up my cousin, you guys locked up my family, F the police, F that.' It really depends on who you ask.

Though most citizens appreciated the positive outcomes of the concentrated police effort, some people whose family and friends were rounded up during the police operation harbored negative feelings. This reflects the influence of perceptions of police (in)effectiveness (i.e., outcomes) and police-citizen encounters on citizen views of police legitimacy.

Echoing Capt. White's previously discussed rationale for what some perceive as the "stupid shit" police do, Deputy Sanchez turns to the controversial practice of stopping and frisking citizens. He explains:

> We might hit a location and we're there for a reason, a purpose. In-
> telligence has told us this is the location to be, and we might stop and
> frisk eight or nine people. Well, you only got one person. That one per-
> son could have committed eight shootings, eight robberies, eight
> homicides. Is that a failure? Ask the people that live there, the good
> people, if they mind the inconvenience of us goin' there and target-
> tin' that area. We go places for reasons.

Resultant crime reductions, citizens understanding the impersonal (or, data-
driven) reasons why police target specific locations, and police acting professionally assuage citizens' negative perceptions of the police.

Technology, implicated in the latter part of the Reform era for alienating
the police from the community, is used in the New Community Problem-
Solving era to justify the allocation of police power and police attention. Though
the tactics are data-driven, they are still person-performed and citizen-centered.
Thus, another key to gaining and maintaining legitimacy with the citizenry is
for police officers to conduct themselves in a personable and courteous manner while fulfilling their data-driven mandate. Deputy Sanchez explains:

> If you ask any policeman or any citizen, at the end of the day, it's
> about how you treat people. I can stop you and say, 'This is the rea-
> son I'm stoppin' you, A, B, C and D. You have the right to stop and
> talk to me, or you don't.' As long as you treat people with respect, at
> the end of it, they can walk away saying, 'Yes, it was an inconvenience;
> yes he held me for ten minutes, but I don't have to worry about a stray
> bullet hittin' me and killin' me through the window.'

The need for police to be perceived as treating citizens fairly remains true regardless of the setting or the reason for meeting them.

Other respondents cite further examples to illuminate the merit of establishing
professional relationships with the community to respond to problems in their
neighborhood. For instance, when questioned about the importance of explaining police tactics to the community and to the police themselves, Chief
Thomas points out:

> It's more important to explain it to the cops, because, not that the
> cops are more valuable than the community, but what's gonna hap-
> pen is the cops are gonna encounter the community first, and if you
> don't get it right with the cops, then you're working backwards.

Before we can expect police to articulate to the citizens their rationale for stopping them, police departments must first implement the training and mana-

gerial components necessary to getting their police officers to understand and value such behavior. The NPD uses technology to maintain open lines of communication with the community. Lt. Crossin demonstrates how these four officers appreciate the value of communicating their rationale to citizens, implement a more specific strategy, and see the results of their work:

> The four [police officers] that are there permanently will give you their personal cell phone number [and say,] 'If you see something out here, or somebody's lurkin' around, call my cell phone and I will be there to handle it.' They've had quite a few good arrests off of that, from people trusting them enough to know they are only a few blocks away and they're comin'.

Lt. Crossin reports that this, along with having his officers go door-to-door introducing themselves, has successfully helped the NPD to regain community trust and has resulted in a decrease in crime in that area. These working relationships with the community members, facilitated by technology and in combination with police intelligence and data, allow police to target more specific locations, individuals, and problems, thereby reducing the amount of actual and perceived crime and disorder problems, thus legitimizing the collective view of the NPD.

Although the NPD has made advancements in the way it relates to the community, the police department and community leaders still look for ways to fortify that relationship and to make the NPD more legitimate. This section has placed the NPD in its greater political context and has explored the fragile relationship between the NPD and its citizens (a vital relationship in CPS). It also demonstrated how a police department implementing a CPS strategy can improve its legitimacy by using technology and data to justify to the community their tactics and their allocation of resources as well as prove their effectiveness in reducing crime and disorder. The intimate nature of the interactions that police have when solving problems with the community requires police to ensure they are perceived as acting professionally and justly.

# The NPD Structure

*"We're gonna push down authority to precinct commanders."*

## Demand Entrance and Demand Management

Newark's bid to reduce violence by focusing police attention on lower level offending includes a shift in the avenues by which the NPD receives demand for their services and in the ways that demand is managed in the organization. Respondents who voice both support for and concern with the direction of the NPD agree that much of the demand for police service has shifted since a time when the Communications Division received demand and allocated it throughout the organization. Many argue Director McCarthy has given the "street boss" (or, precinct captain or sergeant) increased authority to interpret and administer that demand. Chief Thomas characterizes it as such:

> Giving the street ownership to the street boss, as opposed to listening to the boss up in communications. The street boss (usually a sergeant) is quarterbacking his own team. He's not really getting any plays brought in through the sidelines (which would be communications).

This section discusses this shift in the NPD. It describes how, in line with CPS, the NPD receives its demand not only from contacts with the community, but also from calls for service, and how that demand is managed through crime mapping and analysis technology.

**We go places for reasons, intelligence has told us this is the location to be.** As this research discusses, the NPD's shift from the Reform era to the CPS era most strikingly manifests in the new ways the NPD negotiates its relationship with the community. This relationship undergirds many of the other processes involved in organizational change in this study. In this shift, the NPD is moving from a time when they sell their crime-fighting goods to the public, to one in which they consult with citizens and work with them to create the most marketable and useful tools to respond to community needs (see Kelling & Moore, 1988).

Technology (a distinguishing element in the three eras of modern policing) plays a pivotal role in discussions of demand management and in responding to that demand in Newark. For instance, technology in the NPD forms the basis of demand reception and the response to that demand. Traditionally, as in other police departments, demand in the NPD entered (and was administered through) the organization by calls for service to 9-1-1, facilitated by computer-aided dispatch technologies. As Capt. Green remembers:

In the last ten years we had a period of time where calls for service were definitely the priority. Now we've gone away from, as the Director would say, 'Chasing the radio,' going from job to job to job. He's very big on sector integrity, which is having the same people in the same sectors so they get to know the business people, the people who live there, the bad people, etc. So that's a big philosophic change, and that's been in the last two years.

All respondents agree that calls for service are no longer the priority for the NPD. Some speak disparagingly of this shift. Others reminisce on the days of "queue goals" (i.e., time limits by which officers need to respond to and handle calls for police service). Still others laud the move toward what some officers refer to as "intelligent policing." Capt. Goodman disagrees with the new change, stating, "You live and die by your calls for service in the community." She adds, "Response times are certainly not a concern. The boss has made it perfectly clear he's not interested in response times for [less serious offenses]."

Though the NPD still requires officers to respond to serious and in-progress calls for service and relies on communication with citizens (through field inquiries, 3-1-1, community meetings, and tip hotlines), technology most primarily directs demand through the organization and indicates to which places, crimes, and people the NPD should respond. The ample data and demand sources, analyzed using computers, further rationalize police actions. Armed with actionable intelligence that is derived from and explained to citizens, can help justify police tactics and ease tensions with the community. Under this rubric, race, sex, age, or socioeconomic status alone does not drive police response. Whereas the Reform era used technology (i.e., radio cars) to take the politics out of the police and the police out of politics (Miller, 1977), the CPS era uses technology to sterilize the police justification for their response. So, the NPD still "responds" to crimes. The response, however, is no longer simply a reaction to individual crimes or criminals, nor guided by power struggles between minority groups, but rather it is a response to a systematic analysis of geographically and temporally immediate crime and problem areas.

The NPD is moving away from the traditional police response to all calls for police service and toward a clearer understanding of CPS policing. Technologies such as ShotSpotter and the surveillance cameras serve as additional technologies that initiate the demands for police time and resources, and meetings such as CompStat help to manage that demand and to push it through the organization. Although facilitating demand entrance and management, the value of the technological output relies on the merit of the information relayed by contacts with citizens. Whether using informants to take down higher-level players in the drug trade (as reported by Deputy Cardozo), going to community meetings to hear citizens explain their specific quality of life concerns (as discussed by Capt. Phillips and Lt. Vance), or proactively "putting their hands on people" (Capt. Moran), technology's value depends on the quality and amount of information that it processes. As Lt. Dodd tells his officers:

> You're going out tonight, working an area where you had three shootings. I don't care if you're arresting nobody tonight, but if you can talk to fifteen people and find out who they are, what's their nickname, what are you doing here, who do you hang out with, as an FI (Field Interview), that's huge!

Chief Thomas quotes another of Director McCarthy's adages to demonstrate how residents know what the problem is before the police do: "There's an older woman with the pillow who's got nothing else going on but to watch what's going on. So, those are the kind of people you want to befriend because they'll tell you the information." Patrol officers, detectives, commanders, and various technologies process this information and use it to develop strategies and allocate resources. NPD's CompStat process further connotes the preeminent role of this information and technology fusion in guiding NPD's police deployment decisions.

This section has explained the clear shift from a Communications Division-run police department to one that increasingly relies on new technology and data analysis to give precinct-level decision-makers the tools they need to both devise strategies and tactics and to allocate resources. As the NPD continues to negotiate their relationship with the citizenry (assuming they stay on the trajectory posited in this research), they will more specifically enumerate the various channels by which demand enters, and is managed, in the organization. The next sections on the organizational structure and administrative processes of the NPD shed more light on many of these mechanisms and offer additional evidence of an organization coming into the CPS era.

## Organizational Structure and Administrative Processes

Any shift in an organizational strategy should bring the requisite change in how the organization is structured. A change in strategy emphasizes different content areas, divisions, and responsibilities within the organization. A discussion of changing relationships between the patrol and investigative divisions within NPD, personnel hiring and promotional considerations, and the addition or subtraction of other bureaus and task forces evidence changes in NPD's organizational structure that assist in the implementation of CPS.

**O.K., we're going to push down authority to precinct commanders.** Like most police departments, the NPD is shifting toward a CPS strategy while maintaining its quasi-military structure. This makes it difficult to disentangle some of the decentralized activities from the centralized structures in which they occur. This section describes the NPD experience in implementing decentralized processes and in changing part of the organization's structure in light of a profession, an organization, and a subculture that holds tight to the centralized, bureaucratic model of police organizations that has traditionally defined such departments.

NPD's most significant structural change is the centralization of the narcotics division. The formation of the Central Narcotics Division signals the NPD's interest in preventing crime by focusing efforts on all levels of drug distribution. This new division supplements the efforts of the precinct-level Narcotics Enforcement Teams and coincides with a "push down" of decision-making, "sector integrity," and a redistribution of personnel to those high-crime times. The seeming contradiction between centralization and pushing down decision-making reflects the NPD's understanding of the interconnected and expansive drug problem. Their response to this drug problem involves attacking it at the lowest levels (i.e., on the streets), and corroborating intelligence on drug distribution rings that reach far beyond Newark's city limits. Centralization best responds to the latter, and pushing down decision-making authority is best suited for the former. The Central Narcotics Division is intended to detect and to investigate individuals involved in the mid- and upper-levels of drug distribution rings and to coordinate the efforts of the precincts' Narcotic Enforcement Teams and other law enforcement agencies. Again, respondents reveal the distinction and relationship between lower-level and more serious crimes (that is, the need to coordinate the efforts of those working on lower-level offenses with those investigating the mid- and upper-level drug offenders).

In addition to this arrangement for dismantling drug organizations, the NPD also reorganized their investigative units to allow precinct detectives to investigate all crimes in their precinct (except for shooting incidents, which are the only crimes handled by the Major Crimes Unit). The NPD is both centrally and decentrally organized, depending on the seriousness and perceived organization of the crime to which they respond. Units that respond to upper-level drug distribution crimes, shooting incidents, and homicides remain centralized, while less serious drug offenses and most other crimes are handled by decentralized units whose patrol officers and detectives are commanded at the precinct level. At the same time, NPD leaders attempted to push authority down to the precinct level and to instill the idea of sector integrity within the organization. Deputy Nolan explains:

> This administration basically said, 'OK, we're going to push down authority to precinct commanders. As precinct commanders, I expect you to understand what's going on in your area of jurisdiction, and that you can begin to gather the intelligence and then review to make sure it worked. If it doesn't work, change it.' Everybody's need in the city is different; every area in the city is different.

Finally, though not mentioned by any of the respondents, newspaper articles chronicle the tension that occurred between Police Director McCarthy and Chief of Police Campos over the leadership of the NPD. The key point of contention was over who controlled the daily operations (i.e., personnel transfers) of the police department. This resulted in the eventual abolition of the office of the Chief of Police. Flattening the organizational structure facilitated the push down of authority and allowed for clearer, more unified leadership in portraying the new way of doing business in the NPD. A deeper exploration of the department's move toward decentralization follows.

**What we want to do is change the department into the CompStat philosophy.** While the use of CompStat is not new to the NPD, NPD personnel agree that how the NPD uses CompStat is. The new electronic Records Management System and mapping software vastly improved the usefulness of the CompStat process to the NPD. The NPD relies on the CompStat process to receive the maximum benefit from many of the elements of organizational strategy (i.e., function, demand, legitimacy, and tactics). CompStat, viewed by some as a tool for managing an organization, is a pivotal part of the NPD.

Deputy Piza describes the "CompStat philosophy" as such:

> When you are given ownership of a specific area, and when you're workin' in that area, you should be very familiar with that area. You should say, 'I'm gonna prevent crime in my specific zone.' And when every officer takes that approach (and is put in the same spots all the time), and then they're given this support through investigations and D.B. [Detectives' Bureau], that [crime reduction] should come to fruition.

This respondent describes CompStat in reference to what it means for everyday police work in the street. This contradicts common conceptions of CompStat as a managerial process, but also accurately describes the logical implications of this process on the daily activities of police officers. Highlighting the former (and more common) point, Capt. Moran states:

> CompStat doesn't touch our police officers very well. It's more the upper management. The officers don't see directly what happens in CompStat; they really don't have a concept of what the captain goes through, or the sergeant who puts the crime data together and what he's looking for. They don't see the connection between CompStat and what we ask them to do.

He goes on to suggest one way to facilitate officers' understandings of this relationship, saying, "I personally would bring a sergeant or lieutenant to CompStat so they could understand exactly why they're being asked to do things they're being asked to do." The NPD CompStat Unit uses the data analysis and mapping software in the CompStat process to offer guidance to commanders who are responsible for determining the tactical activities of their officers. The underlying purpose of these data and mapping programs is to demonstrate in multiple forms the relationship between low-level crimes, disorder, and more serious crimes.

The NPD's CompStat approach holds precinct commanders accountable, while giving those commanders the authority to act. It also allows them to visualize their problems and receive feedback in the CompStat meetings. Lt. Vance describes the value of the data presentation of CompStat:

> Mapping gives you the most accurate view of what's actually going on. You're seeing dots, you're seeing groups, you know this is where you need to go. Of course you could overlap it with other things, not just crime, but you could put quality of life issues, complaints, arrests, so that definitely has made the CompStat process better.

This researcher observed this mapping process at both CompStat meetings he attended. For instance, the map of one precinct revealed an increase in burglaries, occurring at specific times, and in a limited geographic area. Among other questions, the Director asked the commander about his officers' field inquiries and quality of life offenses. He then asked the GIS Specialist to project on the screen the overlay of police activities and the recent burglaries. Both the Director and the commander (with punctuated proffers from others in the room) suggested a few tactical and temporal changes to make in police activities.

This section explained the role of the CompStat process in helping to push down the problem-response decision-making authority to precinct commanders and demonstrated the ways in which NPD personnel view CompStat. Not everyone in the NPD is convinced, however, that the organization is successfully pushing down that authority to the precinct level. The importance of CompStat and crime mapping to the overall mission of the police department is reflected in this study's survey data. Of those personnel surveyed, 85.5% and 92.8% believed CompStat and crime mapping (respectively) were important or very important aspects of their mission, with a comparatively higher percentage holding crime mapping as very important. This supports the notion that personnel at all levels of the NPD recognize the role of CompStat and crime mapping activities to the department and gives more reason to explore how to better reach these personnel.

Another issue (raised by police personnel) is the cultural impediment to giving managers the authority and responsibility in many of these new decisions. For instance, Sergeant O'Shea notes:

> This police director has empowered the commanders to make a lot of decisions on their own and he has involved them with a lot of the policy making process. But frankly, the problem here is there's just a sort of sense of apathy or indifference. Today, commanders can transfer people within their own commands, they can change their tours, they run their commands as if it's their own little police department. So in spite of all this decentralization that's gone on in the last three, four years now, these guys are just still apathetic.

A decentralized department is one in which both strategic and administrative decision-making is pushed down to the lower levels of the police organization. Again, the importance of middle-management in the police department is underscored. Mr. Craft explains one option the department is exploring to get buy-in from police personnel:

> We're creating a formal evaluation system here. They never had that before, so that will also call them to task. We're tryin' to institute a monthly activity report, so we can actually quantify exactly what you're doin' on a day-to-day, month-to-month basis. You really gotta have that pushed down.

These last two excerpts include information on the department's human resources and the organizational culture. This discussion of police personnel inevitably reverts to a perceived need for more personnel resources and the much-studied impenetrable police subculture.

**The golden rule is having the police officers.** Policing in the CPS era requires hiring and training police officers to be better equipped to interact with the community in the ways discussed in this research. It also relies on effective management of personnel. Themes of "doing more with less" recur throughout research on successful innovations in police organizations, and in this study, it speaks to the ability of police managers to most providently allocate their resources. The mutually conditioning relationship between the police personalities that make up the police department and the police culture influences the ability of a police leader to effectively implement a new era of policing. The recruits a police department hires, the training provided to them, and the skill with which they are managed can change the culture of a department over time.

Police personnel emphasize the relevance of morale, recruitment, training, and economic conditions. Deputy Piza relates:

> It's not only about violence reduction and crime strategies, but it's also about morale building. You hire good people, you're gonna get good cops. Secondly, making sure they're trained well in the police academy, so they start to focus and get steered in the right direction as to what we need them to do when they get on the streets when it comes to fighting crime and their responsibilities and so on.

This speaks to the necessity of recruiting qualified people and giving them the appropriate training to not only more professionally serve the public but to create an organizational police culture that is more knowledgeable to the nuance of CPS. Capt. White notes the effect of not having enough police on morale, as the NPD is expected "to do more with less." This researcher observed the low morale in the precinct houses after tough economic conditions resulted in almost 170 layoffs and nearly 200 demotions in the fall of 2010. Lt. Cross, speaking of the successful patrol operation discussed above, indicts lack of money and personnel as inhibitors to carrying out that operation in other parts of the city: "They've covered the area very well for just four guys, and, if we could do that all over the entire city, we wouldn't have a problem anywhere, but money. Cops, you know." He adds, "The golden rule is having the police officers to do that."

Assignment and promotional decisions also signal to a department's personnel what it views as important to the mission of the police department, thereby influencing the morale and culture of a department. For instance, one respondent notes that personnel who wish to be reassigned from a patrol position to a detective slot believe the road to what they perceive as a promotion to detective is by first working in the Narcotics Enforcement Unit, the Anti-Crime Unit, or the Conditions Unit. This encourages officers to desire these positions and indicates the NPD's faith in the drugs, violence and quality of life triune.

In addition to the usefulness of "cross training" police personnel, Lt. Crossin suggests the following for a successful intensive citizen interaction operation:

> As much training as you can give them, or send them, give them any classes, it's in the person (whether they wanna get along with people or not). I can send people up to that area that are gonna go up there and write a book of tickets every day, lock up everybody they can, but, if you don't have a balance of it, where the people like you and trust you, they're not gonna talk to you if they think you're just the jerk who writes me tickets.

He speaks to the limitations of training and illuminates the proper approach police should take with the community. This helps to explain the absence of the expected positive relationship between more police personnel and improved police service. Police departments do not simply need numbers, they need well-trained and high caliber individuals executing the responsibilities of the position. The issue, as Capt. Phillips sees it, is the tension between the official zero-tolerance policy that many police departments have on the books and the well documented reality that police officers use a vast amount of discretion on a daily basis. He states:

> We do have a zero tolerance policy. That's the bottom line; that's what it is. It's not that we're going to ignore a violation but, there may be violations that you don't cite for if the situation doesn't work. It's just a matter of usin' good common sense I think, in some ways, and I don't know how you teach good common sense sometimes.

The recruitment process, training, supervision, and deployment of police officers and the organizational structure center on the desire to inculcate officers with the ability to properly use their discretion in a nearly infinite number of situations (many of which involve direct interaction with citizens). The ability to use discretion appropriately is a pivotal part of successful policing within a CPS framework and must be considered for police leaders to be effective.

# Summary

This chapter has demonstrated how, within their highly politicized environment and despite (or perhaps because of) a corrupt and violent history, the various elements of the NPD's organizational strategy have shifted toward CPS. Director McCarthy's leadership of the NPD reveals the importance of using technology and the newly established CompStat process to legitimize police activities, enhance community relationships, reduce crime, and change a police organization.

# References

Albrecht, S. & Green, M. (1977). Attitudes toward the police and the larger attitude complex. *Criminology*, 15, pp. 67–86.

The Center for Collaborative Change. (March 2010). Community-police relations [Survey results]. Retrieved from http://newarkchange.org/survey/.

Curry, M. (Director). (2005). *Street Fight* [Motion picture]. United States: Marshall Curry Productions.

Erminio, V. (7 September 2006). Booker taps NYPD ace to lead Newark police [Online]. *The Star-Ledger*. Retrieved from http://blog.nj.come/ledger-archives/2006/09/booker_taps_nypd_ace_to_lead_n.html.

Giambusso, D. (27 April 2010). Newark police director files defamation lawsuit against three 'Newark Choice' candidates. Retrieved from http://www.nj.com/news/index.ssf/2010/04/newark_police_director_files_d.html.

Giambusso, D. & Megerian, C. (10 September 2010). City officials support federal monitor of Newark police department. Retrieved from http://www.nj.com/news/index.ssf/2010/09/city_council_former_police_off.html.

Kelling, G., & Moore, M. (November 1988). The evolving strategy of policing. *Perspectives on Policing*, National Institute of Justice.

Liebman, S. (21 June 2007). Report for action. Retrieved from http://blog.nj.com/ledgernewark/2007/06/report_for_action.html.

Miller, W. (1977). *Cops and bobbies: Police authority in New York and London, 1830–1870*. Chicago: University of Chicago.

Office of Policy and Planning. (23 June 2010). Newark police-community relations strategy [Draft]. Newark Police Department.

Queally, J. (16 September 2010). Newark police union vote 'No confidence' in city's police director after ACLU petition, *The Star-Ledger* [Online]. Retrieved from http://www.nj.com/news/index.ssf/2010/09/newark_superior_officer_group.html.

Schuppe, J (8 September 2006). Newark's new cop director stresses quality of life: Ex-NYPD veteran ties lowering crime to eradicating the drug trade. *The Star-Ledger*. Retrieved from http://www.newarkspeaks.com/forum/showthread.php?t=3068.

Schuppe, J. (22 October 2006a). Hitting Newark crime from 3 angles: Quality-of-life's the key top cop says, *The Star-Ledger* [Online]. Retrieved from http://newarktalk.com/talk/viewtopic.php?p=16503&sid=e39317da8fae2af9b7c0c571d5b34046"http://newarktalk.com/talk/viewtopic.php?p=16503&sid=e39317da8fae2af9b7c0c571d5b34046.

# Chapter 5

# The Boston Police Department

## Introduction

The Boston Police Department (BPD) is famous for its implementation of a community problem-solving strategy in the mid-1990s. During that period, the police worked with a mixture of community groups to drive down youth homicides by 63%. Unfortunately, in the years that followed (i.e., 2000–2006), police department relations with the community fell off and Boston experienced a 160% increase in these homicides. This chapter shows how Commissioner Edward Davis uses the BPD's rich CPS history to re-create a CPS strategy in a now post-9/11, technologically dependent, and financially challenged world. This chapter builds on Boston's policing narrative and demonstrates the value that past good practices could have on the current decisions a leader has to make.

## The BPD Mission

*"The first basic tenet is you gotta go out there and arrest the fuckin' bad guys."*

### Function

About his first full year as Commissioner of the BPD Edward Davis writes, "We enhanced that commitment [to community policing] by ensuring that its philosophy informed all of our decisions and guided all of our actions" (*2007 BPD Annual Report*, p. 3). This research examines the extent to which the CPS strategy influences these police departments' decisions and actions. The analysis of the BPD first considers the BPD's function, before moving on to the other elements of organizational strategy, to uncover evidence of the BPD's stated commitment to community policing. The BPD official mission statement reads, "We dedicate ourselves to work in partnership with the community to fight crime, reduce fear and improve the quality of life in our neighborhoods. Our Mission is Community Policing" (*2009 BPD Annual Report*, p. 2). This section corroborates data from interviews, a community survey, news articles, and BPD archives to explore the BPD's experience in fulfilling their mission.

**The first basic tenet of community policing is, you gotta go out there and arrest the fuckin' bad guys.** The BPD's successes combating youth gun violence in the 1990s epitomized for many the community policing strategy. The BPD, like many police departments, has been, at different times, more and less committed to the community policing philosophy. The St. Clair Commission's Report (St. Clair, 1992) on failed leadership, a stagnant vision for the department, and questionable Internal Affairs investigative practices in the BPD spurred the laying of the groundwork for the BPD's "Boston Miracle" in the latter half of the 1990s. Braga, Hureau, and Winship (2008) then document the end of the miracle. This current research explores the BPD's most recent experiences reestablishing the mechanisms and relationships by which they had successfully fulfilled their mission.

The upper echelon of the BPD clearly understands the multifaceted function of the BPD. In-depth interviews with BPD command personnel echo their mission statement and reveal a community-based, neighborhood-specific, problem-solving function in which the police department, through various tactics, works with the community to define problems (ranging from loud neighbors to gun violence) and create and implement solutions (from removing a bench from an apartment complex to arresting neighbors). The interview data reflect BPD's balance of working with the community to fight crime, reduce disorder, and improve the quality of life. Superintendent Schmidt first admits, "Our mission has always been to protect the public, reduce crime." He then goes on to explain:

> Where I think we're getting better is, we understand we have to deal with all the little issues too, the gang disturbances, the kids in the park, the problems of that particular neighborhood.... Let's address their concerns, whether it's gang caused, or kids drinking down the park, or loud parties, or college kids in Brighton; or is it the Theater District down on Tremont St. with the clubs, or is it some gang neighborhoods. We know what the neighborhoods want by talking to them, going to the community meetings, working with their neighborhood advisory groups, and listening to them day in and day out because if you listen to people as opposed to talk to them, they'll tell you what they want and just adapt your policing to what they want, and that problem solving, community police and problem solving in policing

hotspots, it all works, but the main parts of this is dealing with the community and working with them to solve the community's problems, not just the police problems — the community's problems.

The respondent captures the subtleties of broken windows policing within the CPS strategy. While people often view crime control and community policing as opposites, this quote displays the BPD's recognition of the need to respond to a variety of citizen concerns, with the most pressing concern being public safety. Given the traditional emphasis on crime control through arrest and rapid response to calls for service it is worth noting the baseline acceptance of the need for police to work with the community to police disorder and other low-level forms of community offending.

Another respondent, Superintendent Lee, portrays the BPD's history with community policing as auguring the current iteration of that strategy, which relies on the crime and disorder control function of police. This foundation, he states, brings the BPD to a clearer understanding of the many functions of the police department. He states:

> The first basic tenet of community policing is, you gotta go out there and arrest the fuckin' bad guys. If I'm trying to walk up and down the street and get everyone jobs and alternative programming and they're slinging dope and carrying guns and shooting kids, well, the community is not interested in that. They need to have the crime stopped first. And I think some people confuse community policing with not arresting people. The first tenant, stop the disorder, and that means making arrests, and then talk to kids about alternatives.

Concerning community policing, this respondent portrays the role of an initially strong police presence in creating perceptions of safe and orderly neighborhoods. Superintendent Frank adds:

> An important part of [community policing] is that we arrest criminals, we want people to feel safe in their neighborhoods. That message needs to be promoted among the officers, and I think the additional messages are looking at quality of life issues, problem-solving with the community, and doing prevention work with youth will really start to form nice.

These statements reflect an understanding of the role of citizens' perceptions in forming productive problem-solving relationships with the BPD. They also evidence their mission to reduce crime and fear and improve the quality of life. Deputy Taylor explains:

I don't know what people's perception of crime is in certain neighborhoods, but I think that's important because if they perceive themselves to be safe, they'll be more involved in the community. They'll go outside, they'll go use the park. If they don't feel safe, whether it's real or imagined, but it's still their perception, they won't go out and they won't let their kids out because they just don't feel like it's safe. If they see the police officer and they know the police officer on the beat, if they have a relationship with the district and they feel like they could call somebody like the community service officer, if they have that sort of relationship, that makes people feel better.

Superintendent Lee explains the challenge of getting BPD officers to understand their proper function within the community policing strategy. He states:

I have a challenge, even today, where officers feel we don't want them to make an arrest up there. That's not the case; if an arrest is warranted, it's warranted. I don't need you to arrest just for the sake of an arrest. I think the community sees us more problem solving in dealing with quality of life issues than they do arrest because we talk to them, we survey them. In areas with major crimes going on (whether it's homicides, ton of youth violence) and we'll survey the community and ask them what the issues are, and they'll tell us, abandon cars, speeding cars, people illegally dumping stuff. Jesus, what about the homicide? Yeah, that's a problem, but we got to get rid of these kids that graffiti up the place. So, you know, they'd rather us focus on quality of life stuff too.

The respondent notes that although police maintain the sole ability to enforce the law and to legally arrest a suspected lawbreaker, the community expects the BPD to also assist in maintaining order by dealing with their quality of life concerns. The BPD works with the community to reduce crime and disorder, which enhances citizens' perceptions of their city and of the BPD. A biannual survey[1] of a representative sample of Bostonians (conducted by a BPD-contracted firm) contextualizes these findings (Pulavarti, Bernadeau, Kenney, & Savage, 2007). The 2006 survey asked respondents to state how serious a problem is each

---

1. This survey was conducted just prior to Commissioner Davis' appointment to the BPD. However, the findings are still worth exploring in lieu of data from the yet to be published 2010 community survey (Pulavarti, Bernadeau, Kenney, & Savage, 2007). Also, presenting aggregate level survey data makes it difficult to disentangle the neighborhood level issues and concerns that this paper explores.

of fifteen conditions (ranging from noise to gun usage). The top five conditions rated with the highest percentage as "somewhat" serious or "serious" include: (1) litter and trash lying around; (2) cars broken-in; (3) drug sales; (4) burglary; and (5) vandalism. These problems reflect the variety (and notably nonviolent nature) of problems the BPD responds to in fulfilling their problem-solving, crime and disorder reduction strategy.

This section has explored the definite community-based, crime and disorder reduction function of the BPD. The BPD seeks to work with neighborhoods to define a wide range of criminal and lower-level, neighborhood-specific problems and solutions, and recognizes the relevance of citizens' perceptions and feelings of safety in collaborating with the BPD. These solutions involved a variety of tactics, new technologies, and measurements that support the BPD's mission to work with the community to fight crime, reduce disorder, and enhance the quality of life.

## *Tactics, Technology, and Outcomes*

Superintendent Frank gives a brief history of the BPD's community policing philosophy, reporting that the BPD moved from an arrest-based approach in the 1980s and early 1990s to one where "we really saw the need to expand the way we viewed policing" and "we started to think more comprehensively—enforcement, intervention, and prevention, as well as forming partnerships with law enforcement agencies, the community, clergy, and the business community." Though the strength of and reliance on these tactics and collaborations have changed over time, the BPD's most recent strategies represent a return to the successful efforts of the "Boston Miracle." They include increased formal and informal community contacts, real time data analysis, and violent and disorderly hotspots (i.e., people and places) policing. These epitomize Commissioner Davis's goal to reduce violence and revive community relationships.

**There's more than just runnin' and gunnin'.** Superintendent Miller notes that the BPD, operating with a belief that relationships matter and that "small things lead to bigger things," instituted Safe Street Teams (SST) and a Street Outreach Team (SOT). These teams form productive relationships with citizens in Boston's hotspots of crime and disorder. The SOT is a two-person patrol unit that spends their time proactively interacting with individuals who are among the truly disadvantaged (i.e., mentally ill, street people, drug addicted) and criminal street populations to provide (when applicable) non-arrest responses to underlying problems. The officers build relationships with individual street people and with the agencies with which they work. This facilitates BPD efforts to keep these areas safe and orderly and help to focus police attention on the high-risk people and places that contribute to disproportionately high levels of violence.

Policing low-level offenses against high-risk criminals and in high-risk places without arresting individuals for those offenses assists police in sending signals of neighborhood control and can increase citizens' perceptions of the BPD. Discussing the BPD's response to lower level offending, Captain Garcia states:

> You arrest someone, in some cases you arrest under these circumstances but we're trying to gain in the aggressive panhandling, now you just took that officer off the street for an hour, an hour and a half, if it's a busy day, it's gonna be two hours before you get that prisoner processed and the reports done. The citation takes all of ten minutes and the guy is still in his area, and the same ultimate goal is reached…. It's tryin' to target somebody, the behavior of these individuals; we just try to tell them we don't want this, we're not gonna tolerate it…. Our goal is to address their behavior. For example, for public drinking we do have a right of arrest, but I think it's counterproductive to arrest everyone you see with a drink, and I think we've seen improvement. We don't have the huge numbers. The other thing we've done down there too is using some of the smaller issues to address some of the bigger issues.

This respondent acknowledges the need to respond to these "smaller" quality of life offenses without relying too heavily on arresting individuals. He gives an example of BPD's "Operation Common Cure" that used both a strict law enforcement component and a "little compassion" for individuals' plights in an effort to respond to concentrated levels of crime and disorder. This type of approach has the potential to save officers time (e.g., processing the arrest and going to court) and to more sustainably affect crime and disorder in these locations (by responding to problems, not just incidents). Like the SOT, the SST originates from a similar emphasis on building relationships and taking ownership of areas of crime and disorder.

The SST[2] began in 2007 and borrowed from the earlier ideas of "Same Cop, Same Neighborhood" (or beat integrity) and Commissioner Davis' time as Superintendent in Lowell, MA. Boston's SST are now involved in thirteen neighborhoods throughout the city (i.e., in violent crime hotspots, as directed by crime mapping techniques). Patrol officers in these teams maximize their positive interactions with citizens in high crime neighborhoods by patrolling on foot and bicycle, attending various community functions, and by working with cit-

---

2. See Braga & Bond (2008) for a more in-depth explanation of the Safe Street Teams' Lowell, MA ascendance.

izens to respond to specific problems of crime and disorder. Their visibility serves not only as a deterrent to those who would wish to disturb the evolving control mechanisms in the neighborhood, but as reassurance to citizens who expect to see a police presence and who view the BPD as a legitimate source of assistance. They also serve as necessary forms of formal social control in otherwise disorderly neighborhoods.

Deputy Taylor details the officers' experiences as members of the SST:

> The Safe Street Teams, a lot of our younger, aggressive officers are in that and they're realizing that there's more than just runnin' and gun-nin'. It's getting out there, riding bicycles, talking to people in the busier districts to working with their issues and staying in that spot where they're seeing the patterns and the times that things happen or the people who belong and the people who don't, the crimes that are hap-pening and how they prevent them, how do they help stop them, work with different community groups, whatever issue it may be. But yeah, the younger officers always wants that—they're going to always strive to maybe go to a drug unit or a gang unit or some other unit to do some-thing different.

The deputy's excerpt corresponds to this researcher's observations of a cap-tains' meeting in which the captains in attendance agreed that many young of-ficers are not suited to work with the SST because they do not appreciate the work the teams do. In other words, the captains believe the younger officers prefer the "runnin' and gunnin'" aspects of police work. The deputy's discus-sion also echoes observations from a meeting of the SST commanders who valued having the same officers in the same neighborhoods doing "hotspot policing," "at the problem locations and at the right times." Similarly, the cap-tains enjoyed having officers take ownership of a small geographic location, which, they report, allows the officers to focus on specific problems.

Finally, observations during a walk-along in one of the SST areas revealed the genuine relationships the officer had with various people during the walk. The amount of knowledge that the officer and citizens had of each other's lives and their discussions on various community programs and detailed neighborhood happenings evidence the authenticity of these relationships. The officer gave numerous examples of the payout of the BPD's relationships with that neighborhood. These relationships create knowledge sharing and empathy; they give officers an understanding of the social geography of these hotspot areas; and they facilitate neighborhood-specific, community-based responses to problems of crime and disorder. Captain Garcia details the work of the SST:

They're very proactive. It's a hand-picked group of guys who wanna do some good police work; they give us good numbers, and the key to why it works so well is 'cause these guys are very accountable for what happens in their area.... They're very in tune with what's going on in their sectors, and their sector is not a huge sector because keep in mind they're on bicycles, but it's a pretty big sector; it runs from the downtown crossing right into the district area, so it's about 8 or 10 blocks. We'd love it to be smaller, but that problem, again, the hotspot area, was pretty big, so you can't focus it more on the area. They do focus mostly on the downtown crossing on the later part of the afternoon to the early evening; that's been very effective. If you had that ability at all time, to have a group of dedicated officers, whether they be on bicycles, motorcycles, you name it, Segways if they went that way, any type of mechanism where they're not on a car.... Focusing on those areas where you're having problems really seems to help.

Beat integrity and police collaboration with citizens to define a variety of problems and responses to those problems in areas of said hotspots are features of the SST. The remaining patrol force works under a similar neighborhood and citizen interaction focus. Superintendent Miller reports:

I think it's just talkin' to people, talkin' to the community, and listenin' to what their needs are, because just because we're the police, and we're here, doesn't mean that we know what's goin' on, and what the issues are in different communities, and the thing is, different communities have different issues, especially with a city like Boston which is very divided. Like, in West Roxbury, their needs might be very different than Roxbury is, given the populations in those two areas. So, you have to talk to people and find out, what are their needs, not tell them what you wanna do for them, but tell me what you need from me. This will build a good relationship.... Before we just went and did police work and responded to calls, then see you later! Now it's like, almost, we go to different meetings, different functions, like this [cookout] today.

He continues, discussing the role of quality of life enforcement and the need to place that enforcement within its proper neighborhood context:

I think it's a very positive role because those little things are the ones that bother people the most, although they know around the corner somebody may get shot or whatever, they know that that's gonna happen, but, little things that we have control of, like quality of life things, a dirty lot, or dirty street, or a light that's missin' somewhere, those kind of things are the things that affect people the most. A bad neighbor that's always playin' loud music at all times of the day and night, those are the things that really affect people's lives, and if we take care of that it makes a big difference, and you make a friend in the community. Quality of life is number one.... Every community has their own idea of what quality of life is.

Captain Clarke adds, "It's the quality of life issues that's driving them crazy. Not the things that happen to a particular person, but the things that affect the greatest amount of people." Working with the community to define problems generates a police response to quality of life concerns. Field Interrogation Observation (FIO) forms, Code 19s (also known as "walk and talks"), the Reporting Area Project[3] (RAP), the SOT, SST, attendance at community meetings, a biannual survey of citizens, and data management and analysis technologies assist the BPD's efforts in measuring and implementing solutions to crime and disorder problems (as defined by the community). They also evidence the BPD's efforts to reduce crime and enhance relationships with the community.

The FIO forms and Code 19s are carryovers from the 1990s push for community policing and are meant to increase the quantity and quality of police interactions with citizens. The FIO forms document these interactions and any information gained from the interaction, and Code 19s and RAP provide ways for patrol officers to call in their time to dispatch, making the walk and talk a viable and formally acceptable method of patrol. Technologies used in CompStat, the Boston Regional Intelligence Center (BRIC), and the Real Time Crime Center assist the BPD in measuring the outcomes of their work and in focusing police efforts on high-risk people and places.

Superintendent Frank describes some new technologies and the institution of the BRIC and RTCC:

> The ShotSpotter, identifies locations of gunfire; the development of the Boston Regional Intelligence Center in 2005 as a central depository for analyzing and evaluating and distributing information to the department. Most recently, the Real Time Crime Center, which monitors different locations in the city, has had positive benefits for the department. Cameras in the neighborhoods, things like that have

---

3. The Reporting Area Project expands on the "walk and talks" by assigning patrol officers to small, geographic areas in which they must spend at least one hour of their patrol time interacting with citizens and solving problems.

played a part. I think sometimes they're looked at as these new silver bullets to deal with crime, and I don't think it's that, but it's a good addition that allows for a timely response to some issues of crime in neighborhoods.

Captain Moore explains how the data gathered and analyzed by these technologies help to focus BPD resources on hotspots:

> You know what I think is pretty effective? Hotspots through crime analysis. We have a unit downstairs; they take all that information as it becomes available. That information is sent back to the different commanders, they have their meetings on it. You know exactly where your problems are; you don't have to guess. Anytime something happens, we have that information right from the computer. I open up my computer now and I can tell you what's going on in any parts of the city. The hotspots, know where they are, now let's develop a strategy. What do we need to do here, what's going on here? You got shots fired, got drugs, you got petty theft, you got people stealing cars and stripping them, whatever the problem happens to be, where they're happening at. And you've identified those so-called hotspots. Now you have resources. Put together a plan or strategy, how you're going to deal with it.... I think that whole concept of hotspots, identifying the hotspots and developing strategies and the resources to deal with those problems. And don't forget, always involve working with the community, you still have your community meetings, you still have your crime watchers, you still are working with a lot of your outside agencies, parole, probation, you name it. Depends on what the issues are will determine what resources you need to deal with it. It starts from the top and you have a commissioner that's committed to it, the chief's committed to it, your zone commanders are committed to it, your captain's committed to it. So it goes right down, and then they are held accountable. We have a crime analysis meeting [Comp-Stat], you sit there and you have to explain what you do, if you're having a problem some place, what did you do about it and what do you need?

These technologies give the BPD detailed information on incidents; this information is then used to make decisions about tactics and resource deployment to hotspots.

Respondents discuss other uses for these technologies: computerized report writing that save officers time and in-car mobile data terminals (MDTs) that increase patrol officers' access to information. The time and information gained from these technologies improves the patrol response to neighborhood problems. Lieutenant Harris sums up the incongruity of technology's role in community relationship building:

> Well, I think so much of that [the "community-oriented policing philosophy"] is relationship based. I mean, can we take the information the community gives us and use technology to try to categorize it and sort it and spit it back out in a meaningful way; can we develop strategies through technology? Yeah, I guess so. We can analyze crime trends and crime data and stuff like that so, I don't know. Those things are very valuable, but I don't know that they enhance community-oriented policing more than just the attitude of the officer or again, about discretion of what's he going to do with his time, and the relationships that he forms.

The abilities of these technologies to receive, store and process large amounts of information is indeed valuable to police work. New technologies also give supervisors insight into how their patrol officers spend their time. This new information can then be used to train an officer in how to spend his or her time problem solving and interacting with citizens. Superintendent Schmidt adds, "Technology will help us, but it's really understanding your people, the people you service." Both respondents identify the danger of losing the interpersonal basis of their work and the need for officers to properly use their discretion and form meaningful relationships with citizens. Finally, these technologies help the BPD in reporting their "performance statistics."

For example, the SST track numbers of moving violations arrests, FIOs, and city ordinance violations in reporting changes in Part I and Part II crimes. For the SST, the FIOs and ordinance violations "are used quite a bit because that's their strategy on the so-called 'broken windows,' the public drinking and the panhandling, along those lines," Capt. Garcia reports.

The BPD is still searching for ways, however, to measure the relationship building aspects of police work. As Superintendent Schmidt states, "Most of the things we measure are things that we can count. It's much more difficult to measure the intangibles." Regarding CompStat, Superintendent Miller states, "CompStat doesn't measure the things that we're talking about, community policing type of things, and that's what [one high ranking BPD official] is trying to get to." Superintendent Lee adds:

> It's based on building relationships. Ordinarily in police work, we measure cops on how many arrests did you make, how many tags did

you do, how many motor vehicle stops did you make, how many stops to people did you make on the street where you filled out a field interrogation observation form and you pat for someone (if you thought you needed to) for weapons. Which one of those is most liked by the citizens; when we arrest them, when we give them a parking ticket, when we cost them money on a moving ticket and they got to pay their insurance higher, or when you're walking down the street with your girlfriend and I stop you and ask you questions about whether you committed a crime and pat, frisk you? None. That's what we measure at CompStat. Where are the arrests, where are the tags, where are the FIOs? We don't measure how many community contacts you have, how many positive things have you done for the community, how many community meetings did you attend, how many disputes did you mediate and resolve without law enforcement action being taken, how many friends have you made out there? The minute you pin this badge on your chest, you get all the enemies you need in the world, so my challenge is to try and get my cops to go out there and make some friends.... You make a lot more friends talking to people and being kind, than you do making arrests.... We've never trained cops on that. We've never trained a cop how to walk into a store, cold, say, 'Hello, my name is Officer Jones,' and talk to the store owner and say, 'I'm assigned on here. I'm vested in the community. I want to do what's right to keep it safe here, what do you need me to do to work with you as a store owner?' We don't train them to do that.... So then try and build a relationship with the community when their only experience with a police officer is they're getting a ticket, they're getting arrested, or they're getting tagged, and the cops never come in.... We don't blame the soldiers for war, we blame the cops for crime. So since we get the blame, let's take ownership of it, and it's tough to blame me if you and I are working on it together. And then you realize, 'No, [he's] a good guy, it's not him, it's just these kids. And he's down here, and when I call him he's here, and I've talked to him about the problem, he's addressed it, and, the judges let the kid go, or probation failed, but I feel like the police are a partner with me.' Once we build that relationship then that's one down, we got to hopefully tell two more friends, and two more friends, and two more friends 'til it builds. So I think we have to look at how we look at good cops, how we define a good cop. No one, until recently, have we started defining good cops, the officer who's working with the kids and the community doing community service. We don't give out medals for that. We give out medals for getting guns, and engaging in shootouts and getting kilos; we don't give out medals for taking kids to summer camp, and teaching kids how to write a resume, and talking to a gang kid in a mediation out of not going over and retaliating and trying to get himself focused on positive stuff.

He explains the various interactions the BPD has with its citizens and the effects of those interactions on BPD-citizen relationships. He suggests that new training, departmental recognition, and new ways of measuring police work can facilitate a more neighborhood-based, citizen-focused function.

The BPD recognizes the need to officially measure and reward these community-oriented tactics. Respondents discuss new ways the BPD is exploring to do this. They include encouraging detectives to conduct Code 19s, displaying Code 19 totals during CompStat, and recognizing at CompStat sworn and non-sworn BPD personnel who "have done a good job, or have done something to help with the community," as Superintendent Miller states. These are in addition to the acknowledgments that police departments traditionally offer for the "runnin' and gunnin'" their officers do.

This section explored the tactical, technological, and measurement features of the BPD's deeply held commitment to the community policing philosophy. Specifically, Boston's Street Outreach Team, the Safe Street Teams, proactively responding to problems of disorder using a variety of tactics, beat integrity, citizen interaction, technology and data processes to manage, support, and sharpen these tactics, and explorations into new ways of measuring and valuing the community-related work of the BPD. The following section examines the BPD's relationship with citizens, community groups, and other city agencies in fulfilling its mission to fight crime, reduce disorder, and enhance the quality of life.

# Working with the Community

*"Creating partnerships with the community isn't difficult,*
*it's maintaining it over time."*

## *External Relationships and Legitimacy*

Legitimacy and relationships with the external environment go hand in hand. The BPD's claim of a community-oriented function presumes fruitful working relationships with individuals and groups within the city (or at least an attempt to create such relationships). These relationships are not only a

means to the crime and disorder reduction and quality of life enhancing function of the BPD but also an end in themselves. Data from this study reveal
how the BPD has built on their relationship building mechanisms from the
1990s to find new ways of relating to and working with a number of external
entities.

**Creating partnerships with the community is not difficult, it's maintain-
ing it over time.** The BPD's collaborations with numerous law enforcement
and social service agencies and community and church groups contributed to
the precipitous decline in youth violence in mid-1990s Boston. Braga et al.
(2008) highlight the BPD's challenges in maintaining the successful collaborations
of the 1990s amidst serious cases of internal corruption, a loss of sworn personnel, organizational restructuring, internal conflict in community groups
involved with the Ten Point Coalition, and a subsequent rise in juvenile gang
violence. After this unraveling of the "Boston Miracle," the BPD adapts what
it views as the successful elements of their past strategies to the most recent
environment in which it operates. These renewed relationships with citizens and
continued successful collaborations with a variety of groups signify the BPD's
road to legitimization and lend credence to their use of people- and place-spe-
cific tactics in supporting their stated function to fight crime, reduce disorder,
and enhance the quality of life in Boston.

A survey conducted just prior to Commissioner Davis' tenure at the BPD revealed residents' feelings of no confidence in the BPD's ability to prevent and
solve crimes (Pulavarti, Bernadeau, Kenney, & Savage, 2007). The BPD faced
a series of crises including: arrests of BPD police officers involved in illegal
drugs, accusations of widespread drug use (i.e., steroids) by BPD personnel,
allegations of mishandled internal investigations, rising violence, and increased
feelings that the BPD did not promote and recruit adequate numbers of racial
minorities (Bernstein, 2008; *More Police Problems*, 2008). Upon taking office,
Commissioner Davis, recognizing the need to be more responsive to the community impulse (and charged by the mayor with reducing violence and enhancing community relationships), discussed his commitment to the community
policing philosophy. He described his community policing philosophy as one
that is not only a "specialized program," but one that ensures all units within
the BPD "operate with a community-policing philosophy" (O'Brien, 2007).

Superintendent Frank discusses the BPD's experience with building community
relationships:

> Making sure that you're always working on building relations with the
> community, and building trust; we do a good job on balancing all
> those things, but really, there's no down time in it. It's continuous

work, really. Creating partnerships with the community and other agencies is not difficult, but it's maintaining it over time, and keeping a high level of operation.... It's really 1 or 2% of the population that will take the most time on these type of issues, and working with DYS [Department of Youth Services] and probation, parole, the district attorney's officer, the U.S. attorney's office. Those partnerships are critical in dealing with issues of gang violence.... And then, even working with families, we've started a couple of bodies around the ideas of working with families that are generationally involved with crime, and then, again, the more you look at this, the more complex these issues become, and the more need there is to, I think, expand the way you look at issues of crime and how you should be dealing with them. I think we've taken a job description that I think 20 years ago was more focused on arrests for the most, and really expanded on that; and understanding that, these issues need to be dealt with, but with a wide range of agencies if they can make a difference. We're not there yet, but we're getting there.

The respondent notices the changing strength of the many relationships the BPD has with other law enforcement agencies, social service agencies, community groups, and families. He realizes the BPD's role is not simply to arrest individuals but to work with the community to respond to a range of community issues. Interview and archival data posit other mechanisms that support the BPD in working (and building relationships) with the community: expanding the community service officer within each district, training in the academy, a BPD blog and Twitter site, a Text-a-Tip program, attending community meetings to receive advice and feedback about BPD efforts, and the SST. As Deputy Taylor states, "We can call anything any different programs, we can put all these elaborate names on them, theories and different strategies, but the plan is, working with the community, working with your neighbors, in development, using the resources."

This "relationship-based" focus of the BPD is evidenced more specifically in patrol officers' designated areas of responsibility (or the RAP). As Sergeant Crowley reports, in response to a question on the BPD's responsibilities:

Well, obviously respond to crime, respond to issues within their designated areas. The way it's been set up basically, is everybody has their beat, their areas of responsibility. Not only are they supposed to recognize the criminal aspect of it, but the conditions, and things that cause them. Dealing with some of the business people, property managers, housing, developments, people who run them; find out actually where the problem issue is at and what can be done to make them better. We're kind of reaching out to a lot of community groups.

These improved community relationships not only assist with crime prevention efforts but also help after a crime is committed. For instance, respondents note how positive relationships come into play, after an egregious crime or BPD mishap, to ease tensions in the community and to more quickly rebound from such incidents. Lieutenant Harris states, "I think there's community leaders that we could reach out to explain what happened, to ask for time to correct the situation."

Sergeant Crowley explains how the BPD focus on "high propensity kids" and Impact meetings represent a more law-enforcement bend to these collaborations. They also signal a return to the successful collaborative and "pulling levers" approach of the BPD that led to the "Boston Miracle," reflect a decentralization of power to captains (who are responsible for decisions about how and when to intervene), and again evidence the BPD's attempts to focus on high-risk people and places. When the BPD feels they have "done all we can with the carrot on" these repeat offenders (or, "impact points"), officers, based on information shared at bi-weekly Impact meetings, may use "minor arrests" to get a potential violent crime suspect (or victim) off the street. He states:

> We work hand in hand with the housing officers, the Safe Street Teams, the street workers, the federal prosecutor's office.... We'll work with parole, we'll work with probation, and a lot of these kids are on probation.... Sometimes, our unit doesn't make minor arrests just because of so many things going on. We have a lot of guys tied up with constant minor arrests, but you do it periodically because it might be the trigger that flips the switch for violation of probation and it may seem punitive in nature, but, it's not done just to jam a kid up, it's to jam up a kid who's high propensity kids, a kid who's probably gonna get himself shot. You have these shootings and you kind of know who's involved and individuals most likely to retaliate. If you can get them off, then you sometimes put out those fires. If you have a hard time getting them locked up, and it just starts snowballing.

Though this unit (i.e., the Youth Violence Strike Force) will collaborate with various agencies to provide a "carrot" to known high-propensity-for-violence individuals, it also acts as the strong arm of law enforcement when information leads the officers to believe that putting an individual in jail will reduce the person's likelihood of being a violent offender or victim. Arrest for a minor offense triggers a known offender's violation of probation or parole conditions and, in turn, prevents (or at least delays) a violent act or acts. The YVSF's regular tactical-planning and information-sharing Impact meetings represent the BPD's attempt to institutionalize the "pulling levers" approach of Operation CeaseFire, made famous in the 1990s.

Respondents consistently report the exchange of information that occurs between the BPD and the community and between the BPD and other agencies. This information exchange creates relationships that assist the BPD in doing their jobs and increases BPD legitimacy in the community. The relationships that individual officers make with community members serve as the basis for citizen judgments about the BPD. As discussed above, Superintendent Lee explains how community members who have positive relationships with BPD personnel will be less quick to negatively judge the BPD when scandal occurs.

Though the most recent BPD community survey data are not available, the dearth of newspaper and interview data revealing strained BPD relations with the community suggests that the BPD has built on its community policing foundation and increased their legitimacy within the community by improving working relationships with the community, decreasing violent crime rates, and having the oversight and support of an external citizen review board (Community Ombudsman Oversight Panel, 2009). This section has shown the forms these relationships take in the BPD and how the BPD has reached back to their successful efforts of the 1990s in building relationships with the community. The following section describes issues in receiving and managing demands for Boston police services, and highlights issues in maintaining perceptions of public safety while reducing a reliance on traditional ways of handling this demand.

# BPD Structure

*"That's yours; you're responsible for it; you're accountable for it.
We'll give you the resources to fix it; fix it."*

## Demand Entrance and Demand Management

Increased interactions with the community have the potential to increase the demand for police service through interpersonal avenues of communication. Or they might even raise community expectations regarding a department's rapid response to calls for service as citizens come to believe an officer should always be nearby. This section explores the BPD's experience balancing their community policing philosophy with traditional law enforcement demands on their time.

**It's always a fine balance between answering their radio calls and dealing with issues.** Building relationships with the community takes time, whether it is a patrol officer building a one-on-one relationship with a citizen during a "walk and talk" or a detective attending a multi-agency information sharing meeting. For most patrol officers, the time they have to put in to building relationships is secondary to responding to calls for service. Though training in problem-solving at the academy, "walk and talks," the STT, the SOT, and the RAP encourage BPD officers to take time to work with the community, it remains up to the individual officer's discretion and capabilities to use that time wisely. As a police supervisor, Captain Clarke tells his officers:

> You have a certain amount of time—you have to write reports, you got to answer calls, you got to bring the car over to the shop; there's all kinds of things you have to do, but ultimately, you're going to have a lot of free time. And that's going to determine the kind of police officer you're going to be, is how you handle your free time, the decision-making you make, the discretion that you use, that right there is sort of like the core of the community policing, the rest you just have to put up with.

Additionally, one respondent discusses how technology (e.g., communication and CAD systems) gives supervisors a clearer picture of how their officers spend their time responding to calls for service. This information gives supervisors ammunition to help their officers see that they have the time to partake in these community building activities (when not responding to the radio).

Captain Garcia, however, describes the reality faced by officers who must respond to calls for service while also trying to work with the community:

> You can only be so proactive. My district is a perfect example. We answered 77,000 radio calls last year, it's the most in the city, so that's the reactive. So, the majority of the work of the patrol officers in the cruiser is still somewhat reactive. We're trying our best to shift that over, but it's hard to do it when you have minimum staffing levels, and you have to answer X amount of calls, all day long, and tryin' to get them on some of their free time, which there's still free time available, but the way the free time is broken down, it's not spread out all as much as we would like it to be. It would be great if we just had four hours of calls and four hours of free time. But you get forty minutes of good time, and then 15 to 20 minutes of down time, you continue that throughout the day, and that's where you come up with your 40%. They don't really have as much free time as you would think to

really go out and target some of these things. So, we're still kind of married to the radio response, and the other officers aren't, so even though they'll listen to the radio, and they will get calls from the dispatcher who knows they're in a certain area; he'll call them on certain things; and then another call may come in, they'll jump on that call, because it's in their area of concern.

The respondent acknowledges the common perception that patrol officers have a large percentage of "free time" and points out that how that free time is allocated (i.e., by dispatching officers to respond to calls for service) can determine the quality of the officer's community building responses, regardless of how motivated an officer may be. The demands placed on police time by calls to 9-1-1 rose steadily from 2004 to 2008 before dropping down to just above 2004 levels in 2009. Though the reason for the decline in calls for service warrants further investigation, it is possible that the BPD's renewed reliance on community interactions (in the form of "walk and talks," community meetings, RAP, Constituent Response Teams, and the other programs mentioned) proactively absorbed some of these issues that would have otherwise been handled by the BPD's patrol officers reactively responding to calls for service.

Constituent Response Teams (CRT), created by Mayor Menino in 2009, are collaborations between the BPD and other city agencies aimed at analyzing data on problems of disorder and quality of life to proactively and comprehensively respond to these problems. The SST and SOT represent units whose main responsibility is to proactively interact with citizens to prevent (and respond to) problems. These units have the authority, resources, and time to receive and manage the demand that arises for service in their (geographic and content) areas. Sergeant Crowley explains:

The guys in the blue and whites, the uniform guys, they do it [make referrals to other agencies] to a limited degree, just because they're busy on certain radio calls. They're not really given the same kind of leeway we have in Safe Street Teams. The Safe Street Teams are basically on the bikes; they don't get a lot of radio calls; they aren't being pulled all over the place where the uniforms, got cars, and the service calls are wrapping you up in the one man cars. So, you've got walkin' beat guys; they're comparable to the Safe Street Teams.

The respondent notes the benefit of having officers assigned to the SST and to walking beats where they are freed from responding to many calls for service. Superintendent Lee adds:

Now we have 13 teams of six officers and a supervisor walking in the hotspot areas, all driven by our crime data, and that's it, that's their job. We don't take them and put them in the wagon, we don't take them and put them to watch prisoners one night if we're short. Every night, it's those officers. Now if they're on vacation we don't replace them, but those guys, 'You own it. You own this geographical area, you deal with everything in there. Speeding cars, drug dealing, homicides, you own it all.'

Technology and meaningfully organized data on crime and disorder hotspots served as the initial reason for allocating these resources to those specific parts of the city.

Captain Garcia explains how mapping technologies and direct input from the community guide the BPD's ongoing allocation of resources:

I think we've gotten more into lookin' to proactive type policing where we're targeting hotspots in response to hotspots based on crime mapping and input from other sources, the community, community meetings, and complaints from the various constituents; we tend to target things in response to that.

In addition to units that have the leeway to get involved with the community, the BPD encourages all of its patrol officers to proactively work with citizens. These interactions inevitably place a demand on the officer's time — whether by stopping an individual for a low-level offense in a high-crime area or conversing with a local business owner about problems affecting his patrons. The Reporting Area Project and Code 19s ("walk and talks") encourage all officers to take the time to get involved with the community. Deputy Taylor notes the difficulty in getting the personnel to understand the need to balance the radio and community responsibilities:

We're trying to make them do their Code 19s, get out, talk to people in the community, go to community meetings. It's always a fine balance between answering their radio calls and dealing with issues. But making sure they stay within their sector in dealing with their problem areas, that's what we're trying to instill now, dealing with issues and the really hotspot areas of the city at every district.

This section has shown how the BPD, famously driven by their community policing philosophy, manages citizens' demands for police response to calls for service while also allotting the resources for their patrol officers to proactively respond to citizens concerns. The Reporting Area Project, Code 19s, Safe Street

Teams, Street Outreach Teams, and Constituent Response Teams assist the BPD in getting their personnel to spend more time interacting with citizens. These interactions give patrol officers the time to respond to lower-level offenses and to define neighborhood-specific problems. The final section in the BPD case study explores the organizational structure and administrative processes that may or may not contribute to the BPD's efforts in the CPS era.

## *Organizational Structure and Administrative Processes*

Applying a community policing philosophy that relies on interactions and collaborations with citizens and other agencies should coincide with changes in the structure and administrative processes of a police department. This section explores the role of BPD's Boston Regional Intelligence Center (BRIC) and the CompStat process in increasing information sharing between detectives and patrol officers and in pushing accountability down to the district level.

**That's yours; you're responsible for it; you're accountable for it. Fix it.** The SST are a prime example of patrol officers being made accountable for the problems in their limited geographic area. Individuals in the SST maintain responsibility over their given areas and have the supervisory support to spend their time proactively working within those areas to solve problems. Captains and commanders initially discussed issues of the supervision of the SST (i.e., the ability of commanders to select certain individuals for the specific job). They also mentioned a disconnect between the captains' and commissioner's understandings of the SST mission. Despite these kinks, the teams essentially follow a decentralized model. Similarly, district detectives investigate most crimes within their districts but seem to have a hybrid supervisory and accountability structure whereby detectives are housed in the districts, report to the Bureau of Investigative Services, and "respect what we call the detail to our district" (Capt. Garcia).

Respondents discuss the information sharing capabilities of detectives and patrol officers and recognize that both groups have unique skills and abilities to access and use valuable information about criminals and crime and disorder problems. Superintendent Lee discusses the traditional lack of information sharing between the two groups. He offers a recent example of how a patrol officer on the SST received information from a citizen and then gave that information to the district drug detective supervisor. He reports:

> The challenge there is territorial and a lot of the things [that] can be successful to arrest, or in prosecutions that can help get some people off the street that are interfering with the quality of life is good infor-

mation, so people tend to hoard information. Patrol force would keep it to themselves because they want to make the arrest, detectives would keep it to themselves because they want to make the arrest. I think we've worked hard to try and say, "Look, why don't we all make the arrest so whatever you have for information investigatively, whatever we have information from the person walking down the street, let's work together to get it done." Do we have instances where that's not happening? Sure. But I think we have a ton of instances where it is happening, where the goal is to get the problem out of the area, and there's sense of ownership for both the detectives and a sense of ownership for the officers.

He concludes his example with a prescription also mentioned by other respondents—to reward the patrol officer by involving him in the ongoing investigation (for example, holding an observation post since the area is, after all, one in which the officer already frequents). Another respondent discusses how he will use overtime (when available) to reward patrol officers for sharing information and to give the officers the time to continue working on the case. This develops information sharing between the two groups. Respondents also mention other means of encouraging information sharing between and among patrol officers and detectives that include meetings with detectives and detective supervisors from gang and drug units and representatives from homicide and district investigations, informal conversations that occur after detectives attend roll calls with patrol officers, information shared by the BRIC, and discussions at CompStat.

Captain Garcia explains how the real-time reports offered by the BRIC assist his personnel in getting information from the detectives to patrol officers on a frequent basis:

> The BRIC, the supervisors all read it. We have the detective supervisors, and basically their responsibility is when a flyer comes out that we're lookin' for a certain guy that pertains to our district or even remotely, they'll make up several copies, and they'll mention it at roll call. We don't so much hand it out individually, but we'll put a stack of them on the desk and they'll grab them. Watch out for this guy, watch out for that guy. It happens on robberies, happens on car breaks, or things like that. We get the information to the BRIC; they get back to us a nice flyer, with nice pictures. They'll take the crime mapping portion of it, and put that on the one-piece document. We'll have a description of the problem, a little map of where it's happening, if we have any type of indication of time of day. That gets handed out and

the guys, they'll take that, and it's very helpful. That's what I mentioned earlier, where it took weeks before, we could get that in hours now. In most cases, the very next day we'll get somethin' back from the BRIC. The detectives are responsible for getting that out, and they've done a great job.

When needed, the BRIC can get information to all relevant personnel about a specific problem place or problem person. Then, the avenues of communication discussed earlier help to enrich each other's understanding of a problem. CompStat, Superintendent Frank notes, helps personnel to "coordinate on trends and patterns of investigations" and to "paint the big picture, the broad picture of what is going on" by bringing together representatives from drug and gang units, district detectives, specialized units, and the uniformed branch.

In addition to CompStat's role in facilitating information sharing, respondents also view it as a setting for holding commanders accountable. Superintendent Frank describes CompStat as fulfilling the role of an "accountability process at the district level" and as an:

> Open problem process, not a punitive process, but the expectations are clear on whether it's lookin' to reduce crime by 10% or looking to how we deal with the issue of gangs, how we work with schools, whatever the priority might be for that particular district. There are discussions about what the best way to go about that is, and then make a clear message that once the meeting's over, that you've got to deal with that issue.

Superintendent Martin discusses both the accountability and information sharing function of the CompStat process: "I see it as accountability, but it's also good to share information with folks across the board of what's working and what's not working." All of these factors contribute to the BPD's move toward getting officers to take ownership of specific areas and indicate the BPD's focus on high-risk people and places. As Superintendent Lee explains, officers feel:

> This is my sector, it's like my home. You can't do robberies in my home because it … it affects you personally. And we're starting to see officers who have that personal attachment to that geographical area cause we've told them, 'That's yours; you're responsible for it; you're accountable for it. We'll give you the resources to fix it; fix it.' And when they feel like they got support and they own it, then they take pride in it. We used to do a good job of putting a ton of resources in the areas, and we put out the fire. Whenever the next fire came, we would take those resources and put them someplace else. So, hey, all I'm

doing is putting out fires, that's all I'm supposed to do. Now we've told officers, 'No, put out the fire here, and you make sure it doesn't go on fire again.'

The respondent reflects on the feeling of ownership that officers can feel when they take seriously their areas of responsibility and captures the BPD's view of a problem-solving function (as opposed to simply responding to calls).

## Summary

After falling away from their strong relationships with the community, the BPD appears to have reclaimed its community problem-solving strategy. Under the leadership of Commissioner Davis, the BPD reestablished positive contact with the community, organized teams to respond to lower-level offenses, and worked on giving personnel the resources, authority, and accountability to maintain responsibility in geographic areas. Furthermore, the BPD recognizes the value of increasing consistent information-sharing practices between detectives and patrol officers. Bi-weekly CompStat meetings and the data analysis and preparation capabilities of the BRIC encourage these working relationships.

## References

Bernstein, D. (18 July 2008). Does Boston hate the BPD?. *The Phoenix* [Online]. Retrieved from http://providence.thephoenix.com/news/64929-does-boston-hate-the-bpd/?page=2#TOPCONTENT.

Boston Police Department (2008). 2007 Annual Report. From the Boston Police Department.

Braga, A. & Bond, B. (2008). Police crime and disorder hotspots: A randomized controlled trial. *Criminology*, 46, pp. 577–607.

Braga, A., Hureau, D., & Winship, C. (October 2008). Losing faith? Police, Black churches, and the resurgence of youth violence in Boston. Retrieved from http://www.hks.harvard.edu/rappaport/downloads/braga_final.pdf.

Community Ombudsman Oversight Panel. (2009). 2009 Annual Report. A report to the city of Boston.

More police problems. (19 March 2008). *The Phoenix* [online]. Retrieved from http://thephoenix.com/Boston/news/58283-more-police-problems/?page=2#TOPCONTENT.

O'Brien, K. (7 January 2007). After nearly three decades on the police force in Lowell, Edward Davis has a new job: Boston police commissioner. *The Boston Globe* [Online]. Retrieved from http://www.boston.com/news/globe/magazine/articles/2007/01/07/the_commish/.

Pulavarti, L., Bernadeau, M., Kenney, T., & Savage, J. (2007). The Boston Public Safety Survey Report: 2006. A report by Boston Police Department.

# Chapter 6

# The Milwaukee Police Department

## Introduction

The Milwaukee Police Department (MPD), under the leadership of Chief Edward Flynn, has undergone the most extensive changes of the departments in this study. Described by George Kelling as "the brightest police chief in the United States," the masters degree-holding Chief Flynn came to Milwaukee as a complete outsider and endeavored to change the department from one driven by an entrenched investigations bureau mentality to one that viewed patrol as the worthy backbone of the department. This chapter explores the many ways Chief Flynn worked with the MPD and its citizenry to bring the entire organization into the CPS era. These ways include a devotion to preventing crime and disorder, an overhaul of the department's structure, and the institution of problem-solving processes.

## The MPD Mission

*"To prevent crime and disorder and to reduce the
level of fear in the community"*

### Function

The stated function of the MPD reflects a return to an emphasis on Sir Robert Peel's principles of policing and shows how "new" ideas about policing are simply refurbished concepts of the past. Interview, archival, and survey data demonstrate MPD's official view of its mission. This section explores the current understandings and manifestations of MPD function.

**To prevent crime and disorder and to reduce the level of fear in the community.** Before being sworn in as MPD's police chief, Edward Flynn stated he planned to run a "community-oriented department," discussed his " 'broken windows' approach to policing, in which officers do not neglect minor crimes and nuisances," and emphasized the need to reduce fear and crime (Spice and Borowski, 2007). During his swearing-in speech on 8 January 2008, Flynn invoked Sir Robert Peel's principles, declaring the mission of the MPD " 'to prevent crime and disorder,' " and, he adds, "to reduce the level of fear in the community" (*2008 Annual Report*, p. 2). He also notes the variation in what different people and different neighborhoods will define as crime and disorder problems, signaling a geographic and neighborhood-level view of crime and related problems. His explication of the MPD function clearly arises in the MPD interview and survey data, as well as in other organizational changes discussed later.

Whether discussing the police function, relationships with the community and media, or organizational restructuring, "problem-solving" leavens the language of MPD personnel. The main, self-acknowledged function of the MPD is to prevent crime. Data from this research, however, emphasize the role of preventing disorder and reducing the level of fear in achieving that end. The MPD also notes their role employing CPS as a pivotal piece in fulfilling each of those functions. Tracing the recent history of the mission of the MPD, Captain Mehall mentions strands of "broken windows policing concepts," "CompStat-style policing strategies," and "problem-oriented policing," and states, "We've not let go of targeting the small things. It's just that we've refocused and we've involved community partners and problem-oriented policing, looking for groupings and clusters, related crimes, in addition to focusing on small things." It is not simply a zero-tolerance policy aimed at arresting or citing individuals for every small infraction, but rather, an approach that involves including community members in the process of problem definition and using data on all offenses (including, low-level offenses) to look for clusters or patterns that indicate a more serious problem.

The police function is to work with the community to understand the various crime and disorder problems and to give attention to all offense categories when defining problems and devising solutions. As Captain Richardson states, "That's where the quality of life enforcement comes in. But, it's not just across the board, everywhere. It's specific to solve specific problems." Including the community in an on-going problem-solving process increases citizens' cooperation. It also adds to the amount of information that the MPD has to "focus on the problem people and the problem places," which increases solvability rates and prevents crime (Captain Reed).

Respondents mention that when the community policing philosophy first entered the organization in the early 1990s, the department's unclear understanding of community policing rendered it an ineffective driving force. Of that time, Captain Wilson states his peers thought community policing was "hug-a-thug," and, "If you were to ask ten cops what is community policing, you would get 11 answers." During the same time, Captain Mehall reports that the MPD began operating under the "broken windows theory and targeting the small things" to "prevent larger issues from arising." He and others report that this approach, during the Chief Arthur Jones' administration, was implemented as a strict, "zero-tolerance" approach and that the MPD neglected to fully understand the possible crime control benefits of their efforts. Though imperfectly divined and incompletely implemented, that iteration of the MPD's CPS function laid the groundwork for the MPD's most recent mission under Chief Flynn.

Building on the early attempts to institute a CPS police department, Lt. Johns reports Chief Flynn:

> Implemented a hybrid philosophy. Taking bits and pieces from policing strategies or philosophies that had success elsewhere over time. So we have a community-based, problem-oriented, and data-driven approach to policing. To a certain extent it's a broken windows philosophy in that he wants us to have a highly uniform visible police presence in public spaces; in the public spaces that have historically been prone to historical violent crime, and disrupt the environment. So ... he's allowed officers to use their discretion, to be creative in how they are going to approach certain problems that are occurring in the neighborhood.

The current mission of the MPD borrows from these popular philosophies. This mission clearly relates to the work of the MPD (i.e., building community relationships, problem solving, using data-driven strategies, maintaining police visibility, and combatting violent crime). Importantly, it also aligns with the expectations of the greater Milwaukee community. In late 2007, the *Milwaukee Journal-Sentinel* held a "violent crime roundtable" (which included the mayor, the district attorney, the Milwaukee county sheriff, and a number of representatives of community groups and social service organizations) that advised the incoming chief to nurture productive, working relationships with the community.[1] As the representative from an interfaith, non-profit criminal justice agency states, " 'I think community policing is just absolutely what's got

---

1. This was despite clear agreement among the roundtable that Milwaukee's violent crime problem is a result of various social factors beyond police control (i.e., poverty, unemployment, under-education, and family and cultural issues).

to come to Milwaukee. Real community policing....'" Others agree and mention the need for "community-based policing," "a very close connection with the people," and getting "the neighborhoods to be self-sustaining ... to help the people start helping themselves" (*Milwaukee Quality of Life Round Table*, 2007). These excerpts relate directly to the MPD function of working with the community to solve an array of problems. Chief Flynn reaffirms these points, saying, "Public safety is not a spectator sport. Safe neighborhoods are a result of people and their police working together to create communities capable of sustaining civic life" (*2008 Annual Report*, p. 4).

**Table 6.1**

*The Current Mission of the MPD: What is the current mission of your police department, as you understand it?*

| Response | N | Percent (%) |
|---|---|---|
| Reduce crime, disorder, and fear | 58 | 58.6 |
| Work with the community to reduce crime, disorder, and fear | 17 | 17.2 |
| Reduce crime | 7 | 7.1 |
| Protect and serve | 4 | 4.0 |
| Other | 13 | 13.1 |
| Total | 99 | 100 |

Survey data (N= 99) support a widespread understanding of this MPD mission in the police department. Table 6.1 (above) shows that, of those personnel responding to the open-ended survey question ("What is the current mission of your police department, as you understand it?"), over 75% explicitly cited *reducing crime, disorder, and the fear of crime*. Nearly 20% of those respondents explicitly mention the role of working with the community in fulfilling their function. Regarding the relationship between the three prongs of the MPD mission, survey items explore the extent to which police personnel in this sample agree with statements on disorder, crime, and fear of crime. A majority of respondents agree or strongly agree with statements on the positive relationships between disorder, fear of crime, and the breakdown of community controls. Nearly 85% agree or strongly agree that disorder and fear of crime are strongly linked. Over 90% agree or strongly agree that untended disorder leads to the breakdown of community controls, making the area vulnerable to criminal invasion. Relative to these function-related responses, the statements that are among the lowest percentage of agreement are those regarding the MPD's role in reducing disorder and fear of crime. These results support the MPD's understanding of the positive *relationship* between disorder, crime, and fear of crime (and their stated mission to respond to those), but the survey responses also reveal less support for the MPD's self-acknowledged *role* in reducing disorder and fear. This may suggest that part of the MPD's understanding of its mission is lost where the "rubber meets the road."

This section has demonstrated the consensus among MPD personnel and Milwaukee's citizens that the MPD must work with the community to reduce crime, disorder, and fear of crime. This function is rooted in a general understanding of the positive relationships among disorder and the fear of crime, and in the belief that different communities have different definitions of problems and various capacities to try to lower levels of these phenomena. The next section describes tactics and technologies used by the MPD in fulfilling their function and the manner in which they account for and measure their outcomes.

## Tactics, Technology, and Outcomes

The actual tactics, technologies, and measured outcomes of the MPD should align with their stated function. This section describes these elements of the MPD and explains the extent to which they support or demonstrate the "community based, problem-oriented, and data-driven approach" of the MPD (Lt. Johns). Themes of "shallow problem-solving,"[2] discretion, and new technologies frame this discussion.

**It's really that problem-oriented policing model of SARA.** The MPD works to fulfill their function by utilizing available technologies to retrieve, organize, analyze, and display data about problems and responses and to create open lines of communication with citizens. Crime-mapping, data analysis software, in-car computers, and teleconferencing technology provide the framework for MPD's problem solving. The daily citywide crime briefings (where commanders meet with the police chief to discuss "real-time" crime data) and CompStat meetings use these technologies to conceive of and implement immediate and long-term crime tactics. These technologies are also used to hold supervisors and line personnel accountable when they execute those tactics. As Capt. Wil-

---

2. Braga and Weisburd (2006, p. 149) differentiate between line officer use of traditional tactics and limited assessments "that focus on high risk places, situations, and individuals" and the principled SARA model of problem-oriented policing, which, they argue, should occur at the higher levels of the police organization.

son relates, "Everyday we talk crime, we have the maps and people are held accountable.... Every single day at 9 A.M., we're talking crime."

An exchange during a morning crime briefing exemplifies this process. A number of district captains mentioned auto thefts as a seemingly incorrigible problem. They reported applying various tactics (i.e., checking with scrap yards, increasing patrols, and motor vehicle stops) to respond to that problem. Chief Flynn asked, "What types of vehicles have been stolen from your district?" The captains were unsure. The Chief then asked their new civilian crime analyst to report back with the types of cars being stolen and from where stolen vehicles were being recovered (or "dumped"). Crime mapping, data analysis software, and a computerized records management system were used to reveal target and geographical patterns, giving captains the ability to formulate a more focused approach to interdicting stolen vehicles (i.e., stopping specific vehicles, in specific areas, upon probable cause of a violation). In one district, this approach correlated with a 33% reduction in auto thefts between 2008 and 2009.

The 2009-created Intelligence Fusion Center, the use of SMART Boards to relay real-time information to patrol officers and detectives, and in-car computer technologies that allow individual patrol officers to both maintain contact with the updated information and to run individual license plates, make these data and tactics even more beneficial. These cutting-edge technologies complement the traditional modes of thinking about and conducting police work by allowing widespread access to information (or, "evidence") in near real-time. These technologies organize, store, query, and analyze massive amounts of relevant information far beyond the capabilities of a department's personnel (see Figure 6.1). The scenario above not only highlights the merit of new technologies, but also the MPD's success with shallow problem solving, the importance of police officer discretion, and the MPD's move toward neighborhood-level policing.

Captain Wilson mentions a number of district captains who follow this shallow problem solving approach, saying:

> These captains look at all this data; they don't need to be said, 'Here's the data, here's your plan, and here's the raw data.' They're smart enough cops to say, 'Oh, okay. I'm going to do this or that.' And then we discuss and we adjust based on what works. It is really that problem-oriented policing model of SARA. Not that it's all in theory and in paper, but it is in daily discussions about what I'm doing about this problem, and other people can listen to it. There isn't this fear that you're going to be yelled at. I think if you were to go over and tell this chief, 'I'm going to use pogo sticks,' he wouldn't say a word. And if it

Figure 6.1 MPD Technology and Data

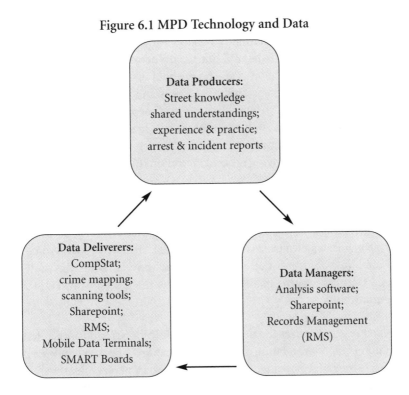

didn't work, the next day, he wouldn't be afraid to say, 'Pogo sticks don't work,' and somebody might suggest a beat cop or something else.

The respondent acknowledges that the MPD encourages their leaders to be innovative and to rely on data to inform their tactical decisions (i.e., to partake in a shallow SARA process). Respondents note the value of a disciplinary process that officers perceive as fair. Now, as the organization moves toward a "values-based organizational culture" (Lt. Johns), police officers are more inclined to interact with citizens, and commanders are more comfortable experimenting with innovative approaches. Citizens and police officers realize "cops are allowed to make decisions" and that the administration "backs its cops to the nth degree when they deserve it" (Lt. Spell). The daily crime meetings give commanders a venue for justifying their actions or explaining how the data from the various technologies guided their decisions.

**Carpet bombing in an area isn't always the proper way to attack a situation.** Respondents discuss the difference between an organization that values officers' use of discretion and those that do not. Inspector Black states of MPD's broken windows policing:

> Part of what had happened in the past was going to an area and bombarding them with a citation or a charge for every thing imaginable. Well, Chief Flynn calls that a crime tax on people, and, if you've got good people in a neighborhood who are hard working, trying to make things right, to get them caught in sweeps and absolute ticketing of everybody that walks through that area, it becomes counterproductive too. We don't do that; we attempt to use some thought in the process now and find out why people are where they are; and there's nothing wrong with giving officers discretion if there's a warning that can be issued to somebody going to work and maybe they got a car and they don't have a front license plate and they should; you don't have to give them a citation; you can have them take care of that problem and help them figure out how, tell them where to go to the DMVs. If it's a stolen plate issue that's different, then we've got do something about that; but there's just different ways to attack the problem. Carpet bombing in an area isn't always the proper way to attack a situation.

This statement recognizes the need for police officer discretion and epitomizes a common (mis)interpretation and (mis)application of broken windows policing as zero-tolerance policing. Paying attention to low-level offenses while patrolling does not mean that all low-level offenses warrant a citation or an arrest.

Even more importantly, when targeting a limited geographical area, data technologies can assist officers in more acutely deciding to which cases of reasonable suspicion they should respond. For example, while riding in a two-person patrol car, this researcher observed officers pulling over (on average) between two and three vehicles an hour for probable cause of various moving and equipment violations. The researcher observed the officers electronically scan individual license plates (either through their Mobile Data Terminal [MDT] or by calling in the license plate). Officers used the rapidly returned information in deciding whether to pull someone over. During a stop for a clear moving violation, the police officers' perceptions of probable cause of a more serious crime (i.e., a sheathed knife in plain view) led to the arrest of an individual in possession of illicit drugs and a knife. Other stops resulted in other serious violations or in written warnings or summonses. Assistant Chief Smith comments on the irony of serious offenders who blatantly violate moving and equipment ordinances. He states, "I've stopped some kids who didn't have a driver's license or who were wanted [for more serious crimes] driving crazy, and that always surprises me cause you'd think that they would abide by the law [to avoid apprehension]." From 2007 to 2009, as a result of the department's focus on stopping citizens, documented subject and traffic stops increased nearly 150%. Traffic stops account for the majority of the increase.

Technology helps officers to focus their tactics and to move away from carpet bombing an entire area. Assistant Chief Jones discusses the strain that such a "zero-tolerance" approach of the past can have on community relations:

> One of the things that detracted from our success in the high crime areas is that the mistake in enforcement policy was that, everything that walks, talks, and moves in that area is going to be stopped and/or cited, and obviously there's people that, for a variety of reasons, are trapped in that neighborhood and are very good people, very law-abiding people that want to support the police, but then they're the ones who are being stopped and inconvenienced at the least or penalized because of where they have to live. So we recognize that, and we're dealing with that now with the data we can get on the real-time basis. We can analyze what officers are making what kind of stops in the particular area, and does it look like they're focusing in on one person or a race of citizens in particular, or something that we need to sit down with that officer and say, 'From what we look at, it appears that you're missing the point here. Part of what your interaction is supposed to be here is to work with the citizens to instill confidence so that they feel comfortable when we have to reduce our force in the neighborhood, that they can still reach out to us and report to us about crimes.'

This excerpt reveals how these technologies assist police officers in the street as they ferret out the troublesome street people from the rest of the street populations. Captain Lyons illuminates these ideas, saying:

> It's a double-edged sword there. They were happy to see the officers in the plagued areas of the city, but then, on the other hand, good citizens were getting tickets as well, so.... Now, under Chief Flynn, it's the quality of ticket. He's always preached that it's the quality of the stop; it's not necessarily the quantity of tickets that you can write at the stop. He made it very clear to officers that you don't have to necessarily even have to write a ticket if you make a stop and deem it not a good quality stop—guns, drugs, or things like that. If it was just a citizen who made a minor traffic infraction, a warning is good enough, and the officers get that, which is huge because the good citizens in the communities that are plagued by violence are actually supporting the police department.

This represents the dilemma police face in balancing their duty to keep communities safe while upholding individual rights. It also touches on a move in the MPD toward not simply counting numbers of tickets, but looking at the quality of those stops and the information gained from conducting the stops that can lead to probable cause for more serious past, present or future offenses that in turn will reduce the rate of crime.

The following finding also supports this. Almost 80% of this survey's sample believes that stopping someone for a low-level offense is an effective way to get information about crime or criminals in the area. Lieutenant Johns echoes this:

> The chief isn't measuring their performance based on how quick they get to a call, but rather what you're doing here 8 hours a day, what impact does that have on our crime rate. That's what matters. He's emphasized a traffic enforcement policy that isn't about the numbers; it's about the number of traffic stops you make, but not the number of citations issued. We're not out there to give people four or five, six citations. We're out there to make traffic stops to engage the community and to maybe turn that traffic stop into a lead towards a shooting that might happen two days from now, or how might that traffic stop end up leading to taking a couple of guns off the street, or some drugs off the street, or something like that.

An exchange during CompStat reflects this intelligence-led focus on individuals. Chief Flynn, in response to a Captain's presentation on violence stemming from a feud between gang sets, states, "Do we know who these guys are so we can pass their information along and harass them?" He is suggesting using police officer and other criminal justice agency (e.g., probation and parole) interactions with these known offenders to find probable cause of law violations.

Police are quite cognizant of the need to both interact with citizens and to do so in a professional manner. The MPD relates officer discretion, the outcome of a police-citizen interaction, and the views that citizens have of police. Captain Mayer states:

> The discretion, that's a huge thing police officers today didn't have before [Flynn] came to office ... [for example] a traffic stop; people think it has to be a citation and it doesn't. It's taking a while and some people are there now, but it's going to take a while. We also have a very young department, very inexperienced. So it's going to take a while before they catch on and realize that they are the representative.

This is the way I learned it when I came out—your decision is what's made out there on the street. If you decide to arrest or not arrest, advise or how you handle it, that's your decision, and your sergeant would support you, provided you made a decision. Now, obviously if you made the wrong one because you intended too, you just don't want to do something here, well, you're going to get in trouble, but if you made a mistake, and you explain, 'This is the way I handled it, this is why....' You were supported because you made a decision.

The respondent gives further support to the idea that the MPD is producing a culture that acknowledges and values discretion. It is not enough to simply tell police officers to use discretion. As the respondent notes, the supervisors and avenues of discipline must also support officers who, in good faith, misuse that discretion. Captain Zest states of those officers still learning the proper use of discretion:

It's a sense of empowerment for them that, 'I have been given this ability to make reasonable decisions and not only enforce the law, but affect crime, and maybe cultivating information or giving someone a warning and letting it be a positive interaction that maybe we can cultivate something in the future from.' It goes towards really turning the citizen's perception of the police force, the positive, as a whole, one person at a time.

Lieutenant Doll adds, "People should fear police if they're committing crimes. If they're driving down the street with an expired plate they shouldn't fear the police. You might get a ticket, but they shouldn't fear the police."

Survey data of personnel's views on the tactics used and knowledge of what the MPD measures (in terms of the outputs of their work) also lend insight into the shifting organizational strategy of the department. The survey data demonstrate a thorough understanding of the stated mission of the MPD to reduce crime, disorder, and fear of crime, but also raise questions about the degree to which the MPD acts on two parts of that mission (i.e., to reduce fear and disorder). Responses to the importance of certain tactics to the mission of the police department reflect a police department whose tactics concur with its stated mission. The top tactics to which respondents assigned the highest percentage of "very important" responses include "crime mapping," "community meetings in which community members and police work together to identify problems and create solutions in their neighborhood," and "patrol officers maintain responsibility over a limited geographic area (i.e., sector integrity)." This indicates the importance of the community-based, data-driven, neighborhood-level problem solving that other data support. Those receiving the highest percentage of "not at all important" include "rapid response to calls for service," the police force representing the racial makeup of the community, and "increasing the number of arrests and citations." The first and third items directly support previous data on the shifting tactics used by the MPD in fulfilling its mission. It is also worth noting, "increasing the number of traffic violations" was not listed among the top percentages for either the "very important" or "not at all important" options. While this may seem to contradict other data that emphasize the role of traffic stops, the confusion might have resulted from the wording of traffic violations, which implies that the MPD values numbers of tickets issued. One might interpret the survey data as supporting the previous data on the value of traffic stops in gaining information on crime. Other tactics used by the MPD include differential police response, saturation patrols, directed patrol missions, foot patrols, park and walks, and bicycle patrols. Each of these tactics plays a part in the community-based mission to reduce levels of crime, disorder, and fear of crime. This section concludes with an exploration of the measurement processes of the MPD.

The measurements of police work should support the stated goals, functions, and tactics of the MPD. While the MPD acknowledges the goals of reducing levels of disorder and fear of crime and the need to improve relations with the community, crime reduction is the ultimate goal of most of the MPD's functions. Lieutenant Star discusses the connection between crime and the fear of crime:

> You can't argue with the overall success that the department has seen in reducing the crime rates. Even though we may say we want to reduce the fear of crime, you reduce that by putting it all back to reducing crime. And how does a police officer reduce crime? He is visible out there and is physically preventing it or arresting the guys who are committing crimes so they can't commit any more crimes. I think everybody knows there's a very, very small percentage of criminals out there that commit the vast majority of crime. If we ever get to the point where we can target those people, get them off the street, I think we would be much more successful than we already are.

He notes that focusing efforts on the small proportion of the population who are responsible for a large percentage of crimes can reduce crime and the fear of crime.

The MPD measures traditional units of police work that include incident reports, arrests, citations, dispatched calls for service, field interviews, vehicle stops, park-and-walks, and clearance rates. These measurements are highlighted throughout the pages of the MPD Annual Reports (with FBI Index crimes taking the spotlight). But, as interview data exhibit, the MPD is also concerned with the outcomes of the measurable activities in which police partake. A memo informing the MPD of the new requirements for CompStat presentations reads:

> Crime numbers will be examined to determine if the issue was resolved, dispersed or the plan was not effective. It is understood that some problems can only be managed, while others can be solved. The plan can produce results, such as arrests, traffic stops and seizures, without a satisfactory outcome. The question is not whether we are expending an effort to solve the problem(s), but rather whether we are effective in our efforts.

While supervisors and even command level personnel acknowledge the importance of the tangible numbers discussed above, the daily crime and CompStat meetings help to create an environment that values the meaning of those numbers and the outcomes that they represent, as opposed to simply counting these numbers as a measurement of line officer production. In both of those settings, the tangibles are used to bring those in attendance to an understanding of the problem, the response to the problem, and an ongoing assessment of outcomes.

Another way the MPD uses data to change officer behavior is through performance measures. Patrol officers in the MPD's Neighborhood Task Force[3] (NTF) have their performance visually displayed during CompStat. Patrol officers' names are placed in quadrants, based on the numbers of arrests, incident reports, subject stops (or, field interviews), and traffic stops (relative to the mean of their shifts). For example, a presentation slide will show quadrants for high and low numbers of arrests and incident reports. Officers who find themselves in the lower, right quadrant are those officers who are below their group's mean number of arrests and incident reports. Officers who consistently underperform are highlighted in red, representing their need for "coaching." Officers in need of coaching have their badge numbers displayed on the screen, while those officers in the satisfactory quadrants have their surnames displayed. This maintains the positive purpose of this unique accountability tool.

---

3. "The mission of the NTF is to provide highly visible, proactive, multi-disciplinary policing presence in hotspot locations aimed at driving down street level crime and disorder" (2008 Annual Report).

The MPD also offers one way in which it measures the quality of the stops that their police officers make. During a CompStat presentation, a representative from the NTF reports that his officers' municipal citations are down, while their felony arrests are up. This suggests that officers are using the proper amount of discretion in arresting wrongdoers while still refraining from "carpet bombing" entire areas with citations. Finally, the CompStat process also includes risk management measures (use of force incidents, pursuits, accidents, and complaints against officers), as well as the supervisors' success in reviewing those incidents. Though there was no evidence of a formal method of measuring improvements with the community (e.g., community survey data), taken together, these exercises support the MPD's commitment to responding to problems and building positive community relationships in a data-driven setting.

Using data to derive, implement, execute, and assess strategies results in more geographically- and target-focused tactics. This information (when effectively produced, conveyed, and interpreted) informs officers' decisionmaking in the street. Departmental processes such as CompStat and the Neighborhood Task Force further ingrain a data-driven, problem-solving, discretion-valuing culture in the MPD. A discussion of the MPD's legitimacy and their relationships with the community follows, giving deeper insight into the MPD's function and tactics.

# Working with the Community

*"Gardener cops, the ones that actually touch the community."*

## External Relationships and Legitimacy

The MPD's move toward neighborhood problem solving exemplifies their response to neighborhood concerns of disorder. Like many big-city police departments the MPD has faced challenges dealing with the numerous and significant minority groups within its city. The MPD's handling of both the Dahmer and Jude incidents exasperated already strained relationships with some of their minority communities. An exploration of MPD's balance between this broken windows policing and positive community relationships belies a widely held perception that the two are inherently oppositive. Nonetheless, the MPD is operating with an understanding of their responsibility for the strained and delicate relationships they have with the community. Increased information sharing and formal collaboration between the community and the MPD, a more transparent and balanced internal disciplinary process, lowered crime statistics, and a relatively calm political environment help to legitimize the MPD with the community.

**Gardener cops and those who cut the grass.** Following the fallout from the Frank Jude, Jr. case,[4] and succeeding MPD's first female police chief, Chief Flynn was brought in to the MPD as a change chief, charged with, among other tasks, enhancing community relations (Spice & Borowski, 2007). One of the ways the MPD responded to that charge was by involving the community in their crime reduction efforts. In January 2008, the MPD created and publicized individualized Neighborhood Policing Plans for each of their districts. The plans' missions were the same: to work with the community to reduce crime, fear, and disorder. The tactics and strategies, however, were based on the specific problems occurring in the diverse neighborhoods within each district. Common community-based policing tactics included enhancing foot patrols, holding stakeholder meetings, park and walks, neighborhood events, distribution of crime prevention material, and meetings with problematic landlords. Traditional broken windows policing efforts (i.e., attacking quality of life violations and signs of disorder) were also used.

Increasing the number of positive contacts the MPD has with its citizens empowers citizens to partake in making their own neighborhoods safe, develops information about crime and problems, and boosts the community's stake in crime reduction efforts. Assistant Chief Jones discusses the role these collaborations play in the crime-fighting efforts of the MPD:

> And not to say that there aren't good, decent, hardworking people living in those areas, but unfortunately they are trapped by economics and certainly intimidated by what's going on around them and wanting to protect themselves and their families. It's hard for them to speak out and to assist us. And through the years, with the shrinking size of our department, I'd say we've had to rely more and more on citizen involvement in terms of block watches, and assisting us to provide us with information ... but through this block watch organizations and officers interacting that way, and having a name to go with a person on the department, they've been able to get intelligence and do some certainly some good work.

---

4. In this case, White police officers were accused of beating Jude, Jr., a biracial male, after they accused him of stealing one of their police badges during a party held at one of the off-duty police officers' homes. MPD officers who responded to the call were also accused of beating Jude. Three of the officers were later found guilty of violating Jude's civil rights.

Capt. Reed adds:

> From the feedback I get, the public views the police department in a positive light for the most part. A lot of the tactics that [Chief Flynn] changed put an emphasis on having the bike officers out there, putting an emphasis on having patrol officers do a lot of park and walks and even the change with painting the squads a different color has made us more visible, even though there's probably less officers out on the street now than there were when he took over (unless you tell the public that, I don't think they'd know that). I think they really believe that there are more police out and that the police are in their neighborhood more often, cause that's constantly what I hear at the community meetings, and I have these people thanking us for checking their alleys, walking up and down the street. So they're seeing the officers more.

Improved community relations, posits Captain Reed, make it easier to obtain volunteered information from citizens. This helps the MPD to "focus on the problem people and the problem places to prevent crime" (Capt. Reed).

Other efforts to increase citizens' views of MPD legitimacy include the Office of Media and Communications "Be a Force" branding campaign and the use of the internet and online social networking (i.e., Twitter) to provide citizens with positive information about the MPD's efforts and achievements. This further enhances perceptions of transparency and gives citizens more information from which to base their views of the MPD. Captain Zest confirms this, saying:

> The community widely accepts us for what we're doing; they know where we're at, they kind of know what we're doing, we're flooding these areas of high crime. They see us out there.... So, we're having an impact, not only us being there, but the street roll calls that we do periodically. We invite the media out there, we are filmed, it gets out there, through all media outlets, keeping people informed of what we're doing and why we're doing it. 'Cause it all builds into the reception or the goal to make people feel safe in their neighborhoods.

Lieutenant Doll adds:

> And I think that end has been extremely successful and part of our message that people out there doing their work is not only—you have several factors, you have a deterrent factor, just being out there on patrol, and then there's obviously, the interdiction factor.... Then there's also the community presence type of thing where the community and

the police work cooperatively together because we have to both be on the same page to be successful on reducing crime.... The department has done a very good job on promoting that—this administration specifically, at putting out the good information about what's happening in the department, how we are helping the community, how the community has stepped up and helped us in a number of areas. It's not just to go out and stop cars and arrest people, but it's during these contacts—not every contact is an arrest or an adversarial situation—it's engaging the community and cultivating information about what's going on in the neighborhood. 'Hey, who's involved in the robberies and shootings here?' or, 'Do you know someone that's carrying around a gun that shouldn't be or that's on the street dealing drugs?' They'll often times come forward and tell us, but now, by virtue of all of the contacts that we have out on the street, we can get that information, and in a couple of instances, it's paid-off real big for us. We just had this situation where some cops were shot at last week, and we've obtained some information just by doing that, where before that we had no suspect information. The coppers went out as part of an enhanced patrol force. But went out and obtained information instead of going out and just making it look like we're going to arrest everyone in the neighborhood to show you that shooting at the police is a bad thing. They get that part of it, and that's a very good thing for both sides, the community and the police.

This excerpt underlines the main reasons for establishing quality relationships with the community (deterrence and detection). It also emphasizes a more productive style of broken windows policing. While many police departments will respond to a crime incident by saturating an area and "arresting everyone in the neighborhood," this respondent recognizes the importance of using those stops to garner actionable information about the crime problem in that area (just as the MPD suggests it champions with other stops). The "zero-tolerance" hue of broken windows policing serves both to create the perception that someone does indeed care about an area and to give police access to valuable information about the crime problems in that neighborhood. Pre-established positive relationships with neighborhood citizens strengthen the police department's ability to create those perceptions and to gain valuable information when needed.

An earlier section discussed tactics that put the MPD in contact with citizens on grounds of reasonable suspicion. The current section has focused on the mutually beneficial police-community relationships that the MPD has nurtured with the goals of crime reduction and improved community relations.

A central theme of each discussion is the manner in which police interact with citizens. Interview data, a 26% decrease in complaints against officers from 2007–2009, and news articles suggest that, except for a few rotten apples, the MPD has taken the appropriate steps in maintaining positive views among the public. Captain Wilson offers insight into a useful approach to police work that should enhance these relationships. He states:

> My father who was a cop, would always say there was two types of cops, those that cut the grass, that's their [limited] interaction with the community. The other cops, were gardener cops, the ones that actually touch the community. And you look at the difference. Look at someone who cuts the lawn—their lawn looks nice, it's cut, and you go to the house next door, where the "gardener" lives there, and you have flowers, you have other things. The difference is the touch, and that's what we're trying to return to, the day of gardener cops.

Captain Wilson distinguishes between cops who take the time to cultivate relationships with citizens and those who do not—Gardeners and Grass-cutters. This distinction is not new to the police profession, but rather it is an understanding of police work that comes and goes with different strategies and in response to various problems and political pressures. The MPD, in its current mission to work with neighborhoods to respond to crime, fear, and disorder, finds it useful to emphasize the role of the department this way.

Broken windows policing in the CPS strategy requires police to be in the neighborhoods interacting with citizens to both enforce laws and to co-produce self-sustained, lower levels of crime, disorder, and fear. With this understanding, a "Gardener's" approach to policing may be best suited to fixing broken windows. Working alongside other city departments and with other community groups and citizens, the MPD as a whole demonstrates its commitment to "gardening." Additionally, the MPD's direct handling of potentially calamitous challenges over the past three years (i.e., deaths caused by pursuit driving, allegations that officers ignored sexual assault victims, troubles with a new police radio system, and officers arrested for drugs and domestic abuse) proved their commitment to transparency and confirmed the strength of their relationship with the community. Lieutenant Johns summarizes the department's overall relationships with its external environment and lends insight into the successes of the MPD:

> The chief has done a great job on the media side of things in communicating our mission, our vision, our policing strategy and philosophy, having a vision and mission, as we do, communicating that

by use of the media, going and speaking to the community leaders. The elected officials are on board, the community leaders are on board, the district commanders have their monthly crime meetings, their neighborhood meetings in communicating that. And when we communicate in advance to say, 'This is what we're going to be doing, this is how we're going to go about doing it, you're going to see a visible presence in your neighborhood.' And we understand that not everybody in a neighborhood that's historically prone to violent crime is a bad person, but you are going to get stopped, and it's not so much as what we do, but how we do it that's been a problem in the past when you have this zero-tolerance kind of approach … everybody got locked up, everybody got a ticket, everybody got stopped. The chief isn't saying that you have to give everyone a ticket. Everyone doesn't have to get arrested. It's having that visible presence to disrupt the criminal environment.… So I think it's a combination of a lot of things. Communicating to the masses of what we're about, how we're going to go about doing it. And when you have less crime … people are aware of the fact that the city is safer. The neighborhoods that were most out of control, are now under control. And it's in no small part because of the fact that the police are there. I think they're less offended by maybe getting stopped a couple of times in a week, but being let go and treated well because they know that that is a, for lack of a better term, a necessary evil to being able to be able to sit on my front porch and not be feared of getting shot, or being a victim of a crime. So our complaints aren't at zero; we still have officers who are maybe too aggressive, or who don't treat some citizens the way that they should be treated. But overall, with fewer crimes, we have fewer crime victims; the community sees us more and it's an overall execution where the officers are treating the people that they're running into better than they might have 10 years ago.

The MPD rebounded from a tumultuous period by working with citizens to apply neighborhood-level crime plans and by increasing information-sharing with other city agencies and community groups. The gains were facilitated within a congruous political context in which the mayor and Common Council supported the MPD's bid to gain legitimacy with Milwaukeeans. Although responding to low-level offenses and stopping high numbers of individuals, the MPD's ability to be perceived as working in the citizens' best interest, the improved working relationships with the community, and the consequent crime declines brought the MPD to a higher level of legitimacy. The final section, on the organizational structure and administrative processes, provides information about MPD's restructuring and the role it played in setting the foundation for the crime-fighting and community-building activities discussed above.

# The MPD Structure

*"The criminal investigations bureau represents the most significant change in the business model."*

## Demand Entrance and Demand Management

The MPD's community-based, data-driven, neighborhood-level, problem-solving function, suggests an understanding of how demand enters—and is handled by—the MPD. This section explains the impact of MPD's increasingly community-based, data-driven mission on their demand processes.

**We basically just went from hitch, to hitch, to hitch.** The technological, data, and community aspects of the MPD mission translate into a demand for services stemming from and managed by these sources. Under a new mission, these technologies and strategies result in different ways of receiving and managing demands. For instance, telephone and computer-aided dispatch systems are traditional sources of demand entrance and management. This, as Assistant Chief Jones reports, resulted in officers going "from hitch, to hitch, to hitch ... [that is,] assignment, to assignment, to assignment, not looking at the long-term things that went on in their squad areas." The community and the MPD still use these technologies to request and deliver police service. However, what police do upon responding to calls for service, the importance placed on certain calls, and the role of data analysis, mapping technologies and crime intelligence meetings distinguish the past from the present.

An understanding of the MPD police role as one of responding to problems, even when responding to calls for service, is the mechanism for the difference. Captain Reed explains:

> You have a lot of people that just have it in their minds that they can't control or affect anything that's going on in the district, that their only responsibility or job is to wait and respond to whatever's coming over the radio and run around. Even in many cases when they respond to what's on the radio, it's a quick solution that they're looking for. If there's ten kids in the street fighting, we can break them up and just get them to run away without us getting out of the car. In many ways, that's acceptable, when really if they're getting out and figuring out

what's going on they might be able to get two mothers involved that are going to settle the problem and they're not going to have to come back two hours later for the same thing. I think it's changed in that mindset to realize that there's on-going problems, that if we address them on a longer-term basis, rather than just looking for the quick fix, we can be more successful and prevent stuff.

The respondent discusses the transition from a department whose police officers are only concerned with clearing (or, responding to) their calls for service, to one in which officers' responses to calls for service involve a view toward preventing underlying problems that may cause or affect the initial purpose of the call to which they responded. This "mindset" is reinforced by various command meetings, highlighted by data analysis and crime mapping technologies, and supported by a Differential Police Response (DPR) unit that frees police time to conduct these problem-solving activities.

In October 2008, following an April 2008 pilot program, the MPD implemented DPR throughout Milwaukee. This program uses limited duty, sworn personnel to respond to these lower priority calls, freeing up time for patrol officers to partake in proactive, community-based problem solving or other traditional police activities. In 2008, the DPR handled more than 15,000 lower priority calls for service and produced a nearly 75% satisfaction rate among surveyed callers (a citizen satisfaction survey was built in as part of the establishment of the DPR to gauge citizens' responses to the MPD's new way of responding to citizen calls for service). In 2009, the DPR received almost 28,000 calls. In addition, the MPD eliminated going to certain calls for service (e.g., unverified burglar alarms), freeing up even more time for patrol personnel.

Captain Mayer, in response to a question on factors contributing to crime decline, speaks about patrol officers' connection to the radio:

That's the sad part of what's happening, even right now in our age of progress. They were still strapped to the radio. Communications division needs to be revamped. There's too much authority for those dispatchers, and they seem to carry a supervisory role, and again, if the sergeant doesn't have the backbone, they're going to acquiesce to what the dispatcher wants and they could go completely against what the captain wants. So, an answer to your question, the single most factor was giving the autonomy to the district captains.

Changing the organizational structure of the MPD, pushing down authority to captains, and the addition of the DPR facilitate the MPD's move away from depending on the communications division in allocating the demands for police service. Changes in what MPD commanders pay attention to and measure also assist this change. As Inspector Black reports:

> This chief has said that it isn't the response time necessarily that's the driving factor here. It's what you're doing when you get to a scene and what we can do proactively to reduce the number of calls for service coming in. Of course priority one calls are priority one calls, and you're going to go to those as soon as possible. In the past we've been kind of driven by response time. Maybe quality was sacrificed for expediency. Even on smaller types of offenses or things that maybe aren't even a crime, but are nuisance problems in the neighborhood. If you don't spend enough time on that, it creates an opinion in the public that you don't care. And once they think you don't care, you're starting to lose them, you know? You're not going to get calls about the problems in neighborhoods coming through as quickly as you would if people understand that you do care. So, doing that, shifting away from that response time only protocol, that's helped us, explaining all of that to the public at every opportunity when there's a meeting. The captains have their monthly meetings for the community. Their community liaisons officers are always out at community meetings and just making sure that people understand what we're trying to accomplish and how we'd like to do it has done a great deal to help us get the message across and start to break down some of those old perceptions.

His statement ties together multiple areas discussed in this research: measurement, tactics, community relations, and demand. It is the police response to those lower-priority calls for service that, he suggests, influence citizens' views of the police. These are the calls, after all, that place the greatest demand on patrol officer time. The DPR handles many of those calls. Patrol officers and community liaison officers represent the department in person and implement the various responses to the demand created by the community and data analysis technology. Calls to, and information gathered by, the DPR are another source of data from which the MPD makes decisions about deployment and strategy.

Lieutenant Spell explains how data and technology help to manage the demand for MPD service:

> Knowing what you're doing and why you're doing it didn't exist until 2008. Why are we in this neighborhood? Well, there's robberies and there's burglaries. And you went out there and you did the same thing. Whether they told you there's robberies and burglaries, there's sexual

assaults and homicides, there's car thefts, or panhandling, you did the same thing. We started looking at crime, we started looking at data. It was amazing. You're here because there's been these burglaries during this time of day, committed by this kind of perpetrator, stealing this kind of item. Okay, now that changes things a little. Focus. These are the blocks, this is what you need to do. That is amazing. These are the vehicles you should be looking for. These are the target vehicles you should be focusing on. You gotta be kidding me! If I would've had that when I was a cop, I would've cut my workload in half. I mean, I can actually tell you this car is stolen more than any other car. Holy mackerel! That's awesome. Focus the data. It's been an incredible transformation. Part of me wishes I could still be a cop, to have all this at your fingertips. The technology, the share-point sites. I could look at my profile. This is how many arrests I've made, this is how many stops I've made, this is how many people I've engaged. The reports I've made. None of that existed when I was a cop. Everything was paper. It got filed God knows where. I could be investigating a burglary at your house, knowing that, or not knowing that next door to you was a burglary yesterday—never would've known.

As the respondent reports, this widespread access to data on crimes, criminals, and places helps patrol officers understand why they are being deployed to the places and crimes to which they are. This "focus" can be viewed as a way in which demand for police service is managed. Similarly, the renewed relationships with the community (i.e., meetings with the community) serve as manner of demand entrance and (as discussed earlier) have the added benefit of enhancing the MPD's relationship to the community.

Captain Richardson sums up the tension between a police department driven by rapid response to calls for police service and one with a more judicious response to demands for their service:

There's been some great community response, and then there's been some not so great community response, as we are concentrating on trying to do problem-solving and trying to be in the neighborhoods more. At the districts we're doing a lot of park and walks to have cops just stop what they're doing, park the car, and get out and walk in the neighborhoods, and do some observation and policing that way. That's really great for people who in that neighborhood they like to see the officers. But the person that was waiting for a cop to respond to their call that's not getting their call responded to now, because that cop's on a park and walk, they don't like it. Now, there's calls for service. When you go from years ... of rapid response for calls to service where people are expecting cops to show up two minutes after they call to now trying to change that, a lot of people don't like that. So, that's been difficult, but I think we're more engaged with the community. We had some really terrible community relations times during our whole Frank Jude era and it's taken a lot to come back from that. There's a lot more community meetings, there's a lot more cops and district people that are going to community meetings or community liaison officers who are super busy. The community has embraced that but they want a cop to come to their door, and they want that cop there now when they call the police, and that's hard for people to get over. You know? Get past.

Even though the MPD may no longer use response times to measure police performance, the community still expects a rapid response. However, the MPD's continued use of community liaison officers, positive community interactions, successes in problem solving, and reductions in crime, disorder, and fear should continue to move the community along with the MPD's new way of managing demand.

## *Organizational Structure and Administrative Processes*

To support the MPD function, in 2008 Chief Flynn created four distinct bureaus (Professional Standards, Administration, Neighborhood Policing, and Criminal Investigations), a Differential Police Response Unit, and a Neighborhood Task Force (NTF). In 2009, a newly-created Intelligence Fusion Center was placed along with five other divisions (Investigative Management, Neighborhood Investigations, Organized Crimes, Sensitive Crimes, and Violent Crimes) within the Criminal Intelligence Bureau (CIB). This move signaled the MPD's commitment to an intelligence-led, neighborhood problem-solving policing strategy. These changes in 2009 coincided with a redistricting of Milwaukee's seven districts[5] along neighborhood lines and crime patterns (2009 Annual Report). This shift in the MPD, the addition of the CompStat process, improving the allocation of resources, and decentralizing some CIB functions are discussed below.

---

5. As of the end of the data collection for this case study, the MPD was transitioning into another redistricting plan in which the city is divided into three geographic areas (North, South, Central) led by a captain.

**The CIB represents the most significant change in the business model.** As discussed later in this section, the MPD was traditionally a CIB-dominated police department. The CIB (as opposed to the patrol unit) was viewed as the preeminent bureau within the MPD. It drove the MPD mission, and the top leaders in the MPD were consistently chosen from the CIB. Reorganizing the CIB and rethinking its place in the overall function of the MPD has personnel, work environment, and tactical implications. While intended to enhance the MPD's service to the community and to improve its neighborhood-based crime prevention strategy, the drastic change also created unease among personnel in the CIB and represented a paradigm shift in the way the MPD works.

One of Chief Flynn's earliest moves was the creation of the Neighborhood Task Force, to which were assigned nearly 200 personnel from the Vice Control, Intelligence, and Patrol Support divisions. It was intended to increase the amount of uniformed police presence in Milwaukee's most crime-infected neighborhoods. Lieutenant Spell reports, the MPD "needs to get those guys [personnel in the specialized assignments] to be cops first and specialists second." At the same time as the creation of the NTF, the MPD established a Differential Police Response Unit[6] (DPR). Together, these moves represented a wiser use of personnel and freed up resources to focus on a more proactive approach to solving neighborhood-specific problems. As Capt. Zest reports:

> Patrol at one point was looked on as kind of a secondary aspect of the department. Patrol generally took assignments, and that was their main focus—going from call to call, and taking care of assignments as quickly as possible, and as many as possible. We've been focusing more on freeing up those squads from taking assignments and giving them more time to actually patrol and reduce crime, reduce fear in the neighborhoods.

The new NTF had widespread support among the Common Council President, the Chair of the Public Safety Committee, the President of the Milwaukee Police Association, and a representative from a neighborhood association. Some within the CIB, however, perceived the move as a "blow to the CIB" (Haggerty & Diedrich, 2008). This sentiment would prove to be a challenge for

---

6. The DPR was an important move in redeploying police personnel and making time for police to partake in a variety of activities discussed in this research. The DPR represented the MPD's move toward making the most advantageous use of limited duty personnel who were otherwise serving the MPD by fulfilling non-police specific clerical functions.

the MPD as it continued to change the organizational structure and environment in which it operated.

While detectives perceive the change as devaluing their work, Lt. Johns states that patrol "is happy to say, 'We're back on the map again, we matter, we count!'" Respondents reflect on the CIB-based tradition in the MPD, in which the organization assigned prestige to personnel in the CIB. They note that the department's penchant for the CIB was manifest in the MPD's strategies and promotional processes. Captain Mayer states:

> This was always a detective-bureau run police department. The detectives, they walked on water, and the uniform people were just the worker bees. It was not really recognized, but it was known that that's where you cut your teeth in order to get a good reputation.

The reorganization was a tangible display of the MPD's interactive, neighborhood focus. Shortly after this move, the transfers of 19 captains and rumblings of a plan to decentralize part of the CIB added to the uneasiness that some personnel felt (Haggerty, 2009). Many of the captains were transferred from the Neighborhood Policing Bureau (patrol) to the CIB (and vice versa), with the intent of "cross-pollinating" leaders and exposing them to various parts of the organization. Department records and newspaper and interview data suggest that this move was intended not only to enhance MPD service to the community but also to influence the provincial culture that had arisen in the MPD bureaus.

The CIB reorganization, the NTF, and the push for decentralizing part of the CIB reflects a previous attempt at breaking away from CIB domination. As Lt. Star explained:

> A lot of the older guys, there's not too many of them left, say, 'This is how we did this, 25 years ago.' We didn't have homicide detectives, we didn't have burglary detectives, we didn't have robbery detectives. You were assigned a district and anything that came into your district, you handled. Some of that was good, some was bad. I think our homicide unit success over the last 20 years has proven that. We handle homicide investigations very well. Do we handle burglary investigations very well? No. Did we handle shooting investigations very well? No. Did we handle robbery investigations very well? Yeah. We did some that was good, some that was bad.

For detectives, the pendulum swings from geographically-based investigations (and structures that support that arrangement) to functionally-based investigations (or, the generalist versus specialist and centralized versus decentralized models). The MPD is moving to a more decentralized model of investigations in which detectives work with patrol officers to maintain a geographic area of responsibility in investigating a variety of crimes in their areas.

Though many in the MPD perceived the CIB's clearance rates to be above national averages, memos from the MPD explain that, except for homicide clearance rates, clearance rates for most other offenses were at or below national averages. And, as Capt. Michaels discusses:

> For years the organization has been missing out on a great opportunity to really endear itself to a lot of the citizens we would normally rely on for support. I mean, because we never clear or arrest anybody who stole a barbeque grill, or broke into the garage, or broke the window out of her car and took their GPS. We're getting so many more of those crimes than the killings and the robberies and that's the point where we're having our touch points with most of our citizens here.

Interview and department archival data show the MPD recognizes that the majority of crimes occurring within their city (that is, the crimes that directly affect the greatest number of people) are the crimes that have traditionally received the least amount of successful effort from investigators. These shifts in the organizational structure and the various processes in which the MPD partakes are a response to this reality. They are in line with their stated function to work with neighborhoods to reduce levels of crime, disorder, and fear. The reorganization also advances MPD's plan to increase the amount of positive interactions with citizens. By having patrol officers and detectives work together on cases, the MPD hopes to raise clearance rates and to proactively prevent and solve problems, thereby increasing the number of satisfied citizens and their relationship with the community.

Survey data shed light on the community-relationship building and personnel information-sharing purposes of the CIB reorganization. Though survey data from this research reflect agreement that patrol officers establish positive relationships with citizens in their districts, there is much less agreement on whether detectives do the same. The same data also reveal a lack of agreement about the information sharing purpose (between patrol officers and detectives) of the CIB reorganization. Only 42% of MPD personnel in this survey agree that patrol officers regularly share information with detectives. Only 26% of those surveyed agree that detectives regularly share information with patrol officers. The data reveal a definite distinction between the level of importance assigned to statements regarding patrol officers' and detectives' responsibility for maintaining a limited geographic area. For instance,

61% of this survey's respondents believe it is "very important" for patrol officers to have sector integrity while only 36% believe it is "very important" for detectives to do the same. A limitation to the survey research and the history effect explain these discrepancies: patrol officers made up the majority of respondents and the survey was conducted before the CIB reorganization was fully implemented.

Along with breaking up bureaucratic "silos," the structural change (and new processes and technologies) created different means of accountability and authority. Captain Reed discusses the MPD's success of new technologies, crime meetings, and pushing authority down to the district level:

> Focusing on the repeat offenders so keeping track of who the people are that are getting arrested for stealing, and when they start stealing them from the same areas again, going back and checking if those people are in custody or not and following up on them and arresting them faster. That's all the stuff that's attributed to that decrease. And a big part of that, which would be what the chief has changed is he's pushed much more accountability down at the district level, holding the district commanders and supervisors responsible for the crime that's occurring in the district. A lot of times, the responsibility for a lot of the crime problems would be placed on the commanders in the Detective Bureau rather than the district commanders. So I think that the commanders at the district level will focus on crime and not all this other stuff that's going on. That's had a huge effect.

Crime mapping and crime analysis technologies used during the CompStat and daily crime meetings focus police work and help to hold commanders and supervisors accountable for the problems in their areas. Additionally, the establishment of the NTF supplies resources to patrol to further assist their efforts to prevent and investigate crime problems.

The new organization of the MPD, in which detectives and patrol officers work more closely together, emphasizes the prevention of crime and disorder problems for both the CIB and patrol bureau. These new processes, then, hold commanders and supervisors in both bureaus responsible for producing the desired effects. The meetings, now on a daily and weekly basis and involving representatives from all areas of the MPD, fortify this process. Captain Wilson and others explain the value of these meetings:

> Our strategies are based on crime and based on what works and what doesn't. In the past we've had these conversations once a month, once every two weeks, and they were separate conversations really—the de-

tective bureau having their conversation over here, districts having there conversations over there. Districts were concentrated on things that probably weren't connected to the entire city. Now the conversation is everyone together, it's every single day, and it's about what's going on right now, not about what happened two weeks ago or three weeks ago. And then everybody works together because collaboration is the key.... So those things where we pump this down to the lowest level, decisionmaking down to the lowest level, deployment decisions, down to the lowest level, so if there is an emerging trend or problem, you don't have to go through all of this bureaucracy to get it done.

The excerpt also explains the benefit of pushing down decisionmaking, resource allocation, and deployment decisions to the lowest levels of the organization.

Respondents discuss the Safe Streets Initiative as exemplifying the pushdown of authority. Under the current structure, captains and even sergeants can decide deployment strategies without needing to have the inspector's or assistant chief's approval. Assistant Chief Smith summarizes this discussion, saying:

What [Chief Flynn] managed to do is that he has not allowed the investigative units to determine a mission of the department in terms of resources deployment. He has brought it down back to a neighborhood level where it should be: each block by block, the district captains, allowing them to have a say in how and where their resources be deployed.

This respondent and others portray the move in the department from one that is driven by the detective bureau to one in which both the detective and patrol bureaus have a say in the driving mission of the police department—a department in which more decisions are made at the lower levels of both bureaus.

Major structural and administrative process modifications to the MPD include the creation of the Neighborhood Task Force (which took personnel from the Criminal Intelligence Bureau and many of the specialty patrol units), a Differential Police Response unit, and Intelligence Fusion Center, the institution of weekly CompStat and daily crime meetings, a move toward decentralizing part of the CIB, and a pushdown of authority to the district level. These influence the manner of police delivery of services and are intended to change the police culture. Most importantly, these changes coincide with a more efficient application of a CPS strategy because they facilitate police interaction with the community, encourage collaboration between two historically separate bureaus (the CIB and patrol bureau), and increase information, free time, resources, and authority at the lowest levels of the organization to allow for more proactive neighborhood-level problem-solving.

# Summary

This section has shown how the MPD's newest methods of service delivery influence the way demand enters and is managed by the organization. These changes also apply to the tenets of a CPS strategy by encouraging a differentiation of responses based on data of neighborhood-level problems and on neighborhood abilities to respond to those problems. Creating the DPR unit and limiting the types of calls that require patrol officers' response combine with the MPD's new data analysis and mapping technologies, as well as community interactions to form the entrance and management processes for the demand of MPD service. These processes, in addition to the other elements of the MPD explored in this study, support the community-based, data-driven, problem-solving mission of the MPD.

# References

Braga, A. & Weisburd, D. (2006). Problem-oriented policing: The disconnect between principles and practice. In D. Weisburd & A. Braga (Eds.), *Police Innovation: Contrasting Perspectives* (pp. 133–154). New York, NY: Cambridge.

Haggerty, R. (22 March 2009). Flynn's police shuffle intended to improve versatility, communication. *Milwaukee Journal-Sentinel*, Retrieved from http://www.jsonline.com/news/milwaukee/42064062.html.

Haggerty, R. & Diedrich, J. (29 May 2008). Police launch new patrol. *Milwaukee Journal-Sentinel*. Retrieved from http://www.jsonline.com/news/milwaukee/29568124.html.

Milwaukee Police Department (2009). 2008 Annual Report.

Milwaukee Police Department (2010). 2009 Annual Report.

Milwaukee Quality of Life Round Table. (18 November 2007). Violent crime, *Milwaukee Journal-Sentinel* [Online]. Retrieved from http://www.jsonline.com/news/opinion/29311989.html.

Spice, L., & Borowski, G. (19 November 2007). From budgeting to crime, Flynn faces challenges. *Milwaukee Journal-Sentinel* [Online]. Retrieved from http://www.jsonline.com/news/milwaukee/29313144.html.

# Chapter 7

# The Los Angeles Police Department

## Introduction

The final case study examines the handoff of the Los Angeles Police Department (LAPD) from the end of Chief Bill Bratton's tenure through the beginning of Chief Beck's. The rich diversity of Los Angeles and its being the nation's most (self-proclaimed) underpoliced big city mean the LAPD faces special challenges fulfilling its community problem-solving (CPS) mission. The city's second-place ranking on the list of largest cities in the United States and its preeminent spot in the history of the policing profession make this study of the LAPD a caricaturization of CPS. The reader will note how the LAPD carries on its historic leadership of the profession as it fights crime, repairs community relationships, and implements the most innovative policing technologies.

## The LAPD Mission

*"To protect the community by reducing the fear and incidence of crime."*

### Function

The stated constitutional, legitimacy, and terrorist prevention aspects of the LAPD mission reflect defining characteristics of policing in the twenty-first century. As part of Chief Bratton's leadership under the consent decree and the events of 9/11, the LAPD has these issues at the forefront of their organizational mission. The now traditional parts of a police department's mission (i.e., crime and disorder prevention and quality of life) are also extensively discussed in this section.

➤ **Keeping the people of Los Angeles safe and helping to provide quality of life.** The Los Angeles Police Department First Quarter Manual (2010, section 103) lists as their mission ("To safeguard the lives and property of the people we serve, to reduce the incidence and fear of crime, and to enhance public safety while working with the diverse communities to improve their quality of life." Interviews with LAPD personnel echo this mission and specify the CPS functions used to fulfill it. Like the other departments, the LAPD confirms reducing the fear of crime, improving the quality of life, and working with the community as conspicuous parts of their mission. Yet, notorious events in LAPD history show how they did exactly the opposite: they ruled by fear, destroyed residents' quality of life, and neglected community mechanisms for managing behavior. This study examines the perspectives of LAPD personnel (who now answer to a new chief, Charlie Beck) to retroactively explore the institutionalization of Chief Bratton's seven-year tenure.

In 2002, Chief William Bratton swore to lead the LAPD off its corrupt and insular path and into the twenty-first century. He vowed to "reduce crime, protect the city from terrorists and reform the character and style of our policing" (Bratton, 2006). The *Los Angeles Times*, in their sanguine endorsement of Chief Bratton, complimented his savvy quality of life strategies and charged him with using technology, community relationships, and problem solving to clear up the criminals both in the streets *and* within the police department (*Los Angeles Times*, 5 Nov 2009). These characteristics of the LAPD epitomize (at least in theory) the New Community Problem-Solving era—driven by data and technology to work with the community to solve problems of crime, fear, and disorder (and including threats of terrorism).

In many ways, the LAPD and its personnel, like the BPD, are building on their earlier conceptions of community policing. Capt. Carlo notes, "[Community policing] is a lot of what people were always doing.... And the people coming on the department today understand it. It's pretty well-rooted here. The roots are there." Capt. Carlo reports "our inroads when it came to really embracing community policing has been a huge change." Captain Shelly suggests community policing has not taken as strong a hold on the LAPD. He states, "There's still people that are hesitant to embrace some of the community policing philosophies. There are some command level officers that still understand it, but a lot don't embrace [it]." He points to a "change in upper management thinking" in bringing about community-oriented changes. Captain Allen, reflecting on the police executives he witnessed over his nearly three decade long career, describes how some have "better attributes towards the community [than others]." He then nominates Chief Bratton the "biggest change" chief. Captain Grimm similarly uses the Chiefs' tenures to demarcate LAPD history. She concludes, "[Bratton] really put his money where his mouth was and tried to give resources to the geographic areas to help promote community policing."

Captain Carlo gives further reasons for the LAPD's change toward community policing. He describes how the LAPD's earlier understanding of community policing conflicted with the typical police recruit's excitement-driven motivations to be a police officer—to "shoot guns and chase bad guys." He believes that the LAPD now does "a much better job as an organization of making people understand community policing is not soft on crime." Captain Allen and his colleagues give examples of the embedded nature of this new CPS strategy of their department. They include managing disorder in Skid Row, the use of Gang Intervention Teams, and other "alternatives to law enforcement" (Captain Carlo). These and other tactics are discussed in the next section.

The leadership of the LAPD's current chief, Charlie Beck, offers more evidence of the institutionalization of their CPS strategy. In his chief's message in February 2010 he writes to his personnel "The goals and objectives by which I will hold you and myself accountable are; [sic] Constitutional Policing; Crime Reduction; Prevention of Terrorist Incidents; Maintaining the Personnel Strength of the Department; and Employee Wellness." He then expounds upon each goal, emphasizing the role of constitutional policing in working with and serving the community. He concludes, "No officer is justified in breaking the law on the grounds of expediency." Chief Beck goes on to describe crime reduction as the "true measure of our strategic hard work: keeping the people of Los Angeles safe and helping to provide quality of life." In this post-9/11 policing environment, it is worth noting that the LAPD is the only department in this study to explicitly and repeatedly mention the prevention of terrorist acts as part of their mission.

The data in this research clearly point to the fear and crime reduction and quality of life function of the LAPD. They also suggest that Chief Beck is leading the LAPD on the trajectory established under his predecessor, Chief Bratton, who led the LAPD under the mandates of the consent decree. As Los Angeles Mayor Villaraigosa noted during Beck's swearing in ceremony, "'For the first time in many decades, what we are asking of this chief is to continue the momentum of reform, rather than to be the first to usher it in.... [He] embodies the new era of LAPD'" (Rubin, 2009). The following sections examine the other aspects of the LAPD's organizational strategy to determine the extent of their institutionalization of a CPS strategy.

## Tactics, Technology, and Outcomes

As LAPD personnel often lament, the LAPD covers an expansive geographic area with relatively few personnel. In 2010, just under 10,000 sworn personnel serve nearly four million people in an area over 500 square miles. The LAPD in this study responds to this reality by working with the community and by using tactics and technologies that focus their attention on specific crime and disorder hotspots. Interview and LAPD archival data also discuss the role of the CompStat process in helping to measure, organize, and assess their tactics.

**First you have a ding, then you have a dent, then you have a junk.** Despite data suggesting the LAPD's mission to prevent terrorist attacks, interview responses on police tactics, technologies, and outcomes concentrate on those activities that pursue the crime and disorder prevention and quality of life improvement portions of the LAPD mission. A review of news coverage, LAPD archival data, and interviews with LAPD personnel discuss the Safer City Initiative in Skid Row and the Gang Intervention Teams within the context of hotspot policing, broken windows policing, and working with the community to reduce crime and disorder and improve the quality of life in Los Angeles.

Skid Row, an area described as "a violent, drug-infested 50-block radius in downtown Los Angeles" (*Our City, Our Duty*, 2006) and harboring nearly 1,400 street people (Blankstein & DiMassa, 2009) epitomized a hotspot of disorderly and criminal behaviors. In 2006, as a result of a series of articles in the *Los Angeles Times*, a "consensus emerged among politicians, public officials, and the public itself: Los Angeles must do something about homelessness" (*Our City, Our Duty*, 2006). The call to action led the city to focus efforts on street and sidewalk cleaning in that area (DiMassa, 2006) and prompted the county to add $80 million for shelter and social service agencies (Winton, 2006). The LAPD responded to that concentration of crime and disorder with broken windows policing. District Attorney Steve Cooley and the probation department complemented the law enforcement component by making it a violation of one's probation to visit Skid Row.

The LAPD's implementation of broken windows policing involved increased patrols in Skid Row and the use of laws against sidewalk sleeping and public urination as a basis for interacting with citizens in that area. This researcher observed the lasting effects of these practices during an observation of a sergeant on foot patrol one warm December afternoon in 2010. People resting alongside buildings and on the curbs lined the (otherwise unobstructed) sidewalks of Skid Row. The sergeant, playing the part of a politician, stopped and talked with people, shook their hands, called some by name and followed up on previous conversations. Many smiled and called the sergeant by his last

*talked to the people as people*

name as they listed their compliments and complaints. For example, a Black gentleman reminded the sergeant about one police officer, "Black Nigger Billy," who was overly invasive and too physically forceful in his patrols of the area. A more complimentary chat followed with the director of one of the many Skid Row missions. They discussed the LAPD's Community Impact Teams (a community and police collaborative intended to address issues of quality of life). In between these chats, the sergeant kindly stopped a man with whom he was familiar. The man was carrying a box of small vases, each containing a silk red rose. The sergeant, using his discretion, scolded him, acting as though the man must have forgotten the crooked use of the small vases—as a crack pipe. The sergeant then requested the man smash the vases and throw them in the garbage.

The Safer City Initiative in Skid Row was not without its detractors. Out of concern for the individual rights of street people in Skid Row, the American Civil Liberties Union (ACLU) of Southern California sued the LAPD for violating the Fourth Amendment rights of those frequenting Skid Row. They argued that the LAPD's arrests for sidewalk sleeping were unconstitutional (Winton & McGreevy, 2006; *Jones v. City of Los Angeles*, 2006). Later, they questioned the constitutionality of searches of street people and their belongings incident to violations of jaywalking, street sleeping, and other minor offenses (Ripston, 2007). These court cases highlight the unintended negative consequences of aggressive broken windows policing: citizens perceive police as acting discriminately against "poor, mostly African American residents" (Dennison, 2007) or "ordinary people whose only mistake was being homeless in the wrong part of town" (Ripston, 2007).

The courts ruled in favor of the ACLU. Chief Bratton, Mayor Villaraigosa and the ACLU then agreed to ban sidewalk sleeping from 6:00am through 9:00pm (to allow for the more conventional use of sidewalks at those times), to prohibit setting up camp near business and residential entrances, and to delineate a section in Skid Row where street people might sleep at night (Khalil & Winton, 2006). The city council, with the support of local business representatives, voted against the agreement. They argued that it would invite even more street people into Skid Row and that it compromises the LAPD's enforcement efforts (Hymon & Winton, 2006). Interviews with LAPD personnel suggest another view of the broken windows policing being done on Skid Row.

Capt. Allen believes quality of life enforcements "really set the tone. Because if you let the small things go, then the big things will follow." He then offers the daytime ban on sidewalk sleeping as an example of broken windows policing on Skid Row:

> You could look at the simple things—there's a city ordinance, [citizens] are allowed to sit in certain hours of darkness and they gotta be done and up and going by six in the morning. Something as simple as that—if that's not adhered to, if the officers don't really take that seriously and [citizens] start settin' up at 5:00 in the afternoon as businesses are open and they don't start breaking their tents down until seven or eight in the morning. That would set a tone really quickly. It's important that the officers are out there enforcin' it. You need to make sure the people who are doin' it are educated as to why it's being done. It's not just us coming through a tunnel and saying hey listen, here's the parameters we gotta work within, please be our partners and help us out and be up and ready to go. It's that constant communication of letting everyone know what the expectations are.

He exemplifies the negotiable yet strict standards of maintaining order in Skid Row. Police consult with the community to set the boundaries of behaviors in their neighborhood. In *this case*, the police then strictly enforce those boundaries (*à la* "zero-tolerance") to "set the tone" that certain behaviors will not be tolerated in specific circumstances (i.e., sleeping on the sidewalk during set times of day).

Other interviewees explicate broken windows policing in the rest of LAPD. They eloquently caution against the misinterpretations that some police have of broken windows policing and defend its suitability. Deputy Chief Cathy relates her conception of the broken windows theory to an old family adage:

> My grandfather used to have a saying that every time he had a little ding in his car he'd get it fixed. I'd say, 'It's just a ding grandpa, it's just a ding.' First you have a ding, then you have a dent, then you have a junk.

She then discusses how the same mechanism of destruction can occur in a Los Angeles neighborhood. She and others also relay how citizens attending community meetings often complained about disorders such as graffiti, transients, and litter, and not more serious crimes. Lt. Braden uses the term "elephant hunters" to describe those officers who wish to arrest the robbers and auto thieves (or, "elephants" as he calls them). The enforcement of "quality of life crimes," he notes, was one of Bratton's five pillars. Finally, each person who discussed the role of quality of life enforcement in the LAPD mentioned the need to engage the citizens (and other city agencies) in a politically sensitive, community-specific, problem- and solution-defining process.

**We're gonna be in the era of dot policing.** The previous section showed how the LAPD used and viewed broken windows policing in a crime and disorder hotspot. This section uncovers the other tactics the LAPD uses to focus on high-crime locations and high-risk individuals. Like the other above-discussed changes (e.g., the move to a community policing mission), the new focus on these high volume people and places took some getting used to. Lieutenant Hamel explains how some of his colleagues came to realize "that [hotspot and problem-solving policing] was gonna be the new new." He describes how as a supervisor he noticed how some people thought they would "wait Bratton out," and not buy into these new ways of improving their "service" and "crime fighting effectiveness." He concludes, "When the chief says you're going to change, well, you're going to change." The LAPD continued on its new CPS path, improving the Gang Impact Teams (GIT) and refining their use of gang injunctions and gang interventionists.

The Gang Impact Teams exemplify the LAPD's inclusion of hot people (i.e., gang members) and hot times into the hotspot, community collaboration, and problem-solving equation. These teams "facilitate the development of long-term gang and narcotics enforcement strategies and provide the increased supervisory oversight and accountability" to the other gang and drug details as required by the consent decree (LAPD, 2004, p. 1). As part of the GIT, the Gang Enforcement Detail's (GED) and the Community Law Enforcement and Recovery (CLEAR) units' crime suppression activities include: establishing a presence in gang areas, deploying uniform personnel during high gang activity times, focusing efforts on the most violent gangs, and establishing and maintaining relationships with law enforcement and community groups. Starting in 2009, the GIT also enjoyed the responsibility of helping the LAPD to organize their gang injunctions.

Gang injunctions define the gang's criminal behavior as a nuisance to the community. They give police the authority to intervene in a situation before a nuisance (i.e., gang members congregating in a restricted [often hotspot] location) becomes a more serious problem. These injunctions require the cooperation of other criminal justice groups (e.g., the district attorney and the courts) and the support of the community. As such, they demonstrate the nexus between hotspots, hot suspects, hot times and broken windows policing. Lieutenant Davis, who claims the "highest arrest rate for injunction violations," depicts groups of youths hanging out in public "smokin' dope" as "kind of like a broken window." He continues, "I recognize that allowing those gang members to congregate will lead to other issues."

The use of gang injunctions is not without its opponents. A 2009 Los Angeles mayoral candidate Carlos Alvarez, for instance, called the gang injunctions "racist," claiming "they have criminalized whole sectors of the city's youth" (*Carlos Alvarez: L.A.*, 25 February 2009). Another community member worried the neighborhood might become a police state (Gold, 2009). The city attorney's director of anti-gang operations discerns this, mentioning how the LAPD's approach to gang injunctions has evolved "to show [the public] that the [LAPD] has more in mind than the 'hookin' and bookin'' tactics of the past" (Gold, 7 June 2009). He impresses the use of discretion, saying "'Don't arrest everyone because you can. Arrest them because it's the right thing to do'" (Gold, 7 June 2009). The LAPD also taps the community by engaging civic activists (including critics of the LAPD) to help deliver the message of improving quality of life through the proper enforcement of the gang injunctions. As Capt. Mark Olvera notes, "'It's all about respect.... That dignity you give them is going to pay you back in the long run'" (Gold, 7 June 2009).

One of the ways the LAPD engages a traditionally outlawed group is through one of their most controversial tactics—gang intervention. Many of the gang interventionists in Los Angeles are former gang members who try to reduce violence by bridging the gap between the LAPD and current gang members. The gang interventionists' background in the gang life legitimizes them with the gangs but draws suspicion from police personnel. This study reveals the historical challenges to the LAPD's adoption of gang interventionists. It also documents the current trends in balancing the tenuous relationships they have with these community members.

Captain Shelly uses gang intervention as an example of how the LAPD's commitment to work with the community has strengthened since the 1980s and 1990s. He concedes, though, that despite their acknowledging it as the avant-garde of policing, some command-level staff only half-heartedly embrace the gang intervention. Also in response to a question on new CPS strategies, Deputy Chief Hannan discusses his success as an early adopter of gang interventionists. As a captain in one of Los Angeles' most violent divisions in 2005, Hannan "[threw] the kitchen sink" at his violent crime problem, using mostly "aggressive suppression efforts" to no avail. He turned to the gang interventionists, who he perceived as an unorganized "bunch of former gang members who didn't like me, and [with whom] I didn't have a whole lot in common." When he reached out to them, they helped put an end to a string of retaliatory shootings. Then-Captain Hannan became "their biggest advocate" and "took a tremendous amount of heat from within the department over acknowledging that these former gang members who were now calling themselves gang interventionists actually were legitimate in some ways."

Some of the "heat" resulted from what Deputy Chief Hannan describes as gang interventionists "[mismanaging] their monies" or "playing as a double agent." Two city reports on the gang interventionists as well as the LAPD experience confirm the difficulties facing the gang interventionists as the interventionists attempt to maintain legitimacy in both the gang and cop cultures (Gold, 28 June 2009). However, the Deputy Chief also reports gang interventionists are now better organized within the official LAPD response to the gang problem. The city also manages them better than they had in the past. As a result of the perceived benefits of gang interventionists, senior-level Los Angeles and LAPD personnel (including Chief Charlie Beck) vowed to keep such programs in place while also providing them with improved oversight and accountability (Gold, 19 November 2009).

This section covered the LAPD's response to what they see as a gang-violence problem—the use of broken windows policing in hotspots and against repeat offenders, as exemplified by the GIT, the Safer City Initiative, and the rebirth of the gang injunctions. Though each initiative came with its challenges, the LAPD worked with the community to build legitimacy and gain their support in implementing these controversial tactics. These issues of community building and legitimacy are discussed later. First, we turn to how the LAPD measures their work and to their views of their organization's use of technology.

**We're using technology better, to strategically strike.** The predominant theme of technology that arises in this study of the LAPD involves technology's ability to organize intelligence and to disseminate it in real-time to better inform police tactical and strategic operations. The LAPD's uses of technology include street cameras in hotspots, in-car cameras, real-time and weekly crime maps, an electronic database, portable fingerprint scans, and smart phones to disseminate this information. As Lt. Davis explains, "We're using technology better … to strategically strike, in dealing with crime." These uses of technology (in a manner similar to that documented in Milwaukee) assist the LAPD in creating and focusing their tactics. They also allow for a more effective and efficient implementation of them.

Lieutenant Davis describes three types of technology used by the LAPD. Firstly, he receives real-time shooting notifications on his smart phone. That way, when a shooting occurs in or near his area he can send officers to locations where retaliatory shootings may occur (e.g., if it is believed that a shooting is gang-related or part of a beef between groups). Secondly, mapping, computer, and electronic database technologies aid in these determinations by providing for the creation and dissemination of daily and weekly crime maps. These maps provide visual trends in hotspots, repeat offenders, on-going conflicts, or relationships between offenders. Captains Allen and Folson argue that these ways of managing offense and offender information help the LAPD to draw the connections needed to deploy tactics that focus on hotspots or repeat offenders. Others note the expedience of collecting and displaying this information at CompStat (discussed later). Finally, Lt. Davis and other respondents find in-car cameras useful in building cases against arrestees whose actions and statements are recorded by the cameras. Similarly, Lt. Hamel would like to see Los Angeles follow what he refers to as the "iron ring philosophy of the London Metropolitan Police," where data centers and cameras capture much of the activity in public spaces.

Captain Grimm and observations of patrol officers offer another way technology makes the LAPD more efficient. Portable electronic thumbprint readers help to instantly identify individuals who otherwise do not cooperate with the officer's request for identification or whom the officer feels is not forthright. This allows the officer to make a better-informed decision about how to proceed with the individual, helping the officer to distinguish the incessant lawbreakers from the rest of citizenry. Other respondents mention the role technology plays in building community relationships. For example, Lt. Braden discusses the ways internet-aided technologies such as Nixle (an application that allows the LAPD to send geographically-specific notifications to citizens), online news media, YouTube, and Facebook connect the LAPD with the community to give them information on a real time basis. He notes Chief Bratton used these technologies to make the LAPD more transparent and to show the public "much more clearly the 95% of cops who are always doing things right."

Some respondents worry not even technology can bolster the LAPD's efforts to continue driving crime down. Lieutenant McColgan, contemplating his shared concern, suggests a new reliance on a traditional investigative technology—DNA. He states:

> It's just a matter of prioritizing your limited resources. If we can find the funds or find a technique that doesn't cost as much and focus on DNA analysis on property crime, God help the criminals. That's the next phase in this quest to decrease crime.

He notes that these crimes more directly affect the greatest amount of people. By enhancing the investigative capabilities of detectives and getting these property criminals off the streets, the LAPD could continue to produce lower crime statistics. Other areas of technological consideration, as offered by interview respondents, include the use of predictive analytics and automatic license plate readers and capitalizing on the younger generation of police officers who are inherently more "technologically savvy" than their more senior colleagues.

This section suggested innovative ways the LAPD uses, and might consider using, technology to better safeguard life and property, decrease citizen fear, and enhance the quality of life for their citizens. The technologies discussed here allow the LAPD to better communicate within the department and with the community to provide a more efficient and effective implementation of their sharpened tactics. A brief discussion of the ways the LAPD measures their work will show to what extent these measurements align with a CPS strategy.

➤ **It's always been about reducing crime—it's the bottom line.** Not surprisingly, as part of Chief Beck's explanation of the LAPD's crime reduction goal, he writes, "This is the true measure of our strategic hard work: keeping the people of Los Angeles safe and helping to provide quality of life." Despite respondents' assertions about the community-based activities of the LAPD, there exists only one formal mechanism for measuring those activities. Many interview respondents offer crime reduction as the primary goal of the LAPD. As Capt. Folson reports, "[Reducing crime] is a primary measure of effectiveness of the organization; reduce homicides, then Part 1 crime." Interviews suggest informal ways of measuring their community-building goals.

Captain Tanner describes a number of ways he and his officers engaged the Watts community. For example, police began going into the local school to read to students every Friday after the school's "Donuts for Dads" program revealed a father to student ratio of 2:11. The reading program gave rise to police involvement in the local Christmas parade and pep rallies to encourage reading. These changes between the police and the citizens, the respondent reports, correlated with an increase in students' test scores as well as a 14% decrease in overall arrests and a 45% decrease in juvenile arrests from 2008–2009. He concedes, "The department measures it in a little more of an anecdotal way. [The chief of staff] knows the relationship that we have with the community here because they get feedback from the community." He believes the reduced crime numbers reflect the enhanced community relationships. Though not acknowledged explicitly by the LAPD, meetings such as those of the Watts Gang Task Force exemplify another type of assessment of the LAPD's crime and disorder fighting and community building activities.

Deputy Chief Alvarez offers an increase in the community proactively assisting the LAPD as another anecdotal measurement of the LAPD's success in interacting with the community. Captain Tanner suggests community feedback makes its way informally through the organization. He states, "I know that I'm doing a good job here because they won't let me leave. Chief Beck has made it real clear I'm not going anywhere. That's probably how it's measured more than anything." Lieutenant Laker suspects the CompStat process reinforces the importance of the crime reduction outcomes of the community-building function. In discussing the process, he states. "Police work now is all about the numbers ... reducing crime. It's the bottom line." He then implies, like Capt. Tanner, that if you can keep crime down, you can keep your job.

Lieutenant Garcia offers one final example of the LAPD's lack of formal measurement of their non-crime reduction-related goals. Lieutenant Garcia is a newly established leader in a unit responsible for providing additional personnel to crime hotspots. She also spent time in the LAPD's community relations division and responds to any community issues that arise in the Central Bureau. Yet she states her unit really only tracks crime-related outputs, including new systems for arrests, citations, and search warrants. She offers the bureau-level forums as an example of how the LAPD engages in community problem-solving. Each of these quarterly meetings takes place between a Chief and leaders from the Black, Asian, Hispanic, or Gay and Lesbian communities. The extent of the LAPD's measurement of these activities, as Lt. Garcia describes, is an "audit" of the meeting, to ensure the setting, parking, and equipment were sufficient for the meeting.

Others agree on the importance of each part of the LAPD mission, but they admit difficulties measuring the activities that fulfill them. As Lt. Braden states:

> Quality of life enforcement is critical because the first line of our mission is to protect the community by reducing the fear and incidence of crime. So, incidence of crime is one thing, go and catch the robber. Fear of crime … that's difficult to measure.

The LAPD steadfastly desires to reduce citizen fear and crime and to increase the quality of life for residents of Los Angeles. Though they acknowledge the merit of all parts of their mission, they have not incorporated formal measures for comprehensively gauging their efforts. The next section further explores the LAPD's community- and legitimacy-building function. Measures from Stone, Foglesong, and Cole's (2009) study of the LAPD federal consent decree support the efficacy of the LAPD's efforts in this area.

# Working with the Community

*"First and foremost is just the transparency."*

## External Relationships and Legitimacy

Though historically more indicative of the earlier, "professional" (or reform) strategy of policing, incidents such as the excessive use of force against Rodney King and the Rampart scandal in the 1990s jolted community and police perceptions of the LAPD and finally fomented the LAPD's path toward adopting a CPS strategy. The previous sections provide examples of how the LAPD works with various members of the community to control problems of crime and disorder. The current section includes personnel's conceptions and citizens' perceptions of such changes. Findings from Harvard University's study of the LAPD consent decree (Stone et al., 2009) and a survey of Angelenos conducted by Loyola Marymount University's Center for the Study of Los Angeles (*20th Anniversary*, 2012) complement this study's original research on how the LAPD views their relationships with the community.

**First and foremost is just the transparency.** The crises the LAPD faced throughout its history (especially those that contrasted with the greater profession's move toward CPS in the 1990s) provided kindling for the LAPD's move toward the new CPS under Chief Bratton. Stone et al. (2009) and interviews with LAPD personnel cite the transparency Chief Bratton provided under the consent decree as important to change in their department. Captain Carlo, for example, states, "We're much more transparent with the community. We provide as much information as we can about what we're doing and how we're doing it." Captain Oneida, commenting on how the LAPD has enhanced its relationship with the community, notes, "First and foremost is just the transparency. Allowing the community to realize [the officers are] people, [educating them] on what the department offers, what the department does." Stone et al. (2009) cite Bratton's commitment to transparency as a primary motivator for the upper levels of the LAPD. However, the question arises of whether such organizational changes can withstand the transfer of a police department from one chief to the next.

Though much of this study examines Chief Bratton's impact on the LAPD, interview and survey data suggest differences in Bratton's and Beck's LAPD. A quinquennial, longitudinal survey of a cross-section of Angelenos (*20th Anniversary*, 2012) has allowed for an examination of changes in citizens' perceptions of the LAPD since 1997. It describes a number of potential areas of difference among chiefs over that time. For example, from 1997 to 2012 the percent of Angelenos giving the LAPD at least a "good" job rating has declined from 78% under Chiefs Willie Williams and Bernard Parks to 75% and 70% under Chiefs William Bratton and Charlie Beck (*20th Anniversary*, 2012, p. 4). Comparing support for the reappointment of Chiefs Williams and Beck, one notes no change (40%). However, support for the reappointment of Chief Bratton in 2007 (56%) is significantly higher than all other chiefs in the survey (*20th Anniversary*, 2012, p. 4). Responses to questions asked beginning in 2002 reveal definite differences between the LAPD under Chiefs Parks and Beck regarding their effectiveness in increasing community policing and civilian review of complaints, imposing more discipline among police officers, and improving police recruitment (*20th Anniversary*, 2012, pp. 4–5). The survey suggests both Chiefs Parks and Bratton were more effective in these areas than Chief Beck. Despite this, Chief Beck still receives a passing grade, with 72% of respondents grading his performance a "C" or above.

The disparities in Angelenos' views of the LAPD under each chief may result from the relative and subjective views of "effective" change over time (which is why this study's recent historical perspective is important in studying police leaders' ability to create change in a department). For example, citizens might perceive changes made in the wake of the infamous Rampart scandal as more effective than the small changes instituted in a stable police department, if for no other reason than the attention each receives. Each of the survey questions compared the LAPD today to the LAPD of 1992 (i.e., the Rodney King incident). So, it is likely that the elements of history and time account for some of these differences. The short amount of time Chief Beck had served as Chief at the time of the survey in 2012 (fewer than three years, compared to five for the others) could also explain the less positive survey results for the LAPD under his command. The greater proportion of "Don't know/Refused" for Chief Beck compared to the other chiefs on these questions supports this notion that maybe the respondents did not feel comfortable judging the LAPD's efforts as it underwent the change from Bratton to Beck.

Interviews with LAPD personnel also validate this. Many respondents discuss Chief Beck's success in maintaining the positive trajectory (i.e., department morale, continued crime reductions and healthy relationships with the community and political leaders). Lieutenant McColgan notes, however, "He hasn't really been tested yet with some crazy incident. In our world—in the LAPD—it seems to happen a lot." This also bolsters the point made earlier about the ability of a police department to shine when it effectively responds to a sensational event. The only crisis noted during Chief Beck's tenure thus far is the persistent threat of being forced to lay off civilian and sworn employees (after, of course, Chief Bratton's personnel gains). These survey results, in the context of this study of the LAPD during both chiefs' tenures, could lead one to believe that the LAPD remains quite effective in the areas of community policing, civilian review, and imposing discipline of police officers—measures relevant to legitimacy and transparency.

The infamous 2007 May Day immigration march melee in MacArthur Park tested Chief Bratton's commitment to transparency and reform. LAPD officers used unjustified physical force after march participants threw rocks and bottles at them. A number of online video recordings showed LAPD officers slamming to the ground or using less than lethal bullets against 24 civilians. Chief Bratton acted immediately to discipline and transfer the deputy chief and commander who were in charge of crowd control that day. Soon after, he created the Critical Incident Management Bureau and began the process of suspending or firing fifteen officers involved in the incident. Eric Garcetti (then-city council president and current mayor of Los Angeles) commented, "'The way in which the department responded was a sea change from the past in taking immediate responsibility, not just along the rank-and-file level, but up the chain of command'" (Reston & Rubin, 2009, p. 2). The 2007 results of the Loyola Marymount survey regarding discipline among police officers and civilian review of complaints reveal over 80% of Angelenos believe Chief Bratton is at least somewhat effective in these areas (*20th Anniversary*, 2012, p. 5). Chief Beck's effectiveness on the same questions in 2012 show a 22- and 25-point slide on each of those measures.

Stone et al.'s (2009) study of change in the LAPD under the consent decree provides further evidence of the LAPD's effectiveness under Chief Bratton. Their survey of sworn officers in the LAPD shows a majority believes the LAPD was better overall in 2009 than it was in 2006. Blacks more so than any other race were more likely to strongly agree with that statement (p. 17). Sworn personnel's perceptions of the effects of civilian review and police officer discipline, however, differ from citizens'. A majority of police officers in 2009 fear being punished for an honest mistake and believe their careers can be negatively affected by civilian complaints (though this is less so in 2009 than in a 1999 survey) (Stone et al., 2009).

Deputy Chief Cathy assuages these concerns, however. She explains, "It's really not the complaints, it's the outcome you have to fear." In other words, honest mistakes should not result in officers being "hung out to dry" as is a common perception among the rank and file. Captain Zachar describes this change as "understanding the human side of policing" and as being in contrast to the "Draconian Parks era." She states, "We still take complaints from all sources, but we now develop or discharge our employees…. We recognize that humans make mistakes." Lieutenant McColgan states that when an officer makes a mistake, "As long as your heart is good, we can train you, but if you make too many of those mistakes, you got a problem, we'll deal with that too."

More evidence of the legitimate actions of the LAPD appears when placing Stone et al.'s (2009) findings on stops and arrests within the context of the above-discussed Safer City Initiative. In explaining the increased likelihood of a stop leading to an arrest between 2002 and 2008, Stone and colleagues note that while the likelihood of a stop ending in arrest tripled or quadrupled in some divisions, it remained constant in some of the notably high crime divisions (including Skid Row). These data show that in fact police officers increased both their stops and their stops resulting in arrest by approximately 150%. These data might be interpreted to suggest police officers in Skid Row were already making many stops (many of which resulted in arrest). Or, given the social and political realities of Skid Row, police used their discretion to *not* invoke their arrest power when they otherwise had the legitimate legal authority to do so (as evidenced in the earlier example of the man carrying the rose-holder-turned-crack pipe). Finally, Stone et al.'s (2009) survey complements previous findings of citizen support for the LAPD. Interviews from the current study link the LAPD's transparency to perceptions of legitimacy (evidenced by respondents' favorable assessments of the LAPD's integrity, fair treatment, and community relationships).

The political authority granted to the LAPD by the civilian board of police commissioners, the local city council, and the mayor aided the LAPD's successes under Chief Bratton. Deputy Chief Hannan remembers the LAPD of the past, reporting, "We were battling with the community, we were battling with politicians, we were battling with outside agencies, we were battling with everybody. We were kind of here on an island." This contrasts to the more recent LAPD in which Lt. Laker notes Chief Bratton might have never reached his goal of having 10,000 sworn personnel in the LAPD without the support of the Mayor and city council. The earlier discussions of the Safer City Initiative and the gang interventionists also demonstrated the collaborative negotiating efforts of the LAPD, the mayor, the business community, the American Civil Liberties Union, social service representatives, and city council. Lieutenant Mc-Colgan comments that Chief Beck, dealing with the financial challenges of 2010, has "managed to keep going what Bratton laid the foundation for and those ties to the city council and the mayor are still strong." As of 1 January 2013, Chief Beck had broken the 10,000 mark in sworn personnel, surpassing his predecessor's goal.

Establishing formal, ongoing relationships with key stakeholders in the Los Angeles community supplement the LAPD's political authority. A representative of Chief Beck meets regularly with members from five traditionally marginalized groups: Hispanic, religious, African-American, Asian, and Gay and Lesbian community members. Lieutenant Garcia describes these community forums as including "the shakers and movers that can get the information out just in case we need it." The LAPD representative works with the community representatives to create an agenda and set a location for the meeting. They often will include a question and answer session and a chance for the LAPD to explain their views on what the *community* thinks is a "hot topic" issue. Signaling the importance of such meetings, Chief Beck has ensured that every bureau has a bureau forum coordinator. Deputy Chief Cathy reports that she used to dread the police bashing that would occur when she attended community meetings, but now the well-attended forums often include gratitude toward the LAPD for the work they are doing.

Finally, the department's continued adherence to constitutional policing under Chief Beck further guides the LAPD relationships with the community, even after the lifting of the federal consent decree. Chief Beck states in a message to the LAPD that breaking the law to enforce the law "brings shame on our profession and alienates the people we serve—the community on whose co-operation we depend if we are to be effective." Lieutenant McColgan agrees that constitutional policing is the driving philosophy of the department. (In fact he was late to our interview because he was coming from a meeting on the LAPD's constitutional policing efforts.) He operationalizes constitutional polic-ing as "making sure that we know what we're doing and [that] we can articu-late that for the people at the Department of Justice and the media."

This section uniquely shows the change-trajectory the LAPD continued after the departure of the change-chief, Bratton. The comparison of multiple years' worth of survey data of community members' perceptions of police chiefs' job performance as well as interviews with command personnel reveal distinctions between the two police chiefs. They also demonstrate the chiefs' shared apti-tude in moving the LAPD toward (which we will discuss in Chapter 9 as) the New Community Problem-Solving era. The consent decree-aided constitu-tional focus, the community-based outreach, and the transparent and deci-sive leadership of the LAPD police leaders in this study offer modern examples of how to police a diverse, twenty-first-century police department. The final section of this chapter discusses changes in the LAPD structure, including how they receive and manage demand for their services and the administrative processes and structures that assist their community-based, geographic focus.

# The LAPD Structure

*"Ask yourself, 'How outrageous can I be?'"*

## Demand Entrance and Demand Management

With responsibility for such a large area, the LAPD must find ways to receive and manage demand for their services throughout 21 geographically based po-lice stations. The sections above shed light on how the LAPD does this. Engaging criminal justice agencies and community groups through regular meetings (i.e., Community-Police Advisory Board, the Watts Gang Task Force meeting, and the community forums) and via one-on-one contacts in the street (as in the Safer City Initiative discussed earlier) sends demand from the LAPD's con-stituents to the LAPD. While building community and enhancing the LAPD's legitimacy with the public, they are also methods of learning what Angelenos want from their police department. The CompStat process (discussed in the next section) and emerging predictive policing technologies help the LAPD to manage and act on that demand. The consent decree requirements and the oversight of the Inspector General and the Board of Police Commissioners provided a framework by which the LAPD could receive and manage demand for their services.

Three elements of the LAPD's demand reception and management emerge in this research:

1. Receiving demand for police service through on-going and participative community meetings and positive citizen contacts;
2. Managing that demand with computer technologies and weekly strategy meetings; and
3. Allowing the consent decree, the inspector general, and the Police Commission to have formal oversight of the police response to such demand.

Together, these three elements helped to change the LAPD. Captain Shelly remembers how as a young officer with the LAPD in the 1980s they were into the "heavy suppression-type policing." He states, "We just stopped everybody that walked up the streets, almost like an occupying army." He posits that this created tension with the community that "percolated into the '92 riots." Chief Bratton, Capt. Shelly reports, moved the LAPD toward a more "intellectual" way of deploying resources and of looking at crime. As a result, police in the historically violent 77th Street Area now have the "luxury" to focus their efforts on quality of life offenses (Captain Shelly). The next section shows how personnel view CompStat as tying together the elements of the LAPD organizational strategy to move the LAPD toward a more fully realized CPS strategy.

## Organizational Structure and Administrative Processes

As in the other police departments in this study, the new CompStat process focuses the organization on its community-based, legitimacy-building mission (or what the top of the organization believes is most important). Deputy Chief Hannan explains, "Asking tough questions" gets police captains to ask themselves, "'How outrageous can we be?'" He attributes recent innovations to the CompStat process, saying, "The innovation of the department has gone light years from where I used to sit as a younger officer." Of course it helps that, as Capt. Carlo notes, "The top guy believes in [community policing] and all of us underneath him at my level understand it and have been a part of it and believe in it and know that it works." Lieutenant Braden notes, "CompStat's becoming part of [the LAPD] DNA." This cultural change and the innovation it encourages suffer, however, when personnel confuse quantity for quality.

Lieutenant Laker and Capt. Tanner noted earlier that CompStat's drive to hold people in the LAPD accountable results in too much attention being paid to numbers. Captain Zachar cautions, "CompStat is just numbers and results driven, but there has to be some human emotion, to see the impacts of [their] work. We aren't just chasing numbers all over the place." Deputy Chief Hannan relays, "I'm struggling with a couple of captains that look at it as just a numbers thing. It's not a numbers thing. It's about strategies, partnerships and problem-solving that can be used in order to impact crime overall." He stresses to his captains that not every strategy they try out has to work, but that they must not give up trying new approaches. Lieutenant Braden seconds this, saying that the CompStat process is about "thinking, trying and testing. We got to accept failure." Deputy Chief Alvarez notes CompStat "is not [about] knowing the numbers, but what do the numbers represent."

Deputy Chief Hannan further explains how important it is that the officers in the "black and whites" (i.e., in the police cars) buy in to the new strategies. Supervisors facilitate this buy-in, he suggests, by teaching the officers "the reason for the strategies." He recalls the challenges supervisors faced with problem-solving "Z-car" officers. The officers would leave their designated areas looking for arrests, dismissing their supervisors' intentions for them to stay in a specific area to solve and prevent problems. Deputy Chief Cathy explains, "Now they say, 'Why? Why do I have to? Why?' It's just a different era, a different generation." The explanatory emphasis of CompStat coincides with younger officers' need to know why.[1] Lieutenant Davis also cites the inexperience of younger officers as a challenge to getting them to enforce violations of quality of life (a key tactic in proactively dealing with problems discussed at CompStat). Like the other respondents, he prescribes giving the officer "direct direction" (or, get them to "see what you see," as Capt. Oneida states). A number of respondents note that the now base-level acceptance of new tactics and strategies facilitate officers acceptance of the new way of doing things.

The LAPD's use of CompStat and "cross-pollinization" also facilitated change among other levels of the LAPD—to increase the collaboration between police officers and detectives. The detective-supervisor cross training programs give police sergeants who desire to learn about the work of detectives the opportunity to work with a detective who wants to learn more about the sergeant's activities. Captain Zachar refers to this as "cross-pollinization." Deputy Chief

---

1. This also coincides with the earlier section's discussion on transparency and using multiple media tools to get the police department message out to the public and to help explain the police department's reasoning for what might otherwise be perceived as controversial changes.

Hannan's example of getting Z-car police officers to buy in to proactive policing notes, "What the officer really values is what do my peers think about me."
Captain Zachar discusses the detective and supervisory levels, similarly suggesting, "If you have someone teaching you that's your peer, you're more likely
to learn."

Deputy Chief Cathy fondly remembers an uncharacteristically engaged detective who would attend the officer's daily roll call in the 1990s to advise officers on their incident report writing skills. Today, CompStat brings "more
accountability, more involvement with the officers, better exchange of information, better communication. Detectives are in roll call all the time." Deputy
Chief Alvarez notes that prior to CompStat these relationships were more "per-
sonality driven," rather than engrained in the process of investigating and preventing crime. Captain Grimm confirms this, describing the relationship
between detectives and patrol officers as the "best it's ever been." She reports
CompStat holds detectives accountable "for clearance rates, for filing rates, for
actually being the support mechanism—the feedback mechanism—for the
patrol officers." Deputy Chief Chuck reports a barrier to these relationships: budget
constraints. Budget limitations forced Chief Beck to reduce overtime, extend
furloughs, and layoff civilians. They also gave the chief a reason to move 220
people from specialized units back to operations (e.g., patrol), as Chief Flynn
did in the Milwaukee Police Department. Noting the preeminence of patrol
in the LAPD, Deputy Chief Chuck states, "The black and whites will always
be the last thing to go, and that'll never go."

Lieutenant Yatchski believes "It's unanimous [the command staff] love Comp-
Stat. They see it as directing and impacting what's going on and holding captains
accountable, and causing the captains to change their behavior and change what
happens out on the street." He also questions, however, the need to meet on a
monthly basis and the burden of preparing for such frequent meetings. Captain
Grimm describes how the earlier version of CompStat (called FastTrack) was an
"inquisitorial and dictatorial one-way conversation" but that the CompStat process
implemented under Chief Bratton "truly became a showcase for best practices
and holding command staff accountable." Deputy Chief Chuck tells his personnel, "CompStat shouldn't be anything that anyone fears." Lieutenant Hamel, who
has been involved with the FastTrack and CompStat accountability processes
since their inception, reports, "[FastTrack] was kind of a bully club and there
was nothing positive coming out of it and there was really very little frank discussion of what was actually successful and working and what wasn't working."

In addition to their positive reviews of the CompStat process, interview
respondents offer some constructive suggestions. Lieutenant Yatchski acknowledges, for example, that while it does get personnel engaged, "it doesn't

really make us do anything different than we would anyway," since professionals naturally acknowledge and address any problems that arise. Deputy Chief Cathy, a proponent of CompStat, adds she would like to see it be "more of an exchange" and an interaction between captains who might have dealt with similar problems, rather than simply a question and answer between the chief running the meeting and the captain accounting for their activities. Captain Carlo supports this, stating, "I would like it to be more about best practices," about learning what others did to solve a similar problem in other areas. Lieutenant Braden, though "pleased with the maturation of the CompStat process" and admitting that it has become part of the department's DNA, believes that Compstat's focus on immediate results prohibits the creation of long-term solutions.

The current changes in the CompStat process represent more, substantial changes throughout the LAPD. As seen above, these include increased collaboration between detectives and patrol officers, a culture more open to innovation and openness to risk of failure, and an emphasis on explaining to police personnel the reasons for their activities. It also influences the department's allocation of personnel. For example, in response to an analysis of gang and prostitution incidents, Chief Bratton mandated that detectives from the Vice and Gang Units change their traditional Monday through Friday work schedules. Now, they would be expected to work those times when such crimes were occurring (i.e., nights and weekends). As Lieutenant Hamel described, "We'd be shifting the crime pattern much more so than adjusting for the sports seasons of our children." This shift suggests a police department that allocates resources based on an analysis of crime problems and one that values the intervention effects of responding to crime clusters (in this example—hot times).

This acting and explaining in response to analysis helps within the department (as portrayed above) and with police relationships in the community. As Captain Shelly notes:

> We're a more open department, a lot more working hand-in-hand with other community departments, other agencies. Back in the 1980s, when I first came on, we were institutionally arrogant; it was the LAPD way or nobody's. We couldn't learn from anybody; we didn't do any outside training; we didn't exchange ideas.

Chief Bratton, Captain Grimm reports:

> Had a connection with the community where they believed that transparency was the hallmark and they also believed that because he was

holding us accountable. When we did go in the public forum, the confidence level was high.… Our word was good.

These personnel report the palpable changes they experienced working with the community as the LAPD increased its transparency. Captain Carlo admits that not everyone is going to like or trust the LAPD, "but if nothing else, [the LAPD is] responsive."

Chief Alvarez offers a summary of what these changes mean for the LAPD. He describes the LAPD as moving from an "autocratic" department to one that values "participation and allowing things to change." He gives an example of how Bratton brought in consultants who met with several officers throughout the LAPD to help establish the best supervisory method of the Gang Impact Team. He states that the "open discussion" of that change alone was "monumental," that they could "speak [their] mind" and see change come from it. He concludes, "The shift has been one that now people are engaged at all the levels, not as much as we would like them to be engaged at the sergeant rank and below, but definitely lieutenants, captains and above." Captain Tanner states that Chief Beck continues the transparency of his predecessor. He offers the example of Chief Beck holding "very open and frank meetings" with the area captains. Again, there is the sense that these are more than *pro forma* meetings. Captain Tanner reiterates that Chief Beck and his staff repeatedly took steps to do what they could to change various issues he had brought to their attention.

Captain Shelly notes an additional way that Bratton's personnel reallocation strategy influenced the LAPD. He reports that when Bratton came in:

> He didn't really look at seniority when he moved people around. He put people who he believed was the best fit, and that wasn't necessarily who would have been promoted in the old system. That infused a lot of good ideas, people weren't afraid to challenge the status quo and bring in new ideas and try to push the envelope in different directions. That was one of the biggest changes I'd seen.

He also adds, "The younger officers that are coming on have a different understanding of police work. They've grown up under this new LAPD and they embrace [the community policing] more."

# Summary

The LAPD steadfastly desires to reduce citizen fear and crime and to increase the quality of life for residents of Los Angeles. Though they acknowledge the merit of all parts of their mission, they have not incorporated formal measures for comprehensively gauging their efforts. The comparison of multiple years' worth of survey data on community members' perceptions of their police chiefs' job performance, as well as interviews with command personnel reveal distinctions between the two police chiefs. The maturation of the CompStat process exemplifies the LAPD's many cultural and administrative shifts toward the CPS era.

# References

*20th anniversary of the 1992 Los Angeles riot survey* (2012). Center for the Study of Los Angeles, Loyola Marymount University.

Blankstein, A. & DiMassa, C. (27 January 2009). Homeless deaths on Skid Row have decreased. *Los Angeles Times* [Online]. Retrieved from http://articles.latimes.com/2009/jan/27/local/me-skidrow-deaths27.

Bratton, W. J. (11 May 2006). LAPD Chief Bratton: We've changed. *Los Angeles Times* [Online]. Retrieved from latimes.com/news/opinion/commentary/la-oe-bratton11may11,0,7078215.story.

Carlos Alvarez: L.A. mayoral candidate (25 February 2009), *Los Angeles Times* [Online]. Retrieved from http://www.latimes.com/news/local/la-me-mayorqa-safety-alvarez25-2009feb25,0,6505462.story.

Dennison, B. (6 May 2007). Does Bratton deserve five more years? *Los Angeles Times.* [Online]. Retrieved from latimes.com/news/opinion/commentary/la-op-bratton06may06,0,4316520.story.

DiMassa, C. (12 July 2006). Sharp debate on Skid Row efforts. *Los Angeles Times* [Online]. Retrieved from latimes.com/news/local/la-me-skidrow12jul12,0,695621.story.

Gold, S. (7 June 2009). With crime in decline, a fragile sense of hope, *Los Angeles Times* [Online]. Retrieved from http://www.latimes.com/news/local/la-me-southla-rollout7-2009jun07,0,280768.story?page=1.

Gold, S. (28 June 2009). Gang interventionists distribute food, prayer—and a sense of change, *Los Angeles Times* [Online]. Retrieved from http://www.latimes.com/news/local/la-me-southla-gang-liaison28-2009jun28,0,7737990.story?page=1.

Hymon, S. & Winton, R. (21 September 2006). Attempt to settle Skid Row suit fails, *Los Angeles Times*, [Online]. Retrieved from latimes.com/news/la-me-homeless21sep21,0,2482226.story.

*Jones v. City of Los Angeles*, 444 F. 3d 1118—Court of Appeals, 9th Circuit 2006

Khalil, A. & Winton, R. (20 September 2006). Bid to settle homeless suit causes no celebration on skid row. *Los Angeles Times* [Online]. Retrieved from latimes.com/news/local/la-me-homeless20sep20,0,3048047.story.

LAPD (2004). Gang Impact Teams-Established, Special Order No. 7. Office of the Chief of Police, Los Angeles Police Department.

LAPD (2010). 2010 Los Angeles Police Department First Quarter Manual. The Los Angeles Police Department.

Lawrence, R. (2000). *The politics of force: Media and the construction of police brutality.* Los Angeles: University of California Press.

Los Angeles Times. (5 November 2009). Hail to the chief: In praise of Bratton, 2002. Retrieved from http://www.latimes.com/opinion/la-oew-brattoncc5-2009nov05-htmlstory.html.

Our city, our duty [Editorial]. (5 March 2006). Retrieved from latimes.com/news/local/la-ed-homeless5mar05,0,4431202.story.

Reston, M. & Rubin, J. (5 February 2009). Los Angeles to pay $13 million to settle May Day melee lawsuits, *Los Angeles Times* [Online]. Retrieved from http://articles.latimes.com/2009/feb/05/local/me-lapd-settlement5.

Ripston, R. (12 March 2007). A police state on Skid Row. *Los Angeles Times* [Online]. Retrieved from latimes.com/news/opinion/commentary/la-oe-ripston12mar12,0,248684.story.

Rubin, J. (3 December 2009). LAPD Chief Charlie Beck sworn in, for a second time, in ceremony at headquarters. L.A. Now Southern California—This Just In, Los Angeles Times. Retrieved from http://latimesblogs.la-times.com/lanow/2009/12/charlie-beck-sworn-in-as-lapd-chief.html.

Stone, C., Foglesong, T., & Cole, C. (May 2009). Policing Los Angeles under a consent decree: The dynamics of change at the LAPD, A report by the Harvard Kennedy School.

Winton, R. (27 September 2006). Drug offenders to be banned from Skid Row. *Los Angeles Times* [Online]. Retrieved from latimes.com/news/la-me-skidrow27sep27,0,7451435.story.

Winton, R. & McGreevy, P. (19 April 2006). Appeal of Skid Row ruling is urged. *Los Angeles Times* [Online]. Retrieved from latimes.com/news/local/la-me-skidrow19apr19,0,826699.story.

# Chapter 8

# Moving Towards a
New Policing Era

This chapter first describes the process by which the magnitude of change in the police departments was analyzed and then presents the analysis of each department's shift toward the Community Problem-Solving era, breaking each down into the various elements of organizational strategy.

## Magnitude of Organizational Change

As explained in Chapter 2, this section borrows from Moore, Thacher, Hartmann, Coles, and Sheingold (1999) and Eck and Stern (1992) to discuss Newark's, Boston's, Milwaukee's, and Los Angeles' manifestations of the CPS strategy by positing the extent to which this research reveals definite changes in the elements of organizational strategy as discussed in Chapter 1 (i.e., legitimacy, function, organizational structure, administrative processes, external relationships, demand entrance, demand management, tactics, technologies, and outcomes). Each department reflects varying degrees of the magnitude of implementation of the CPS strategy, as evidenced by changes in the specific elements of organizational strategy. Though Chapter 1 discusses the many dimensions of each element, this research focused on only the most salient dimensions that arose in the various data sources. Our assessment of the police departments' magnitude of change must be interpreted in relation to the dimensions of those elements that emerged in this study.

The magnitude of change regarding the police departments' organizational strategies is assessed based on the discussion of each of the elements in Chapter 1. Previous research has posited the various characteristics of a police department's organizational strategy, generally, and has specifically explicated various aspects of police organizations following a CPS strategy. Table 8.1 places the elements of the police departments' organizational strategies in one of five categories: Low, Low-Medium, Medium, Medium-High, or High, based on the degree to which this research uncovers the police department's manner of change and the degree of perceived institutionalization of change in each element.[1] For example, an assessment of a low magnitude of change in the external relationships element of a police department's organizational strategy means that this study uncovered few robust data on the police department's moves toward social, political, and economic conditions that would indicate an assured attainment of that element in a CPS organizational strategy. This mode of assessment allows the reader to understand the most salient experiences of each police department alone and (when understood in the context of the research findings in Chapters 4, 5, 6, and 7) make comparisons between departments as they relate to the specific elements of organizational strategy.

Then, after each discussion of the department's magnitude of organizational change, Table 8.2, Table 8.3, Table 8.4, and Table 8.5 show the individual police department's key shifts relating to the elements of organizational strategy. Again, these tables reflect only the most conspicuous factors that arose in this study's exploration of the department's change in the elements of their organizational strategies and are simplifications of general trends in the police departments (from where they were coming and to where they show signs of heading). The tables show that none of the police departments in this study had the exact experiences or views of how best to police their communities. However, a display of the actual changes in each department as they relate to a CPS organizational strategy gives practitioners a base from which to formulate innovations in their own departments and offers researchers particular shifts in police departments that may warrant further analysis when exploring their own areas of inquiry.

# Newark Police Department

The undulations of Newark's policing experiences in the CPS era are well-documented and include, at different times, implementations of certain elements of the CPS organizational strategy (e.g., foot patrol tactics, decentralized decision making administrative processes, and team policing) (Kelling, 1981; Skolnick & Bayley, 1986; Liebman, 2007). This study reveals important steps in the beginning stages of institutionalizing the CPS strategy.

---

1. We calculated the overall magnitude of change in each department by assigning a number to each of the categories (Low=1, Low-Medium=2.... High=5). We then calculated the mean for each department and assigned an overall magnitude of change (rounding down from .5 and rounding up from .6).

## Table 8.1
*Magnitude of Organizational Change*

| Element | Newark | Boston | Milwaukee | Los Angeles |
|---|---|---|---|---|
| Legitimacy | Low-Medium | Medium | Medium-High | High |
| Function | Medium | Medium-High | Medium-High | Medium-High |
| Organizational Structure | Low-Medium | Medium-High | High | Medium |
| Administrative Processes | Low-Medium | Medium | Medium-High | Medium |
| External Relationships | Medium | Medium-High | Medium-High | High |
| Demand Entrance | Low-Medium | Medium-High | Medium | Medium |
| Demand Management | Medium | Medium-High | Medium-High | Medium |
| Tactics | Medium | Medium-High | Medium-High | Medium-High |
| Technology | Medium | High | Medium-High | Medium-High |
| Outcomes | Low-Medium | Medium-High | Low-Medium | Low-Medium |
| Overall | Low-Medium | Medium-High | Medium-High | Medium-High |

Chapter 4 discussed the illegitimizing effects of NPD's relationship to politicians and citizens. It also explained the NPD's most recent attempts at regaining legitimacy with the community and reported on a community survey that suggested the NPD was making strides in this area. To that end, technology is used to organize relevant data regarding community problems, to allocate police resources, and to communicate this information to citizens. This serves as an objective justification for why police act in certain locations and is important in Newark where they use aggressive order maintenance policing (i.e., blue summonses) to interact with citizens to prevent more serious crimes. Additionally, the NPD is maintaining and improving working relationships with a number of community groups and law enforcement agencies. Though the NPD's magnitude of change regarding its relationship to the community is associated with a medium degree of organizational change, the NPD still has a low-medium magnitude of change in its legitimacy.

Though NPD's interview and survey respondents mention fostering respect with the community and enhancing the quality of life in Newark, violent crime is indeed the NPD's top priority. The NPD emphasizes quality of life enforcement as a road to preventing violent crime. When performed correctly (i.e., professionally and courteously) and effectively (that is, resulting in a crime decline or enhanced quality of life), these interactions can positively influence citizen perceptions of the NPD. Interviews with command staff, survey data from line personnel, and observations of CompStat meetings reveal the NPD's championing of quality of life enforcement as a means of interacting with citizens in high crime areas. This suggests a high degree of organizational change regarding broken windows policing tactics within the CPS strategy. However, interviews with NPD personnel (as discussed in Chapter 4) reveal that the NPD must include ways (e.g., training and supervision) to get their personnel to see the precise purpose of these interactions (i.e., to send a message about neighborhood control and to gain information about criminals and problems in specific areas). Using citizen interactions and formal meetings with the community to define neighborhood-specific problems of crime and disorder will further embed high functional and tactical aspects of the CPS strategy. Until then, the NPD reflects a medium magnitude of organizational change regarding their function and tactics.

Additionally, the NPD's use of mapping, data analysis, online social networking, computerized records management systems, the community survey, and a considerable reliance on measuring quality of life offenses mark a move toward the CPS strategy; however, they have room to explore more definitive ties to technologies and measurements that more closely relate to the relationship-building and quality of life-enhancing ideals of the CPS strategy (for example, a systematic assessment [e.g., survey] of citizens' perceptions of their police department and of neighborhood levels of crime and disorder, or using technologies to organize citizen groups and to inform those groups of neighborhood problems). Because they have not yet fully explored these more definitive ties, the NPD receives a low-medium degree of organizational change related to how and what they measure, and a medium magnitude of change relating to their use of technology.

This study examines the NPD's administrative processes and organizational structure, focusing on the relationship between the patrol and investigative divisions, personnel hiring and promotional considerations, changes in bureaus and task forces and the ability of the NPD to push down authority to the lower levels of the organization. The NPD approach to responding to their drug and gang problem through the Narcotics Enforcement Teams and Conditions Units at the neighborhood level and the Centralized Narcotics Division signify a recognition of the need to respond to problems at the localized level by organizing efforts and combatting the upper-levels of drug distribution rings and gangs. Additionally, the NPD gave precinct detectives the authority to handle all crimes (except for the shooting incidents), and through the "CompStat philosophy" pushed authority down to the district captains that encourages them to implement more area-specific responses in their districts. Similarly, the use of blue summonses to cite citizens for lower-level offenses encourages patrol officers to interact with citizens for such offenses, giving them more discretionary patrol time. Until future examinations bear out the institutionalization of these changes (and even though the NPD has taken specific steps toward the CPS strategy), the administrative processes and organizational structure of the NPD's organizational strategy is associated with a Low-Medium magnitude of change.

Lastly, there is a definitive move in the NPD away from relying on the Communications Division in placing demands on police time, and toward using data on crime and disorder problems to allocate police resources. This move is used by the NPD to give precinct commanders information that assists them in making tactical decisions and in allocating resources, and shows that the NPD is undoubtedly on the appropriate path to implementing a CPS strategy. Nonetheless, until the NPD finds ways to organize the other elements of their CPS organizational strategy (i.e., external relationships, measurements) in support of their demand processes, the NPD in this study is associated with a low-medium magnitude of change with regard to their demand entrance and a medium magnitude of change regarding their demand management.

To conclude, the NPD represents an organization that, despite encountering obstacles, is working diligently to bring about a solid implementation of the CPS strategy. The NPD's politically-motivated and violence-driven history sets it behind the other police departments (in this study) in moving toward that strategy, and demonstrates immediate changes that can take hold in an organization during the early stages of implementing a CPS organizational strategy. Table 8.2 summarizes the specific moves in the elements of the NPD's organizational strategy.

**Table 8.2**

*NPD's Changes in Organizational Change*

| Element | From—To |
|---|---|
| Legitimacy | Perceptions of corrupting relationships between the NPD and local politicians |
| | A community survey, crime reductions, & a belief that politics is being taken out of policing help to legitimize the NPD |
| Function | Fighting crime; building community relationships |
| | Fighting crime; responding to an array of problems; improving community relations; enhancing the quality of life |
| Organizational Structure | Police Director and Police Chief; no NET or Conditions Unit |
| | Abolished the office of Police Chief; organized criminal investigations based on geographic reach of crime (i.e., Centralized Narcotics, NET, & the Conditions Unit) |
| Administrative Processes | Punitive CompStat process |
| | Problem-solving CompStat process that moves accountability to captains; weekly intelligence meetings |
| External Relationships | Established community outreach programs |
| | Task forces with other LE agencies; increased community outreach |
| Demand | Reliance on calls for service to 9-1-1; queue goals |
| | Differential response rating for calls to service; moving focus from Communications Division; no attention to queue goals |
| Tactics | Zero-tolerance policing; car patrols; arrest |
| | Emphasis on interacting with citizens; blue summonses; FIO |
| Technology | No computerized records management system; no MDTs |
| | Crime mapping and analysis; computerized RMS; MDTs |
| Outcomes | Crime reduction; arrests and citations; queue goals |
| | Crime reduction; a community survey; quality of life citations; FIO reports |

# Boston Police Department

Commissioner Ed Davis was brought into the BPD over two insiders (the heads of the investigative and patrol units[2]) to control Boston's crime rate and to restore the BPD's working relationships with the community. Drawing from his experience as Superintendent in Lowell, Massachusetts, Commissioner Davis vowed to return the BPD to a neighborhood-level function, indicative of a CPS organization. This section shows how the BPD used newly-created units, cutting-edge intelligence analysis systems, and a renewed focus on positive community interactions to reestablish their relationships with the community in fighting crime and disorder in Boston.

Commissioner Davis affirmed his commitment to having the "community-policing philosophy" inform all the actions and decisions of the BPD. The data show that the BPD does in fact work with the community to define a wide range of problems and respond with a variety of solutions. Though the BPD functions to reduce crime, it also works to lower the fear of crime and enhance citizens' quality of life. For this study, the BPD's function reflects a medium-high degree of change. The following sections show support for both the crime-fighting and community-building function of the BPD.

Proactively increasing contacts with citizens forms the basis of many of the BPD's tactics. The Safe Street Teams, the Street Outreach Team and beat integrity exemplify ways that the BPD proactively and sustainedly interacts with citizens. Bicycle and foot patrols and mandated "walk and talks" enhance these operations. The state-of-the-art Boston Regional Intelligence Center, the Real Time Crime Center, and mobile data terminals maximize the payoff from these tactics by organizing data and disseminating large amounts of useful and timely information. These data are used to assist in deployment decisions and to hold police personnel accountable. This research finds that along with index crimes, city ordinance violations and a bi-annual public safety survey, the BPD is looking for ways to measure and acknowledge the community-building efforts of its personnel. The BPD's tactics and measurements, as evidenced in this study, are associated with a medium-high magnitude of change, while their use of technologies reflects a high magnitude of change.

Additional ways in which the BPD works to build problem-solving relationships with law enforcement and community groups include Constituent Response Teams, Neighborhood Advisory Councils, Operation CeaseFire, and

---

2. It is worth noting that prior to the appointment of the new commissioner, these two leaders were seen as having professional differences in carrying out the BPD's function, which possibly contributed to the Mayor's decision.

district-based violence prevention meetings. Maintaining beat integrity (through their Reporting Area Project) and making officers responsible for interacting with citizens in crime and disorder hotspots (e.g., "walk and talks" or Code 19s) instills this relationship-building function in police officers and, when done appropriately, lends legitimacy to the BPD in the community. The community ombudsman's oversight of the BPD's external complaint process gives further authenticity to the BPD's efforts to build community relationships and legitimacy. For these reasons, this study finds the BPD's legitimacy reflects a medium degree of organizational change, while its external relationships evidence a medium-high degree of change.

Increasing the interactions police personnel have with citizens necessarily leads one to inquire how demand will enter and be managed by the organization. Once personnel receive information via the various above-mentioned collaborations, what avenues do they have for managing and acting on that demand for their service? Using communication and CAD technologies to better grasp how patrol officers spend their time gives the BPD and their personnel the ability to see exactly how much time an officer has to get involved in community-building activities. The Code 19s ("walk and talks") deepen the BPD's commitment to freeing officers from responding to calls for service and encourages them to positively interact with the community. Furthermore, the Safe Streets Teams, Street Outreach Teams, and the Reporting Area Project are ways of getting police officers to proactively respond to individual areas' concerns, allowing them to work within those communities' already-established avenues for responding to local problems. The use of technology to organize and interpret large amounts of data further manages the officers' time by offering information on which to act and provides additional accountability for solving problems. Together, these efforts allow the BPD to manage emergency calls for service as well as the on-going neighborhood-specific problems affecting citizens and evidence a police department whose organization is implementing a medium-high magnitude of change regarding the demand entrance and demand management elements of the CPS strategy.

Finally, a discussion of the BPD's structure and processes reveals how the BPD's BRIC and CompStat process increase information sharing processes within the organization and push accountability and authority down to the lower level of the police department. Respondents describe the CompStat process as helping personnel see similar trends across districts and as holding district captains accountable for crime in their area. These indicate a problem-solving element at the higher levels of the BPD. At the lower levels of the organization, mostly informal interactions and the use of daily information from the BRIC encourage both the patrol and investigative units to work together in

### Table 8.3
*BPD's Changes in Organizational Change*

| Element | From—To |
|---------|---------|
| Legitimacy | The community losing faith in the BPD as a result of scandals and rising violence |
| | Regaining citizens' trust by re-instituting effective community collaborations; external oversight of the BPD's complaint process |
| Function | Emphasizes violent crime |
| | A renewed focus on building CPS relationships |
| Organizational Structure | No patrol officers or sergeants assigned specifically to CPS |
| | Approximately 13 Safe Street Teams doing CPS in crime and disorder hotspots |
| Administrative Processes | A distinct Intelligence Unit and Office of Research and Evaluation |
| | Formed the Boston Regional Intelligence Center and Real Time Crime Center |
| External Relationships | The unraveling of collaborations with other criminal justice agencies and community groups that defined the "Boston Miracle" |
| | Revived those collaborations (e.g., CeaseFire, Impact, SST) |
| Demand | Reliance on calls for service to 9-1-1 |
| | Established proactive avenues by which demand enters and is managed by the organization (e.g., SST, Street Outreach Team, Citizen Response Team) |
| Tactics | Lack of formal time for officers to solve problems with citizens. |
| | Mandatory "walk and talks" and the creation of the SST and SOT |
| Technology | A need to organize the varied sources of intelligence and data |
| | The BRIC and RTCC |
| Outcomes | Crime reduction; citizen surveys |
| | Crime reduction; citizen surveys; increasing efforts to recognize officers' efforts at working with the community |

maintaining responsibility for their geographic areas. Also, the establishment of separate units whose sole responsibility is to community problem solve illuminates the BPD's buy-in to such a strategy. This research finds that these and the other elements of organizational strategy assist in getting personnel to take ownership of their areas, thereby positively contributing to a police department's adoption of the CPS strategy and demonstrating a medium-high magnitude of change in its organizational structure, but a medium degree of change in its administrative processes.

The BPD's popularly successful past with community policing set the foundation for this study's exploration of the BPD's current attempt to rebuild these CPS relationships. As summarized in Table 8.3, new technologies, external oversight, significant units dedicated to CPS, and more favorable attitudes toward intra-organizational and community collaborations strengthen the necessary elements for the BPD's shift toward CPS.

# Milwaukee Police Department

The MPD's most recent enterprise in implementing a CPS organizational strategy stems from the efforts of an outsider chief and follows a brief period of tumult that weakened relations between the MPD and the community. This provided an opportunity (and an expectation) for change. As Chapter 6 displayed, Chief Edward Flynn capitalized on this chance to implement historic change in the MPD.

In his swearing-in speech, Chief Flynn made no secret of his desire to bring change to the MPD. The citizens of Milwaukee, as evidenced by the *Milwaukee Journal-Sentinel*'s Violent Crime roundtable, were ready for change, and the MPD recommitted itself to building working partnerships with the community. To assist in these efforts, the MPD relied on increasing their attention to lower-level offenses, working with the community to problem-solve, and using technology to provide meaningful data to guide and focus their efforts. The data reveal a decisive understanding of the CPS focus of the MPD (and, therefore, a medium-high magnitude of change in the MPD function). Shifts in their tactical efforts support this.

Using data to drive tactical decisions (with an emphasis on stopping citizens for lower-level offenses), the technologies used in the CompStat process, daily crime briefings, and the Neighborhood Task Force clearly represent a police department that implements the CPS strategy. These meetings, department archives, uses of technology, and observations show that the upper levels of the MPD understand the purpose of these moves. The exploratory survey data suggest a similar understanding at the lower levels of the MPD as to the value of these technologies, sector integrity, and formal meetings with the community. Data sources also show an evolving understanding of the nature of discretion in the daily activities of police work, which is vital to properly implementing broken windows policing. Evidence is lacking, however, of the appropriate measurement mechanisms for gauging the MPD's success in fostering these relationships and enhancing the quality of life for Milwaukeeans, as is implied by the CPS strategy. In toto, these reveal a strong adherence to CPS principles that will continue to move the MPD toward an even greater implementation of this strategy.

These tactics and technologies, along with a more transparent disciplinary process, lower crime numbers, and an amicable political environment also work to instill legitimate relationships with the community, indicating an organizational adoption of CPS. These tactics, executed with the community's well-being at the forefront, increase citizens' views of the MPD by demonstrating the MPD's success and focusing efforts on the specific problems (i.e., locations and people) that the community believes warrant police attention. The "gardener's" approach to policing, then, fits with the MPD's intention to implement broken windows policing within the current strategy. For these reasons, the MPD is associated with a medium-high magnitude of change regarding their external relationships, legitimacy, tactics, and technologies, and a low-medium magnitude of change in their outcome measurements.

The changes discussed thus far require (or at least are assisted by) consequent structural and administrative procedural changes. Specifically, the creation of the NTF, the new CompStat process, the Intelligence Fusion Center, the Differential Police Response unit, redistricting, the CIB reorganization, decentralizing certain investigative units, and daily crime meetings create the structure and environment for the MPD's CPS strategy. These changes free up police time, encourage a cleaner intelligence-sharing process, increase interactions between the MPD and the community, move accountability to the district level, and focus efforts at the neighborhood level. They represent the MPD's high degree of structural change and medium-high magnitude of changes regarding their administrative processes.

Finally, the shifts in the MPD's other CPS elements suggest a natural shift in the manner in which demand enters the organization. The MPD's proposition to move toward a community-based, data-driven, neighborhood-level, problem-solving strategy, and the organizational changes discussed reflect a move toward freeing up patrol officer time from responding to calls for service and increasing the amount of positive interactions the MPD has with its citizens. Demand, then, has a greater chance to enter the organization through

## Table 8.4
*MPD's Changes in Organizational Change*

| Element | From — To |
|---|---|
| Legitimacy | A series of cases in which police officers misused their power; the MPD had gotten away from positively interacting with citizens |
| | Neighborhood Policing Plans, community outreach, & favorable political conditions lend legitimacy to the MPD |
| Function | Emphasizing community relations; reducing violent crime |
| | A data-driven approach to CPS to reduce levels of crime and fear and to enhance the quality of life |
| Organizational Structure | Centralized detectives; no Intelligence Fusion Center or Differential Police Response unit; beefed-up specialized units |
| | Move toward decentralizing detectives; created the IFC and DPR; took personnel from specialized units to create the Neighborhood Task Force |
| Administrative Processes | No CompStat process |
| | Problem-solving at weekly CompStat; daily crime briefings |
| External Relationships | Lack of community outreach |
| | Online [and social] media campaigns; implementing the NPP |
| Demand | Reliance on calls for service to 9-1-1; no structured DPR |
| | DPR; data drives decisions on deployment and resource allocation |
| Tactics | Zero-tolerance policing; arrests and citations; investigate crimes |
| | Uses real-time data to inform decisions to stop citizens for low-level offenses; emphasize discretion and adherence to values |
| Technology | No coordination of data or geographic mapping technologies |
| | IFC; SmartBoards; daily and weekly crime mapping |
| Outcomes | Crime reduction; enhanced quality of life; arrests and citations |
| | Crime reduction; a citizen satisfaction survey; solving and preventing problems |

these informal and formal community contacts, instead of through calls for service to the MPD. Furthermore, new technologies throughout the MPD and in patrol cars place data-driven demand on the MPD as their discretion and analysis see fit. Demand entrance, then, is associated with a medium magnitude of change, while the ways the MPD manages demand demonstrate a medium-high magnitude of change.

The MPD's history reflects a gradual move toward the CPS strategy and varying levels of broken windows policing over time. This previous experience readied the MPD and the community for more productive working relationships with each other. This study shows, then, the MPD's ability to institute rapid and substantial change toward a CPS organizational strategy. Table 8.4 shows some of those specific shifts.

# Los Angeles Police Department

Long known as the country's premier crime fighters, the LAPD's venture into a CPS strategy was led by one of the nation's most famous police leaders—Chief William Bratton. With the violence of the Rodney King incident and the corruption of the Rampart scandal in the minds of Angelenos, and guided by a consent decree, Chief Bratton brought the nation's third-largest local police department into the CPS era. It appears, too, that these changes have withstood the transition to Bratton's predecessor and current police chief, Charlie Beck.

At the start of his seven-year tenure, Chief Bratton vowed to change the way the LAPD operated both internally and externally. By most measures, Bratton made a number of substantial changes. Chief Beck continued Bratton's legacy by reaffirming the LAPD's commitment to constitutional policing, crime reduction, and increasing the quality of life for the people of Los Angeles. The understanding and implementation of this function, as evidenced above, suggest a medium-high degree of change in the LAPD.

The tactics and technologies work together with the LAPD's external relationships to increase the LAPD's legitimacy within the community. The LAPD's focus on constitutional policing (and Bratton's commitment to transparency in responding to allegations against his officers) gave the LAPD the social capital it needed when implementing the controversial Safer City Initiative. LAPD respondents also noted the need to focus on hot people and hot places (as denoted by computer mapping and analysis technology) when preventing a "ding" from becoming a "dent" or a "junk" (see Chapter 7). Regular community meetings (e.g., Bureau community forums and the Watts Gang Task Force), the oversight of the Police Commission, the mandates of the consent decree, and Chief Bratton's adept political skills created legitimate processes and support for the LAPD. As it relates to the CPS strategy, the LAPD shows a high degree of change in its legitimacy, a medium-high degree of change in its tactics and technology, and a high degree of change in its external relationships. Aside from the external Loyola Marymount survey (*20th Anniversary*, 2012), the LAPD repeatedly admitted having few formal ways of examining the outcomes of their efforts. Generally, crime is the bottom line. For this reason, the LAPD's measurement of outcomes is associated with a low-medium magnitude of change.

Cultural shifts in the use of CompStat, Bratton's and Beck's transparency, and a focus on creating relationships between investigators and patrol officers symbolize the LAPD's organizational structure and administrative processes. Respondents consistently noted both chiefs' esteem for transparency within the organization (e.g., CompStat and one-on-one meetings with Chief Beck) and externally (for example, Chief Bratton's handling of the May Day melee). CompStat and other weekly briefings assist in this transparency, encourage personnel to share information, and help officers understand the reasons why they are asked to engage in certain activities. However, we uncovered few physical changes to suggest specific differences in the ways the LAPD is structured or administered. For the mostly qualitative differences displayed here, we designate the LAPD as showing a medium magnitude of change.

Lastly, the changes in the LAPD's community relationships and in the CompStat mentality of the organization bring about a shift in how the LAPD receives and manages demand for their services. Citizen input at department-sponsored meetings (e.g., Bureau community forums and the Watts Gang Task Force) and positive contacts with citizens while on foot patrol are some ways in which the LAPD has increased the CPS methods of demand entrance. CompStat, weekly briefings, and the computer-assisted analysis of crime, disorder, and personnel data further assist in how demand is managed throughout the LAPD. Regular meetings with the Police Commission and the oversight of the Inspector General also guide how the LAPD handles demand for police service. Without any detailed evidence of a formalized way of receiving and managing demand, this aspect of the LAPD is associated with a medium magnitude of change.

As this study's largest, most under-policed city (25.7 officers per 10,000 population in 2010, compared to 32.0 in Milwaukee, 32.5 in Boston, and 46.7 in Newark), the LAPD faced special hurdles in implementing a CPS strategy. Nonetheless, as a whole, the LAPD, under the leadership of Chiefs Bratton and Beck, has made strides toward increasing the department's legitimacy in the community and imbuing the organization with a sense of transparency.

## Table 8.5
*LAPD's Changes in Organizational Change*

| Element | From—To |
|---|---|
| Legitimacy | The Rampart scandal; Rodney King aftershocks in minority communities |
| | Perceptions that the LAPD is increasing their use of community policing and civilian review; transparent discipline; improving recruitment |
| Function | Rule by fear; viewed community policing as soft on crime |
| | Prevent terrorist attacks; constitutional policing to decrease crime and increase quality of life |
| Organizational Structure | No special assistant for constitutional policing; more officers in specialized units |
| | Created the special assistant for constitutional policing; moved officers out of specialized units and placed them on patrol |
| Administrative Processes | Confrontational FastTrack process; little transparency with officers |
| | CompStat process; transparency |
| External Relationships | Lack of reciprocated community outreach; "battling" with the community and politicians |
| | Bureau community forums; support of prominent community groups and politicians |
| Demand | Little discussion on how to respond to community concerns |
| | Data-informed decisions; CompStat process |
| Tactics | Zero-tolerance policing; arrests and citations |
| | Uses of real-time data to inform decisions on where to go and whom to stop; engage the community; discretion and assistance when responding to low-level offenses |
| Technology | No coordination of data or geographic mapping technologies |
| | Geographic, predictive mapping technology; "dot-policing" |
| Outcomes | Crime reduction |
| | Crime reduction; an (external) citizen satisfaction survey; informal assessments by community members at regular meetings |

After two of the most egregious acts of police brutality and corruption book-ended the last decade of the twentieth century, the LAPD started on a new era of policing during the first decade of the new century. Table 8.5 shows some of the moves the LAPD made during that time.

While discussing the nature and magnitude of specific shifts in each of the police departments and offering specific manifestations of those changes in each department, this and previous sections also lend insight into the current state of cutting-edge policing in urban areas. The final chapter provides information for police departments moving in similar directions, offers an overview of the New Community Problem-Solving era, and concludes with considerations for future police researchers and practitioners.

# References

*20th anniversary of the 1992 Los Angeles riot survey* (2012). Center for the Study of Los Angeles, Loyola Marymount University.

Eck, J. & Stern, D. (1992). Revisiting community policing: A new typology, Paper presented to the National Institute of Justice.

Kelling, G. (1981). The Newark foot patrol experiment. Washington, DC: Police Foundation.

Liebman, S. (21 June 2007). Report for action. Retrieved from http://blog.nj.com/ledgernewark/2007/06/report_for_action.html.

Moore, M., Thacher, D., Hartmann, F., Coles, C., & Sheingold, P. (1999, March). *Case studies of the transformation of police departments: A cross-site analysis*, Harvard University. Retrieved from http://www.hks.harvard.edu/criminaljustice/publications/cops_csa.pdf.

Skolnick, J., & Bayley, D. (1986). *The new blue line: Police innovation in six american cities*. New York: The Free Press.

# Chapter 9

# Leading Police in the New Community Problem-Solving Era

## Introduction

The impetus for this research came from a desire to explore the police organizational experience in what we assumed was the Community Problem-Solving era of policing. Kelling and Moore's (1988) elements of a police organizational strategy helped us to organize the vast amount of varied data we collected. We also chose as a starting point for our exploration the principal police tactic of broken windows policing (for reasons discussed in Chapter 1) as an assumed tactic of each of the police departments.

As mentioned in the first chapter, the exact definition of community policing is elusive. The way that the police and the policed understand this type of policing has often resulted in confusion and missteps. As evidence of this fact, many police departments have a community policing or problem-solving officer or, in larger departments, a community policing section of some sort that incorporates officers that are working on "community policing" as distinct from the mainstream work of that of the rest of the police department. Instead of re-orienting the focus of the entire organization to understanding and sharing the responsibilities for safe communities (Scott & Goldstein, 2005), the departments often maintain the status quo of reactive policing and treat community policing as a distinct activity. This model, which is extremely widespread, does not allow for the full adoption of community problem-solving policing by either the community or by the police. Although many of the concepts that underpin community policing are the result of social research that was done from the 1960s onward (Roberg, Novak, & Cordner, 2009), the dissemination and general practice of many of the ideas resulting from that research has not "stuck" completely in actual practice.

181

Our research provided valuable examples of police leaders trying to get these ideas to stick in their departments. In doing so, our otherwise open-ended exploration discovered many points about change and the police profession. We hope that you can reflect on what you have learned from those cases as you further consider your own research and practice agendas. We would like to further discuss two of the more pertinent and obvious findings from our research. Firstly, the importance of having a strong police leader in bringing substantive and rapid change to a police department; and, secondly, the need for organizational restructuring. We close with key characteristics of the current state of policing that are so vital to policing in the twenty-first century as to warrant a new era. We creatively refer to this era as the New Community Problem-Solving era.

# Leading Change

The police research agenda that began in the 1960s birthed many of the axioms police researchers and practitioners subscribe to today: "Every police department does hotspots policing; The police engage community members in problem-solving; Crime analysis is an integral part of our police operations." Indeed, these are important tactics in the pursuit of healthy communities. Surveys of police departments, however, suggest that the policing innovations championed by academics for the past five decades (and implemented by the forward-thinking chiefs in this book) have not taken hold on "mainstreet America." Indeed, the challenges faced by these astute leaders (and the recent histories of the departments presented here) suggest this is likely the case. One might say, "If the leaders in *these* departments entered such conventional departments, then what does a typical police department look like?" Some statistics help us to answer that question.

A survey of Police Executive Research Forum-member agencies (an arguably biased sample in favor of innovation) reveals that 63% of them use hotspots to respond to violent crime (PERF, 2008). While Law Enforcement Management and Administrative Statistics (LEMAS) data show 56% of all police departments train their officers in at least eight hours of community policing, only 21% actively encourage problem-solving activities (Telep & Weisburd, 2012). Even the forebearer of problem-oriented policing, Herman Goldstein, lamented in a 2004 interview that his life's work had not made as much of a change in the field of policing as he would have hoped. Telep and Weisburd (2012) also report that only 13% of police departments identify hotspots through computer analysis. Finally, just under 60% of police agencies with 100 or more sworn personnel claim to follow some version of a CompStat process (Weisburd, Mastrofski, Greenspan, & Willis, 2004). While pieces of these innovations may be making the scene in the police profession, it appears the pillars of reform era policing (i.e., random routine patrol, retroactive investigation, and rapid response to calls for police service) might be holding steadfast in many police departments. The cases in this book can be seen as being among the preeminent examples of a department's move in the Community Problem-Solving (CPS) era.

## Entrepreneurial Police Leaders

The experiences of the police departments in this study, as relayed by many of the interview respondents, are located within the context of their executive police leaders. When giving a brief history of their police department, respondents delineate their organization's focus in terms of the executive police leader in charge at the time. For example, in giving a brief history of his time at the NPD, Deputy Nolan recalls, "I came on [the force] under former Director Sylester.... By 1995, the department was (disciplinary-wise) somewhat out of control, so we brought in Director Santiago.... As time goes on, there's a change in political leadership, there's a change in police leadership." Respondents repeatedly point to the police leaders in this study as affecting the various elements of the police departments' organizational strategies.

Skolnick and Bayley (1986) implicate multiple aspects of police executive leadership in successful police innovations. In fact, like Stone, Foglesong, and Cole (2009), we find that the chiefs' leadership is an "essential element of every part of this story" (p. 10). Our research adds to the past research by demonstrating the utility of bringing in reform police chiefs from the outside (as did all the police departments in this study). Domanick (2010) refers to each of these leaders in their current capacities as "entrepreneurial police leaders." Upon further examination of his list, one notes that nine of the ten chiefs on his list were brought in from outside of the organization. As we saw in the chapters above, bringing in proven entrepreneurial outside police leaders gave them credibility with their personnel, created an anticipatory environment of change, and gave these new members of the department the ability to enlist the police departments' already established and respected leaders. For these police departments coming off of various departmental and community crises, the outside entrepreneurial leaders acted as a reset button.

These entrepreneurial outside leaders were also open to innovative ideas from within and outside their department. Internal self-surveys serve to gather information about the strengths and weaknesses of the organization, give personnel an avenue by which to have their voices heard, and present police leaders with a sense of personnel's ideas, views, and values. Such surveys (and other outlets such as the MPD's Leadership in Police Organizations blog[1]) show rudimentary aspects of shared leadership and hint at an important avenue in implementing a CPS strategy. From the outside, it is clear that each of these leaders studies the policing research as it relates to their responsibilities and even consults and works with leading police academics.[2] The leaders' and organizations' commitment to innovation (including new ways of working with the community to solve problems) is also evidenced in the organizations' changes in organizational structure.

## *Organizational Restructuring*

Research (Bayley & Skolnick, 1986; Kim & Maugborne, 2003; Moore, Thacher, Hartmann, Coles, & Sheingold, 1999) examines the affects of police executives on other facilitators (and inhibitors) to implementing organizational strategies. One of the more salient change features in this and the current research is the leader's ability to change the structure of the police department. The police departments in this study created new entities and processes within their organizations to facilitate change and to respond to what would have otherwise been inhibitors to CPS organizational change. Examples from each department include, the improved (and in the MPD's case, new) CompStat process, internal department surveys, the NPD's High Risk for Violence list, Fugitive Apprehension Teams, and Violent Enterprise Strategy Task Force, the BPD's Boston Regional Intelligence Center, Real Time Crime Center, Safe Streets Teams, Street Outreach Team, and Constituent Response Teams, the MPD's Neighborhood Task Force, Differential Police Response, and Intelligence Fusion Center, and the LAPD's Safer City Initiative, Gang Intervention Teams, and Bureau Community Forums. These moves produce the physical and infrastructural changes that facilitate such policing.

The organizations' leaders used CompStat to instill a problem-solving mentality at the higher levels of their police department, hold commanders accountable, and transmit the values of the command staff to other police managers. Chief Flynn introduced CompStat to the MPD. Director McCarthy

---

1. Leadership in Police Organizations trains interested MPD personnel to be leaders in their respective positions. It is based on the principle that all personnel can be leaders in their organizations. It is another way of infusing the organization's values to their personnel.

2. Though not explicit, this study discusses some of the results of each department's and police executive's involvement with various researcher-practitioner partnerships.

in Newark instituted marked differences in how CompStat proceeded under his direction. In addition to holding CompStat only as needed, interviews with personnel (and observations of CompStat meetings) describe the process under Director McCarthy as less confrontational, more about problem solving, and focusing on the officers' increased interactions with citizens for minor offenses. The police executive leaders make efforts to reinforce their views on the trajectory of their police department (for instance, by continually reminding officers in attendance of the purpose of the CompStat exercise) and guide the CompStat meeting in the problem-solving process (that is, by asking pointed questions about and commenting on their commanders' actions, responses to problems, and reasoning).

The entrepreneurial leaders' organizational-change goals of the CompStat process are facilitated by changes in their organizations' structure and the activities in which the organizations are involved. In this study, the organizations' structure and activities portray CPS as a saturating, organization-wide strategy (not simply a specialized unit as part of the organization). The NPD's HRV, FAT, and VEST emphasize their violent crime efforts, but in conjunction with the Narcotics Enforcement Teams, Conditions Units, and the decentralized investigations of some crimes, these systems further the CPS strategy of the NPD by recognizing the multiple levels of (and by targeting efforts at) the crime and disorder problems facing its citizens. Similarly, Boston's SST and SOU, and the MPD's NTF and DPR, represent structural changes that facilitate a CPS strategy.

An important part of these changes involves what personnel in this study referred to as "cross-pollinization" or "cross-training." Perhaps the most obvious example of this is Chief Flynn's switching the heads of the Criminal Investigation Bureau and Patrol Bureau in what was, the reader will recall, a traditionally CIB-run organization. Chapter 6 also discusses the MPD's recent move to decentralize investigations and to reallocate some responsibilities of the patrol and detective bureaus. The move was intended to make better investigators of all police personnel and to facilitate information- and responsibility-sharing between the two groups. Informal (and formal) training sessions, as suggested here, facilitate an institutionalization of these behaviors (i.e., housing detectives in precincts, weekly meetings, joint roll calls, and rewarding patrol officers by involving them in investigations in which they offered valuable intelligence). We further discuss this and other challenges to policing in a CPS era below.

## Current and Future Challenges

While offering smart ways of changing a police organization, department personnel also implied challenges to implementing a CPS strategy and suggested ways of improving the police profession. These include the need for better intra-department collaboration, the delicate balance between enforcing laws or local ordinances against disorderly behaviors and individual rights, and the department's ability to measure and reward the types of behavior that support their organization's strategy.

**Investigative-patrol collaborations.** A number of idioms come to mind when assessing the traditional lack of information-sharing relationships between these two groups (for example, "Robbing Peter to pay Paul," "The left hand doesn't know what the right hand is doing") (Haggerty & Diedrich, 2008). Too often, detectives stick to their retroactive investigations of crimes, and patrol officers hold tight to their routine patrols and rapid responses to calls for service, with little collaboration (and even opposition) to prevent crime. The cultural and operational relevance of this was discussed in Chapters 4–7. This hurdle persists despite reliable research on the inefficacy of traditional police activities. For example, the RAND study of investigators (Greenwood, 1979) found that police solve most cases not through the kind of reactive, post-crime investigator processes that many believe is the meat and potatoes of detective work, but through the activities of patrol officers, the public, and routine clerical processing. Additional studies (Tien, Simon, & Larson, 1978) have shown us that there are more efficient ways to prevent and to solve crime than are currently being used.

Patrol operations, for their part, are not without blame. With the advent of 9-1-1, some of the most fundamental police roles began to inexorably change. Police became rapid responders in the expectation that citizen satisfaction would rise if police arrived more quickly and more crimes would be solved. Now, the police were just three digits—9-1-1—away. We all held our collective breath and waited for far greater efficiencies in policing. Unfortunately, they didn't happen. Several studies, first in Kansas City and then in Jacksonville, Peoria, Rochester, and San Diego found that rapid response was only responsible for solving 3% of serious crime. Further, citizen satisfaction was not based on response time but rather, the expectation of response time (Kelling & Coles, 1996; Spelman & Brown, 1984). Instead of increasing efficiencies, 9-1-1 actually made greater demands on police resources and more deeply entrenched them into a reactive, rather than a preventive, model. This reactive policing is the functional equivalent of medical doctors waiting until you get a disease and then treating it instead of trying to prevent disease through inoculations, advising of health risks, dieting, not smoking, and exercising regularly. The police departments in this study have made moves to counter these common issues, suggesting a reliance on getting these two groups to work together to prevent crime on an ongoing basis.

Another layer to the challenge of increasing the partnerships of patrol and investigative divisions is the need to align the structures of authority and accountability throughout the organization. Police departments must find the balance between supporting officer discretion and maintaining strict accountability. Commanders have the ability to apply innovative strategies while being held accountable for failing to adequately explain their failures. Likewise, patrol officers should be encouraged to use their discretion in carrying out various tactics, and should expect to be held accountable for the improper use of that discretion. A traditional police organization's structures and processes do not always facilitate this, and that can lead to frustration. As one BPD captain stated, "Accountability without authority is hell." Yet, in the NPD, one sergeant reports that when managers were given the freedom and authority to "run their commands as if it's their own little police department," the managers remained apathetic toward taking on the responsibility. As police departments move towards sharing responsibility and participative decision-making, police leaders should keep in mind what structural and cultural changes they might make to ensure that the proper authority is given to the personnel who will be accountable for fulfilling the mission of their departments.

**Interacting with citizens.** The November 2010 and February 2011 issues of *Criminology & Public Policy* provide commentaries and analyses of the efforts of local police departments in policing crime and disorder through hotspot and broken windows policing. Articles within these issues explore questions about how police allocate resources, how police carry out these tactics, and how police affect levels of crime and disorder. The research presented in our book contributes to the understanding of the strengths, challenges, and activities facing police today (specifically, issues of police discretion, accountability, the use of quality of life citations, ways of informally and formally training personnel, and necessary measurements for police departments).

Though the police departments in this study continue to emphasize their role in arresting criminals and fighting crime, they explicitly discuss the need to maintain legitimate working relationships with citizens and the role broken windows policing can play in fulfilling both of those functions. In moving from a traditionally held zero-tolerance approach to responding to lower-level offenses, the police departments illustrate a more thoughtful and informed approach to interacting with citizens who violate such offenses and cite other reasons for stopping a person for such an offense (reasons that move beyond simply citing or arresting an individual). These beliefs are reinforced by the police executives at daily and weekly meetings with commanders (e.g., daily crime briefings and CompStat). Possible beneficial outcomes of professionally interacting with citizens on such grounds include improved community relationships, increased information-gathering capabilities, and reduced levels of crime.

The notion that stopping citizens for quality of life and low-level offenses can improve community relations assumes that officers are trained in the proper use of discretion, that the responding officers professionally interact with citizens, and that the police department transparently and thoroughly investigates citizen allegations of officer wrongdoing. Citizens' perceptions of police department legitimacy are likely to increase when these interactions concur with overall crime declines. This research shows that police personnel view their departments' response to lower-level offenses as a means of increasing law abiding citizens' views of their police departments and as an effective stepping-stone in the fight against crime. Earning and maintain legitimacy with the community is an essential piece to successfully implementing a CPS strategy.

Each department studied here would benefit from including more in-depth trainings on the merit of professional citizen interactions, the role that quality of life offenses play in the community (and as regards the police function), and ways to use those interactions to observe or gain information on potential involvement in other more serious crimes. Though this research reveals that CompStat and other administrative functions facilitate the upper-level command staffs' grasp of these concepts, survey data reflect a less thorough understanding of these mechanisms at the lower-levels of the police organizations. Getting police officers to understand these points should move them away from viewing their response to such offenses as simply a numbers game in which arrests and citations are the end. The key, as this research shows, is getting officers to see what is behind those numbers.

CompStat has proven an excellent venue for getting command-level personnel involved in a problem-solving process. Given the closeness of the lower levels of the police department with the community, it makes sense that they should play a pivotal role in a department's overall problem-solving activities. Our respondents suggest their departments find ways to use CompStat or CompStat-like processes to do this. They suggest having regular attendees bring a subordinate to a CompStat meeting and inviting line officers to CompStat to acknowledge them for their community building or information gathering endeavors as ways of reinforcing the organization's views (Moore, 1992). For their part, supervisors must learn about the value of their officers' interactions with citizens and acknowledge what they indicate (and do not indicate) about the work their officers do. This brings us to the final challenge that arose in this research—the measurement issue.

**Measuring and rewarding police activity and outcomes.** As the experience of the MPD shows in Chapter 6, the process of encouraging police officer discretion and using multiple data sources to inform their decisions guides officers in the proper use of their discretion. It also offers impersonal, standard ways of correcting officers who improperly use their discretion. The proper use and oversight of that discretion is vital to police in the CPS era. Just as citizens expect investigations of their complaints of officer wrongdoing to be fair and thorough, police personnel need to perceive the same. Thorough investigations and reasonable repercussions show police officers that their department backs them when needed, coaches them when necessary, and will punish them when warranted, while still encouraging officers to use their discretion as part of a CPS strategy.

As BPD superintendent Frank states, we must "empower the officers at the front lines to be problem-solvers within the community." To this end, departments should implement new measurements and outcomes that are in line with (and facilitate) the CPS strategy. The above-mentioned issues involving supervision of police and holding them accountable speak to the ways a police department measures their personnel's efforts and outcomes. As respondents note, "If it doesn't get written down on paper, it never happened" (Lt. Spell), and, "You have to be able to tell [officers] how that [change] affects their experience, how that affects their job performance, how they're going to be judged on it with meaningful metrics" (Lt. Harris). People work based on what gets counted, documented, and rewarded.

Creating new outcomes and measurements can change the work environment for a police department's personnel, assist the department in making tactical decisions, and can even shield the police department from accusations that would hurt their legitimacy with the community. Prime examples from this study include surveys of both department personnel and community members, the departments' emphasis on quality of life in various crime meetings, citations for low-level offenses (or city ordinance violations), Milwaukee's documentation of traffic stops in which no action at all is taken (to monitor and prevent possible racial discrepancies in police decisions to stop citizens), and even community meetings where citizens are given a chance to present problems and commendations to officers. This section and book now conclude with some final thoughts on why the current police era merits a new name.

# The New Community Problem-Solving Era

Some police academics believe the police profession has moved into a "New," "Intelligence-Led," or "Homeland Security" era defined by an orientation towards preventing terrorism, an emphasis on intelligence gathering, and the need to prevent and detect less inter-personal forms of offending (such as white collar crime and cybercrime) (Oliver, 2005; Stephens, 2005; Treverton, Wollman, Wilke, & Lai, 2011). Their sentiment is correct—the current policing milieu has changed. Anti-terror, intelligence gathering, and new forms of offending do help to define the current policing era. However, the essential elements of the dominant police organizational strategy have not changed. The profession as a whole has yet to fully realize the tenants of the CPS era. And though this is admittedly not a prerequisite for moving into a new era, a more exact title will better orient police researchers and practitioners as they study and engage in the practice of policing. For these reasons we suggest paying homage to the prior policing era while also acknowledging the important changes of the professional environment by naming the most recent era of policing the New Community Problem-Solving era. This New Community Problem-Solving era is defined by an alertness about the potential for terrorist attacks, a contemplation of the different types of offending that affect our citizens, and, most pervasively, the influx of data and technology. The budgetary constraints placed on municipalities and the police are less definitive aspects of this era but are worth noting.

Indeed the LAPD, MPD, and BPD created new bureaus and networks for sharing information on potential terrorist activities. The LAPD even incorporated their anti-terror function into their mission statement. However, there was no evidence in our study that the police organization or police personnel had adopted a motivating homeland security strategy. Stewart and Morris' (2009) survey of police chiefs in Texas and DeLone's (2007) examination of the 50 largest police departments' mission statements also suggest little acknowledgement by chiefs or their departments' missions of a predominant homeland security bent. Nonetheless, law enforcement's attention to anti-terror activities is an important part of the New Community Problem-Solving era. Training in, funding for, and public fears regarding potential terrorist attacks make it a defining characteristic of this era.

Police regard for the less conventional methods of offending (for example, white collar and cyber crimes) is a similarly important, but not propulsive, trait of the current era of policing. Police know those crimes exist, and they are sometimes brought to police attention, but, as a whole, there are few substantive changes within the police departments to reflect a wholesale adoption of this police function. Where such innovation does come into play (at least in the departments studied here) is in using technology to respond to traditional types of offending. For example, one respondent in Los Angeles discussed how they might use a localized DNA database to help solve burglary and other property offenses that usually have very low clearance rates. These departments also exhibited primitive steps to using online social networking sites to gather evidence on street criminals.

The most drastic element of the New Community Problem-Solving era is police access to data and technology and the marriage of them both. Proponents of an Intelligence-Led era (Treverton et al., 2011) are right to follow this aspect of the police profession. Data collection, organization, analysis, and dissemination technologies assist the departments in all facets of their organization. They allow supervisors to explain the who, what, when, where, why, and how of their actions to their officers and to the community. Doing this clarifies for those involved the reason and merit of the tactic and facilitates a shared understanding of their mission (and how they will respond to it). This was an important element for respondents in our study and a useful practice for the police executives. It will be the basis for future comprehensive change in police organizational strategies.

New technologies and greater access to data also give personnel better information in deciding when and how to interact with a citizen. They facilitate more finely tuned tactical executions and assist the department in holding its personnel accountable. For example, the tactic of interacting with citizens (on the basis of a low-level offense) to garner information of more serious wrongdoing is grounded in the fact that individuals involved in serious illegalities are often involved in other, less serious offending. The challenge for police, then, is to focus on those people and places that account for the most serious offending. Data on crime, disorder, and officer activities help the police to do this and can serve to sterilize police interventions from what might have previously been accusations of racism, political payback, or other extra-legal factors. The Christopher Commission in 1991 pointed this out, arguing, "computer-aided studies ... and statistics yield their own truths independent of after-the-fact opinions or reconstruction" (p. iii).

A presentation by Chief Flynn in Milwaukee exemplifies this level of empiricism (https://www.youtube.com/watch?v=Hu8q8WONzFI). During his over 45-minute PowerPoint presentation, Chief Flynn responds to criticisms of racial profiling in traffic stops by presenting data on crime and deployment locations and the statistical relationships of the two. Technology and data worked together in multiple ways throughout the police organization to bring this about:

1.  A mutually conditioning relationship between police data on crime and disorder problems and the location and nature of the police intervention. Data are collected, stored, and analyzed by sophisticated computer technologies.

2.　The interventions might include a problem analysis with community input or sending automobile patrol officers to the area to engage low-level offenders. (Let's assume officers are deployed to a high crime area to prevent a street robbery problem.)

3.　When the officer observes a moving violation in the neighborhood, the officer puts the license plate number into their mobile data computers (MDC). The computer shows them that the individual car is not registered. The officer pulls the vehicle over and runs the driver's license in the MDC database. The driver is wanted on a warrant. The officer makes an arrest.

4.　The MPD continues to gather these data. They analyze them and present it as shown in the above YouTube clip, which they will post on their Facebook and department webpage.

In this very basic and typical example, various technologies used multiple types of data to help police determine the shape of their intervention. The data and technology had both operational and legitimizing purposes for the MPD.

This is just one of the myriad examples of how technology and its ability to use data influence the everyday, community problem-solving operations of police work. Technology and its ability to gather and present data also affect the images that society have of police, police transparency, supervision, accountability, demand for police service, our understanding of a crime or disorder problem, how police relate to its citizens, and how they measure the work they do. Consider how smartphone applications, facial recognition technology, online social networking, data analysis software, and any number of the other increasingly ubiquitous technologies are changing our everyday lives and it becomes obvious that the role of technology is *the* defining characteristic of the New Community Problem-Solving era. As we continue to experience human interaction through technology and become ever so reliant on the many technologies in our lives it is even more incumbent on twenty-first century police leaders to intelligently and constitutionally harness the power of technology in fulfilling their longstanding community problem-solving strategy.

# Closing Thoughts

The context in which leaders lead and police police in the New Community Problem-Solving era bears mentioning. We briefly point out some further items to consider in any discussion of the current policing climate. They include labor unions, competing priorities, budgetary constraints, police culture, politics, inadequate resources, lack of skills, and inertia.

## Labor Unions

Organized labor in policing is an issue with which police chiefs must contend. It is not that organized labor has done anything wrong, but in many instances the existence of a labor contract, which has evolved over the years on a quid pro quo basis, may hobble efforts to make substantive changes to facilitate new ideas in community problem solving. As an example, take hotspot policing. Hotspots of crime may be in areas outside of regularly assigned beats and patrols. If the existing collective bargaining agreement has language on beats and patrols, which is not uncommon, it may be difficult to re-allocate personnel resources to hotspots unless it happens on an overtime basis. Paying of overtime is not a sustainable solution because of the burden it puts on the police budget and in turn, the taxpayer. The normal route would be to re-negotiate the contract. This is a slow process and may not be able to be put on the table until the current contract begins to expire and a new one is negotiated.

Another example was experienced when one of the authors was a police chief. A workload analysis was done, and it was found that there were many more calls for service and more crime occurring on the day shift than on the midnight shift. In the particular department there were three main shifts: days, evenings and midnights. Because of negotiations that had taken place in prior years, the contract restricted the placement of officers to around 33% on each shift. Therefore, the department could not assign officers to solve community problems and still have enough officers to answer calls for service. Eventually, some accommodations were made through negotiations, but it took much longer than it should have to solve some simple problems.

In reading about the experiences of police as they move toward this New Community Problem-Solving era, a police leader must note the inevitable conversations that will arise with union representatives. Fortunately, in a survey conducted in 2004 (Kadleck & Travis), there was generally a large overlap in what unions and police chiefs saw as important in community policing. It is not the intention of the authors to blame administrators or unions for issues experienced in implementing community policing. Both groups work in the same, often unyielding organizational structure. It is important to know, however, that labor relations are often a large factor in getting to a point where specific types of policing can occur and work well.

## Competing Priorities and Budgetary Constraints

Chief Flynn has stated, "All my community policing grants turned into fire trucks, and homeland security became the monster that ate law enforcement" (Czerwinski, 2009). What Chief Flynn is referring to is his belief that the federal government should be investing in resources at the local level to prevent lapses in homeland security rather than invest so heavily in reactive things like fire trucks. It is a fact of life in state and municipal police departments that the major source of funding for municipal governments is taxes. As taxes go up, taxpayers become unhappy. To avoid this, municipal governments almost always have to prioritize how to spend their funds. Roads need to be paved, buildings need to be maintained, school systems need to be operated, and police departments need to provide public safety. Where the tax dollars are allocated directly affects a police department's ability to not only deliver basic services but to make organizational change. When we talk about making changes in an organization that has held on to the status quo and which exists in a bureaucratic setting, it is sometimes necessary to make personnel and infrastructure changes. Negotiation to do this costs money because of the quid pro quo nature of labor relations. Decentralization of the type noted in this book incurs expense. Educating police officers and technology are parts of the budget that are not always seen as high on the priority list in the world of competing departmental budgets in a municipality.

It is a fact that States, counties, and cities bear the largest burden of policing in the United States (Saffell & Basehart, 2001). It is incontrovertible that New York City alone, currently at 36,000 sworn officers, employs almost three times the number of agents than the entire FBI. Nearly 90% of the money to police and house prisoners comes from state sources. As mentioned above, most local governments use tax money to fulfill the police role in their communities. That funding stream is a relatively stable source and does not change dramatically from year to year. When innovation or change needs to be funded, local governments often depend on federal grants to augment their base budgets. In this way, the federal government gains input into the general direction that police head in as far as programs like community-oriented policing, crime and geography, problem-oriented policing, or anti-terror efforts. This input can shift priorities and places local issues in the hands of the federal government.

## Police Culture and Politics

As Wilson observed (1978), police organizational types are shaped by the communities in which police work. Wealthy communities spawn police departments that are service oriented; poor communities give rise to what Wilson called the watchman type of policing; and urban areas and bigger cities experience a legalistic leaning to their policing. There are additional factors other than the external environments and demographics previously discussed that color the attitudes of police.

In his book, *Understanding Police Culture* (1998), John Crank says that a quote on an off-duty police officer's t-shirt prompted him to write the book. The quote was: "You wouldn't understand, it's a cop thing." Other commentators, such as Manning and his dramaturgical explanation for police behavior (1997) and, earlier, Goffman (1959, 1963, 1967) discuss the symbolic communication and roles that exist between a society and its police. Writers like Muir (1979) and Niederhoffer (1979) also explored police culture and how it is formed by intrinsic and extrinsic factors that shape the interplay between police and their communities. Other observers of police culture looked at it from different perspectives. Elizabeth Reuss-Ianni (1993) examined the interaction between the street cops and management cops and how that affects their jobs and their communities. Yet another perspective was found in Kevin Gilmartin's *The Brotherhood of Biochemistry* (1990), in which he examined psychosocial and biological reasons for police behavior and community interaction.

Procedural justice, or the legitimacy that a community places in its police department, is a consequence of how police interrelate to the populations with which they work. How they add value to people's lives, reduce the fear of crime, lower crime itself and, very importantly, how they accomplish those tasks, all shape how communities view the police. If the public are really the police and the police are the public (Reith, 1948) then it would seem logical that the two have to work as partners in fostering efficacy in neighborhoods and feeling of legitimacy in the public. The leaders in each of the departments here faced tenure-defining challenges related to perceptions of their police and how to imbue their organizational culture with the appropriate attitudes and behaviors toward the public.

In his book, *Urban Politics, Crime Rates and Police Strength* (2004), Stucky examines the connection between crime and formal social control (such as the funding of police employment by political entities). Politics in this sense goes to the very heart of the social fabric of communities and how political views and actions might actually affect crime rates by causing racial disenfranchisement and reducing the efficacy of police within communities. In each of the four cities in this book, there was a political will to accomplish policing success and thereby increase the quality of life in the respective communities. Although police operate within organizations, they are, in turn, affected by and operate as a consequence of a larger societal and political culture. Recollect the study of each city in this book and it will be apparent that politics and culture are inseparable.

## *Inadequate Resources, Lack of Skills, and Inertia*

Inadequate resources, lack of skills, and inertia go hand in hand. Because of the limited resources available for advanced training, the skill level of police administrators remains at current levels. The lack of knowledge results in a lack of energy in the organization. The organization is left running on the inertia of the status quo. Policing, like medicine, and other complex areas of endeavor, is not someplace where you want to do on-the-job training. A comprehensive knowledge base is necessary to make and sustain the changes necessary to elevate policing to its highest levels of accomplishment and service to society.

Unfortunately, the places a chief could go to gain knowledge beyond the rudiments of basic police work taught in the academy are limited (Jenkins & DeCarlo, 2014). There is generally no college required to become a police officer and usually no requirement past an undergraduate degree to become a chief (Reaves, 2010). In addition, advanced, specialized schools on the newest police topics and methods are extremely limited and amount to less than a dozen for over a million police officers in over 18,000 departments nationwide. Yet, we know the many benefits of increasing educational standards in policing (Aamodt, 2004).

The police leaders presented in this book collaborated with researchers and advanced their own training beyond the academy in policing methodologies. Resources through additional funding or perhaps the creation of a national police command college to train administrators in advanced policing and policing's role in society is paramount and vitally important to change the course of policing. The inertia of the status quo is formidable. Increasing police leaders' access to the best available skill set will help give them the necessary tools for bringing their departments and the police profession into the New Community Problem-Solving era.

# References

Aamodt, M. (2004). *Research in law enforcement selection.* Boca Raton, FL: Brown Walker Press.

Blomberg, T. (2011). *Criminology and Public Policy,* 10:1.

Braga, A., (Ed.). (2010). Reducing homeless-related crime [Special section]. *Criminology and Public Policy,* 9:4, pp. 807–896.

Czerwinski, J. (2009). The monster that ate law enforcement. Retrieved 6/5/2014, 2014, from http://www.hlswatch.com/2009/01/14/the-monster-that-ate-law-enforcement/.

DeLone, G. (2007). Law enforcement mission statements post-September 11. *Police Quarterly*, 10, pp. 218–235.

Gilmartin, K. (1990). The brotherhood of biochemistry. In H. Russell & B. Allan (Eds.), *Understanding Human Behavior For Effective Police Work*. New York: Basic Books.

Goffman, E. (1959). *The presentation of self in everyday life*. New York: Anchor Press.

Goffman, E. (1963). *Behavior in public places*. New York: Free Press.

Goffman, E. (1967). *Interaction ritual*. New York: Pantheon.

Goldstein, H. (1977). *Policing a free society*. Cambridge, MA: Ballinger.

Greenwood, P. W. (1979). The Rand criminal investigation study: It's findings to date. Santa Monica, CA: Rand.

Jenkins, M., & DeCarlo, J. (2014). Educating police executives in a new community problem-solving era. *FBI Law Enforcement Bulletin, May*(5).

Kadleck, C., & Travis, L. (2004). Police department and police officer association leaders' perceptions of community policing: Describing the nature and extent of agreement. Washington, DC: National Institute of Justice.

Kelling, G., & Coles, C. (1996). *Fixing broken windows: Restoring order and reducing crime in our communities*. New York: The Free Press.

Manning, P. (1997). *Police Work, The social organization of policing* (2nd ed.). Prospect Hill, ILL: Waveland Press.

Muir, W. (1979). *Police: Streetcorner politicians*. Chicago: University Of Chicago Press.

Niederhoffer, A. *Behind the shield: The police in urban society*. New York: Doubleday.

Oliver, W. (2005). The era of homeland security: September 11, 2001 to.... *Crime and Justice International*, 21, 85, pp. 9–17.

Reaves, B. J. (2010). Law enforcement management and administrative statistics (LEMAS). Washington DC: Bureau of Justice Statistics.

Reith, C. (1948). *A short history of the British police*. London: Oxford University Press.

Reuss-Ianni, E. (1993). *Two cultures of policing*. New Brunswick, NJ: Transaction.

Roberg, R., Novak, K., & Cordner, G. (2009). *Police & society*. New York: Oxford University Press.

Saffell, D., & Basehart, H. (2001). *State and local government: polictics and public policies* (7th ed.). New York: McGraw Hill.

Scott, M. S., & Goldstein, H. (2005). *Shifting and sharing responsibilty for public safety problems*. Washington D.C.: Office of Community Oriented Policing.

Spelman, W., & Brown, D. (1984). Calling the police—citizen reporting of serious crime. Wasington DC: National Institute of Justice.

Stephens, G. (2005). Policing the future: Law enforcement's new challenges. *The Futurist*, March/April, pp. 51–57.

Stewart, D. & Morris, R. (2009). A new era of policing?: An examination of Texas police chiefs' perceptions of homeland security. *Criminal Justice Policy Review*, 20, 3, pp. 290–309.

Stucky, T. (2004). *Urban politics, crime rates and police strength.* New York: LFS Scholarly Publishing.

Tien, J., Simon, J., & Larson, R. (1978). *Alternative approach in police patrol: The Wilmington split-force experiment.* National Institute of Law Enforcement and Criminal Justice.

Treverton, G., Wollman, M., Wilke, E., & Lai, D. (2001). *Moving toward the future of policing.* Santa Monica: Rand.

Wilson, J. Q. (1978). *Varieties of police behavior: The management of law and order in eight communities.* Cambridge, MA: Joint Center for Urban Studies.

# List of Abbreviations

| | |
|---|---|
| ACLU | American Civil Liberties Union |
| BPD | Boston Police Department |
| BRIC | Boston Regional Intelligence Center |
| CAD | Computer-Aided Dispatch |
| CLEAR | Community Law Enforcement and Recovery |
| CIB | Criminal Investigations Bureau |
| CPS | Community Problem-Solving |
| CRT | Constituent Response Team |
| DB | Detectives Bureau |
| DPR | Differential Police Response |
| FAT | Fugitive Apprehension Team |
| FIO | Field Interrogation Observation |
| GED | Gang Enforcement Detail |
| GIS | Geographic Information System |
| GIT | Gang Impact Team |
| HRV | High Risk for Violence |
| LAPD | Los Angeles Police Department |
| MDC | Mobile Data Computer |
| MDT | Mobile Data Terminal |
| MPD | Milwaukee Police Department |
| NET | Narcotics Enforcement Team |
| NPD | Newark Police Department |
| NTF | Neighborhood Task Force |
| QOL | Quality of Life |
| RAP | Reporting Area Project |
| RMS | Records Management System |
| SARA | Scanning, Analysis, Response, Assessment |
| SOT | Street Outreach Team |
| SST | Safe Street Team |
| VEST | Violent Enterprise Strategy Task Force |
| YVSF | Youth Violence Strike Force |

# Index